D0613007

RARY

DEMCO

THE NEW REALISM

Detachment is one of the marks
of Civilization . . .
along with Wonder

—Sister Susan John
Solitary nun and artist

THE NEW REALISM

A FRESH BEGINNING IN U.S.-SOVIET RELATIONS

Roland S. Homet, Jr.

Braddock Carnegie Library
419 Library Street
Braddock, PA 15104

A Cornelia & Michael Bessie Book
An Imprint of HarperCollins*Publishers*

THE NEW REALISM. Copyright © 1990 by Roland S. Homet, Jr. All rights reserved. Printed in the United States of America. No part of this book may be used or reproduced in any manner whatsoever without written permission except in the case of brief quotations embodied in critical articles and reviews. For information address HarperCollins Publishers, 10 East 53rd Street, New York, NY 10022.

FIRST EDITION

Designed by Alma Orenstein

Library of Congress Cataloging-in-Publication Data

Homet, Roland S., 1932–
    The new realism: a fresh beginning in U.S.-Soviet relations/
Roland S. Homet, Jr.—1st ed.
      p. cm.
ISBN 0-06-039125-1
    "A Cornelia & Michael Bessie book."
    Includes bibliographical references and index.
    1. United States—Foreign relations—Soviet Union. 2. Soviet
Union—Foreign relations—United States. 3. United States—Foreign
relations—1989– 4. Soviet Union—Foreign relations—1985–
I. Title.
E183.8.S65H67 1990   90-55060
327.73047—dc20

90 91 92 93 94 CC/HC 10 9 8 7 6 5 4 3 2 1

Contents

PART THREE   External Relations

PART FOUR   The View Ahead

Foreword

The historical facts in this account are as accurate and comprehensive as diligence can make them, up through the end of 1989 when the manuscript was finished. History moves on, however, and nowhere more insistently than in the rapidly shifting landscape of inner-Soviet and U.S.-Soviet affairs. Events both scheduled and unscheduled, coming after my completion date, are bound to have altered the face of the landscape we are watching.

But this is not a book about landscapes. It is instead an attempt to understand, and portray, the subsurface dynamics that can transform landscapes—as surely as the San Francisco earthquake of 1989, in its own way, remade the face of the Marina district. It is the dynamic stresses within and between the two superpowers, and our understanding of them, that will determine the face of the landscape we experience in the coming decades.

R.S.H., Jr.
Washington, D.C.

Preface

America has won the peace and lost control of it. Both elements reflect the same success. We have succeeded in our postwar aims of thwarting Soviet expansionism and rebuilding a concert of nations. From now on it is those nations that will set the pace. America can still play the lead, if it chooses, but from within and not from on high as it has done for the past two generations. The symphony conductor, if that has been our role, must re-emerge as concertmaster.

There is no sign as yet of this taking place. Neither public attitudes nor governmental policies in this country are oriented toward such a change. It can be difficult, of course, for anyone to step down from a position of pre-eminence. But it is necessary now for America to do so, both in consequence of its past successes and because no future alternative lies open. Either we will adapt ourselves to changed circumstances or we risk having important national interests displaced.

I have had some experience of what this may mean. In 1978 I was part of a U.S. negotiating team that blocked a Soviet-proposed UN resolution endorsing the censorship of Western news. We had no appropriations from Congress with which to fight this initiative, and no military or covert means of persuading the non-aligned nations to withdraw their sponsorship. The only course open to us was reasoned exploration of the common interest. On that basis, we drew up a counter-proposal to establish a clearinghouse for global information needs and resources—in effect, uniting the world community rather than pulling it apart. Our motion carried, by a vote of 156 to nothing, the Soviets joining in when it became apparent that there was no place else for them to go. The French Elysée operative in UNESCO drew me aside at one point to ask if I realized that we might shortly succeed in "taking the Third World away from the Soviet Union." My answer was to muse aloud with him about "whether we would know what to do with them if we got them."

The Third World was not of course ours to keep on that occasion, any more than the Soviet Union became permanently chastened by our diplomacy. All we Americans could really do, while the Soviets were exerting themselves so insistently to undermine our values, was to hold out against the day when they would no longer feel obliged to do that. This was the crux of the Cold War struggle, which at its height could lead us both into mythologizing our rivalry—we painting the Soviets as conscienceless despots, they showing us as greedy monopolists. The caricatures at least made it easy to judge who was on what side.

Then came Mikhail Gorbachev, not as an isolated individual but as a product of the forces of Soviet reform we had long awaited. In the four-year period of Ronald Reagan's second term as president of the United States (1985–89), he and General Secretary Gorbachev together began moving away from myth-driven posturings to a relationship based on realism. Gorbachev's so-called "new thinking," with its assertion of a mutuality of East-West interests, was backed up by arms-reduction proposals and reform initiatives in both domestic and foreign policy that moved a good distance toward changing the face of our familiar "enemy."

In a sense this has made things more difficult. We had learned more or less how to deal with an all-out enemy, but what were we to do with a rival whose policies could sometimes conflict and sometimes coincide with our own? The next phase of global ordering, it now seemed, would be characterized by ambiguities and lit by half-lights, requiring choices and distinctions to be made that we had not schooled ourselves to draw.

An effective American leader for this coming period will have to be one who is ready both to enter the orchestra and to pitch an ear to the tone of the other instruments. For this purpose it may be that Mikhail Gorbachev has done us a favor. By raising as boldly and dramatically as he has the question of who the Soviets are and what their mission is in the world, he is obliging us to ask the same—probably overdue—questions about ourselves. He and the new realities he partly represents are challenging America to move in its own international relations not only beyond myth but beyond pragmatism, to a new definition of our global interests and capacities. The implications of that process can be every bit as far-reaching as those of the immediate postwar period, bearing in mind the changed circumstances that have come about since that time.

The postwar period was extraordinary in at least two senses. It was a period of unchallenged American pre-eminence in all domains—military, economic, political, even cultural—and it was also a period in which the United States for the first time in its history committed itself to enduring structures of world order. America came as a result to dominate those structures, including the United Nations and the North Atlantic Treaty Organization, to a degree that could only thereafter subside. While the dominance lasted, it meant that America could control almost any outcome it chose, simply by shifting its weight in the desired direction. It is a tribute to the statesmen of the period to note how often they refrained from exercising that power, in the interest of rebuilding a more balanced world community.

Still, the environment of the late 1940's was one in which American interests and capacities could be seen as virtually without limit. We might choose to exercise restraint, or encourage others to take a lead, but America was the ultimate peacemaker; and this engendered attitudes and expectations that are with us to this day.

Pragmatism alone is not a sufficient release from the obstacles that have resulted. Pragmatism, or the art of the possible, can do little more by itself than triangulate a mid-point among prevailing prejudices—and it is those prejudices, unreexamined, that now stand in our way. It once seemed clear to us, for example, that any appreciable strengthening of the Soviet economy would build up that government's capacity to work mischief in the world, and should therefore be resisted; we limited our exports, and export credits, accordingly. Now, however, a new Soviet government gives signs of wishing to join, not wreck, the world economy. The tempering opportunity this may present, to bring about a long-term moderation in Soviet global behavior and thereby to benefit U.S. and global security, is not something that was conceivable 40 years or even ten years ago. Now it is here and compels a rethinking of long-settled premises.

American leverage is something else that needs to be reexamined. Two generations ago, if we wanted to withhold goods or services from the Soviet Union, we could count on other supplying nations to go along. Either we ourselves were the only substantial source of supply, or we could exert such a powerful influence on the others that they would follow our lead. For a number of years now, that has not been the case. There are today many other potential suppliers for almost any export, and the countries that can provide it are also capable of forming their own views about the Soviet Union. If they now perceive Soviet policies as moving toward harmonization with the world community, the fact that we may see things differently is not going to empower us to impose our differing view. The Soviet gas-pipeline controversy of the first Reagan term, in which America had to back down from its attempt to enforce a collective Western boycott, made that clear, as did the unsuccessful Soviet grain embargo of the preceding Carter term.

But if American interests have shifted and its policy leverage has dwindled, what remains? Curiously, perhaps, the answer is a chastened and more effective leadership. We may have lost the capacity to lead unpersuasively, but not the capacity to lead by persuasion.

No other power or power bloc can today claim that capacity—not the Soviet Union or China, whose processes of reform are too self-engrossing; not the European Community, whose preoccupations also are mainly internal; not Japan, whose energies reach everywhere but which stands for no idea more composing than Darwinian exertion. America alone still stands for something richer—for harmony and freedom, for unity in diversity, for orchestrating the choir. There lies the opportunity ahead.

It is not an opportunity from which Americans can afford to abstain, even though our history may incline us in that direction. For all of its first 200 years as a nation, our country has known only two ways of relating to the world: isolation or control. Until 1949 and the North Atlantic Treaty, America stood apart from the turmoils and the intrigues of the old world it had left. Then, one day, when no one else was capable of doing so, it took charge. For the next 30 years or so—the "American Century," as some described it—we governed. The record of that period is inevitably mixed, but for an untutored country we did well. We succeeded in our major aims; we were not diverted into self-aggrandizement; and by our labors we disabled ourselves from continuing as world governors. Now it is no longer possible for America either to control the world or to withdraw from it. We must learn instead to mediate, to understand, and to persuade.

The challenge this presents is not a new one, indeed, it is as old as our country. It is the challenge to act on the basis of American interests, and of American capacities, as they present themselves to us from time to time. George Washington's famous Farewell Address, in which he counseled his new nation to abstain from entangling alliances, was grounded in this perception. Washington said:

> The nation which indulges toward another an habitual hatred or an habitual fondness is in some degree a slave. It is a slave to its animosity or its affection, either of which is sufficient to lead it astray from its duty and its interest.

That advice is as useful today as it was when it was delivered in 1796.

Toward the Soviet Union in particular we must develop today some tenable alternative to sworn enmity or close friendship. The USSR is neither the "evil empire" of Ronald Reagan's first term nor the intimate collaborator of his second. It is instead an independent actor, with interests of its own, some of which will be congenial to us and some of which will not. We can neither banish nor ignore that independent actor, and we are limited in our ability to control its behavior. That may be frustrating, and doubtless will be, unless we revise our expectations.

This will mean giving up the crude images and sharp opinion swings that have characterized American public attitudes toward Russia and the Soviet Union throughout this century. First, the Russian Tsar was considered a "despot" or "tyrant"—as he still usually is, in crossword puzzles—so that the 1917 Revolution was broadly welcomed by American opinion. The ensuing Communist government then came to be seen as hostile and menacing; for several years we would have nothing to do with it. In World War II, when our two countries joined as allies against Hitler's Germany, *Life* magazine took to declaring that the Soviets "look like Americans, dress like Americans, and think like Americans"; their secret police was just "a national police force similar to the FBI." After that came the Cold War, and a sharp shift of attitude back against the Soviet Union. Now as the century closes there is another thaw, whose reach and effect have yet to be discovered.

The time ought finally to have come for America to settle on a single, consistent, great-power approach to its rival. A great power, history teaches, has neither permanent friends nor permanent enemies; it has durable interests and changing opportunities. It makes judgments on the basis not of sentiment but of informed self-regard. Thus, for example, regardless of how far the Soviet Union becomes "reformed" internally, so long as it remains heavily armed it will be capable of intervening in or intimidating a variety of countries around the world. How America chooses to relate to that capacity—what initiatives we will take, by ourselves or with our allies—ought in future to be a matter of objective calculation, ungoverned by feelings of friendship or dislike.

The Soviet Union simply is, as we are, a factor in world affairs. We have the chance in the coming years of improving our great-power relationship—provided we can determine, by wise and patient assessment, the distance that should separate our differing endeavors. It will be the part of America's maturity as a nation to develop and to practice that skill.

The change will not come easily, as I in a sense have again experienced. I originally had it in mind to write this book in a way that would show very little of my own opinions or ideas, but would offer the views and insights of recognized authorities. I would weave the connections, at a safe editorial distance. As the project went forward I was encouraged to think of it more and more as a conversation with politically literate readers—with the people, in effect, whose attitudes tend to shape what our government is disposed and at liberty to do. There are many fine books by or for specialists, I was told; why not write one for generalists? Eventually I took to this suggestion, and found myself drawn to it. But it has obliged me to adopt a different stance, to find and to use a different voice. The shift of perspectives has taken some time.

The book began as a series of discussions I organized and moderated for six years (1984–89) among American specialists on the Soviet Union, American policy makers, and American media correspondents. We would meet periodically in Washington for informal sessions, twelve to twenty people around a table, and would invite the specialists to lead off on a selected topic of current Soviet policy. A brief introduction—almost always by two specialists, to insure balance—would be followed by discussion. I would take notes and produce a summary set of minutes, which after correction by the participants would become a record of our consensus.

We chose our participating academics, 27 in number, with one eye to their distinction and another to their balance. No one who had served as a senior adviser to a president or secretary of state of either political party was included. For the rest, we had some who identified themselves as liberals, some as conservatives, most as neither. We consciously combined our specialists to avoid any impression of imbalance, while focusing our main attention on the caliber of their contributions. We and our political and media audiences were invariably well served.

In the Congress, we met on differing occasions with both party caucuses, with the bipartisan leadership of the House Foreign Affairs Committee, and with the full Senate Intelligence Committee. In the Executive, we met regularly with an interagency national security group, drawn from the White House, the Departments of State and Defense, the Joint Chiefs of Staff, and the Central Intelligence Agency. Regular meetings were also held with selected senior print and broadcast correspondents from around the country who follow U.S.-Soviet affairs. On other occasions, we invited political counselors from the Soviet, Chinese, European, and Japanese embassies in Washington to sit in on public sessions with our specialists. Altogether we held some 50 separate meetings over the six years, covering 27 different topics.

These topics dealt always with one or another aspect of the changing Soviet reality. There are, of course, groups in Washington and elsewhere that seek to promote a particular U.S. policy position on these matters. We did not, and this (we were told) was one reason our meetings were well attended. We aimed instead to acquaint the policy and media communities with the best current evidence of what the Soviet reality is, and then to let political

preferences work their will. We said for example that the United
States can have any trade policy it wants, for any reason or for no
reason; but if the reason chosen to curtail trade with the Soviets
is to bring them to their knees, then one should know that the
evidence is against that happening—indeed, that there is a strong
consensus on this point among all independent specialists, regardless of their political views.

To the Senate Select Committee on Intelligence in particular,
we said that this kind of grounding is essential. That committee
asked our advice about the kinds of factual questions the U.S.
government should be pursuing, and we drew for our answer on
Washington's Farewell Address. "We as a country," we said,
"should be asking questions about the Soviet Union that bear on
U.S. interests and that illuminate Soviet capabilities, constraints
and interests. 'Interests' for both countries are not the same as
affections or antipathies." That is the perspective we sought to
carry with us throughout the specialists' project, and it is what I
have taken as my starting point for this generalists' book.

PART ONE

Overview

1

Realism and Reflection about Soviet Change

The Russia entrusted to Mikhail Gorbachev in 1985 was unproductive at home and counterproductive abroad. Despite generations of prodigious sacrifice the Soviet experiment was falling progressively behind in all major categories of accomplishment—economic, technological, diplomatic, even military if the respect gained by arms was considered. The Soviet Union was making no headway in Afghanistan and was spending large sums on subsidies to countries like Cuba and Ethiopia whose stars were never bright. Domestically, morale was faltering as jobs were often make-work and rewards in terms of consumer goods were patchy: "We pretend to work and they pretend to pay us," was the presiding joke in this workers' society.

Gorbachev set out to restore morale, at first by a great show of energy and direction. He showed up in the streets and factories, he delivered fresh-sounding speeches and appointed fresh-looking officials, and he trumpeted an increasingly insistent note of reform. At times he seemed to be lifting the whole Soviet enterprise up by its elbows. He attracted attention, he generated hope, and he gained some time for substantive measures to be developed and take hold.

With the economy, whose over-centralization had roots going back to the Tsarist period, reform would have to reach very deep.

Russian black bread, as an example, which is served as a luxury
to patrons of American restaurants, was apt in the Soviet Union at
this time to be served by a farmer to his pigs—not as a sign of scorn
for capitalist decadence, but because the Soviet-subsidized price of
the bread made it cheaper to use for this purpose than other feeds.
Other anomalies abounded, such as a very high level of family
savings coupled with an almost total unavailability of new apartments, quality food, or consumer conveniences. Life was, for most
people, a dreary struggle 70 years after the Revolution carried out
in their name and 40 years after the Great Patriotic War conducted
for their sake.

The new General Secretary saw the problem as one of insuf-
ficient initiative. He moved in several ways—farm leasing, bureaucratic reduction, and a limited licensing of private enterprise—to
shift the structure from a command economy to one driven by
contract relations. This was not to be a full market system, on the
Western model, but it was to point in that direction and to combine the energies of enterprise with the policy guidance of the
central authorities.

To make the new stimulus work, Gorbachev judged it necessary to introduce social reforms as well, aimed at bringing out the
initiative of Soviet men and women and of curbing administrative
restraints on that initiative. He sought in particular to make an ally
of the intelligentsia, a class of people with no direct counterpart
in American society. These sparkplug intellectuals, who had seen
their hopes in Nikita Khrushchev drained by the intervening
Brezhnev years, were cheered by the personal decision of Mikhail
Gorbachev to release from house arrest the noted physicist and
independent thinker Andrei Sakharov. More signs of freedom
were to follow, among them the film *Repentance,* displaying to
packed houses the cruelty of the Stalin regime and its continuing
hold on the national consciousness; a declaration by Gorbachev
that there should be no "blank pages" in Soviet history; and a
reasoned exoneration of Nikolai Bukharin, a Revolutionary leader
and the victim of one of Stalin's "show" trials in 1937.

At a wider level, the months after Gorbachev's accession saw
a progressive easing of the restrictions in all major categories of
what Westerners would call civil liberties: freedom of the person,
press, assembly, religion, and travel. New non-official advocacy
groups for reform of one or another aspect of Soviet life were both

permitted and encouraged. Political prisoners were released, and emigration permitted, in large numbers. Gorbachev even honored the Russian Orthodox Church on its 1,000th anniversary, and arranged for it to move its headquarters back to Moscow. None of this was in service of Western-style liberty, with the individual at the center and the state serving him; but it did add up to a kind of directed license, aimed at revitalizing the "Soviet way of mind" within the contours of a markedly less oppressive state.

To bolster those aims, and to round out his domestic agenda, Gorbachev elected also to strike for governmental reform. Part of this took the shape of law revision, designed to secure a government that would obey its own laws and leave individuals free within those laws to follow their own initiatives. Part of it sought also by systematic restructuring to open the way to new blood and fresh minds within the government. Gorbachev presided for this purpose over a highly publicized "town meeting of the air" in 1988—a Communist Party Conference at which open arguments and even criticisms of Party performance were voiced for the first time in memory. The old guard was not immediately removed from office by this means, any more than all elements of the law reform package were at once adopted; but a process was set in motion whereby results of this kind—inconceivable before—began to become conceivable.

A key element in this process was constitutional revision. The Soviet Union had had several constitutions and had never found them confining. Now Gorbachev proposed by a strengthening of the legislatures, or *soviets*, to give them a supervisory handle over the executive, and by the introduction of contested elections to hold governmental and Party leaders accountable to the public. Constitutional changes to this effect were adopted in late 1988, although it was not at once clear how far-reaching the reforms would be in practice. Nothing in their provisions was designed to undo either Party control over the state or state control over the economy. The emphasis in the Soviet system would still be on order, not liberty. But if by Western standards the changes did not amount to democratic pluralism, they did constitute and sustain a new social diversity that might evolve in a more democratic direction.

The words used by Mikhail Gorbachev to describe his domestic initiatives quickly became familiar to news audiences around

the world: *perestroika, glasnost,* and *demokratizatsiya.* The third
of these, an imported term, had shallower roots in Russian political history than the other two. *Glasnost* comes from the Church
Slavonic and means "voiceness," or publicity (not "openness," as
it is sometimes mis-translated). There may be a spiritual
resonance to the word, a sense of transparency, which could have
some personal significance for Gorbachev in that his mother
raised him in his early years as a Christian. Within the context of
the overall political culture, however, *glasnost* means chiefly candor-for-a-purpose. It has what specialists call an "instrumental"
value within the prevailing system of state socialism, along with
the potentiality of evolving one day into something more trans-
formative.

Perestroika is usually translated as "restructuring," and applied by Western analysts to changes in the Soviet economy. Soviet
usage is not so limited, however. Gorbachev's own book, published
in 1987, used the title *Perestroika* to describe the whole of his
domestic and international agenda. The word has the wider con-
notation, experts tell us, of "reformation"—very much in its
churchly sense. The Soviet Communist system can be understood
as a kind of church, with leaders and a system of governance that
are not working well. Its appeal has been dwindling among its
parishioners, and its missionaries have been losing rather than
gaining converts. The Polish Solidarity spokesman Adam Michnik
says that what Gorbachev is really attempting is a counter-reformation, aimed at preempting rival energies like those of Solidarity. The metaphor helps to draw our attention to the fact that the
Russia of today, like the Roman Catholic Church of earlier times,
never experienced a Reformation or a Renaissance until, perhaps,
its necessities required it.

That lends some force to the long-run prospects for Soviet
reform. Change in the Soviet Union, as Gorbachev perceives it, is
not just an option but a requirement. The problem lies in getting
enough fellow Soviets to agree. *Perestroika* gets good support from
intellectuals and from women, both beleaguered classes. It enjoys
less certain backing among farmers and workers, to whose futures
it appeals but who face the near-term prospect of reduced job
security and purchasing power. Those who accept the challenge of
private enterprise have had to run the gauntlet of entrenched dis-
taste among their neighbors for any form of profiteering: Russians

of all classes have long preferred the values of community over individualism, of consensus over competition. Within officialdom, forces in the government and Party bureaucracies who oppose *perestroika,* or greet it with "positive inertia," do so not only for reasons of self-preservation but also to safeguard these aspects of the traditional culture. The military, who have gone along with reform like good soldiers, feel some unease about their potential loss of status in the society. They, along with many patriotic civilians, place a high value on the quality of disciplined leadership. Gorbachev personally has earned their respect for this quality, but the transitional instabilities spawned by reform—among restive nationality groups, for example, and in declining production patterns—are broadly disquieting.

Against those discouragements stand certain emerging characteristics of Soviet society, which together may be shaping a new constituency in favor of change. The old Russian peasant mentality is fading and a new, more urban or middle-class independence is appearing, accompanied by information flows and transactional complexities that make the old authoritarian practices of Soviet governance increasingly difficult to maintain. This augurs well for change in the long run, and helps to distinguish Gorbachev's opportunities from those of the predecessors with whom he is most often compared—Peter the Great and Nikita Khrushchev, two reformers whose modernizing impulses did not long survive their tenure. The problem for Gorbachev is that the "bottom-up" transformations of his day may be coming either too slowly to support his "top-down" innovations or—in some cases—too swiftly to avoid a backlash from conservatives.

Navigating the crosscurrents between these hazards has become a special attribute of Gorbachev's leadership. Unlike his celebrated forbears, Gorbachev has both pushed and paused, demanded and awaited support. He is a consensus shaper and mover, never too far out ahead of his Party colleagues. Unlike Boris Yeltsin, an activist dismissed from the leadership, Gorbachev has chosen to move "at consensus speed, not ultra speed." He is a proposer who knows he cannot always dispose. So he has engaged in tactical retreats as well as advances, keeping his reputation largely intact as a winner. In these respects Gorbachev has come across as a Franklin D. Roosevelt of Soviet Russia, both leaders serving as radical saviors of their inherited economic and political systems. As with Roosevelt's New Deal, not all elements of Gorbachev's *perestroika* are likely to be adopted or to survive— though many of them certainly will. The initiatives of reform will solidify over time into the accomplishments of reform, through changed social attitudes that *perestroika* will have helped to set in motion: "Reformation" in this sense will be experienced as a changed way of mind. How much of the change will take place during Gorbachev's time in office is less and less the controlling question, as qualified observers have come increasingly to believe that the underlying dynamics of *perestroika* are irreversible.

That is not to say that there are no alternatives to Gorbachev as the manager of reform. The modernization of traditional cultures is always a hazardous undertaking, as the late Shah of Iran certainly discovered. Opinions are bound to vary as to where the balance should be fixed, and as to how rapidly it should be moved along. There is some prospect accordingly of a more conservative successor government at some point, one that would usher in change less jarringly. As social patterns continue to unfold, however, and the change in attitudes proceeds, that government too would be obliged eventually to let the reform movement resume, broadly along the lines opened up by Mikhail Gorbachev.

The key determinant in all this is what scholars like to call *political culture:* the sum of values and habits and expectations that shape a nation's institutions. That is what now is changing in the Soviet Union, in a way that will ultimately yield the economic and social and political reforms being sought. Human rights and democratic practices and entrepreneurial initiative are the flowers in this process, not the soil; they will blossom only after, and as a result of, the transformation of the culture. Mikhail Gorbachev, as chief cultivator, has worked with diligence inside this framework—although he too seems sometimes to chafe against its limitations.

His first policy direction was one of acceleration, or *uskoryenie:* Do what you're doing, but do it more rapidly. The line soon became more rounded, but it retained some of its raucous or hectoring edge, as when bureaucrats were berated publicly though their cooperation was needed for reform. Gorbachev's speeches, proposals, and even claims of performance were frequently out ahead of his accomplishments; they sounded like the barking of a sheepdog at a slow-moving flock. He tended on occasion to set millennial goals for reform and then to accompany them with accountants' timetables: The Constitutional revisions of 1988 were pushed through to adoption with almost no time for public reflection, and the economic structure of the country was first set down for overhaul by 1991, which no one could consider realistic.

Historians suggest that this pattern fits the traditional view of Russia and the Russians as a "mobilization society," whose movement can be stimulated only by laying out vast and improbable goals. Stalin's forced industrialization and Khrushchev's deforestation of whole republics are cited as examples. Yet this tactic may no longer be so effective with the changing, more self-determinant, Soviet society on which Gorbachev must rely for the realization of his reforms.

The transformation of the Soviet way of mind is bound to be the work of decades. It will take at least until the 21st century for the economic change of direction to begin to take full hold, if it does; for *glasnost* to enlist the sustained participation of citizens other than intellectuals and dissenters; for legal and governmental reforms to gain a durable place in the Soviet political system. If Gorbachev keeps insisting on earlier returns, he could start looking like someone who cannot deliver.

Already some of the more pivotal issues of reform, like pricing freedom and the treatment of nationalities, press independence and criminal justice, have had to be deferred. Five years into the Gorbachev reform era, there was not much new food on the table or housing for the family or consumer goods for the pent-up savings and expectations of the average person. As many had been saying for some time, "you can't eat *glasnost.*"

Yet it is also the case that you can't dream bread. Soviet society needs a new conceptual direction and it probably has to be declaratory to begin with. There have been marked changes already in attitude and orientation since the reform campaign began. Even if these do not currently amount to a full-scale revolution, the changes in direction are meaningful. There are both top-down and bottom-up elements in the transformation. And the nature of the social changes, on which a future evolution can take root, are very significant in the setting of Soviet history, even if they do not now match what has begun happening in the more Westernized societies of its Warsaw Pact neighbors.

The language of Soviet reform shows this. There is less liturgy now, and more common speech, in the calls and exhortations that issue from the podium. People are being invited to witness and take part in the proceedings. An elderly woman in Yaroslavl who watched the 1988 Party Conference on television told the press that she wept at what she saw: "My brother disappeared under Stalin. One night they came and he was gone. And to think that now people can talk so freely."

The talk, it must be said, is not always disciplined. There is little sense of give-and-take sometimes between the partisans of differing positions, each of whom is likely to adopt an absolutist line. The 1989 nomination meetings for candidates to the new Congress of People's Deputies often dissolved into pointless shouting matches between rival factions. Reformers have been as guilty of this as conservatives, and even Gorbachev for all his political astuteness is not beyond slipping into a preemptive form of speech. At the 1988 Party Conference, when the country and the auditorium were awaiting the fresh winds of debate, Gorbachev began the proceedings with a standard five-hour speech.

But Gorbachev knows the sorry state of Soviet political argument and how much it needs to be improved. To a group of editors concerned about ethnic disturbances in Armenia, he acknowledged that "we still lack the culture to conduct the debate and respect the viewpoint of a friend, a comrade. . . . We will mature." At the Party Conference he told his colleagues, "there is no need to fear [uncongenial] opinions, there is no need to overreact and lapse into extremes at every turn of the debates." "It is important now," he added, "in the period of humanization of all aspects of our life, to learn the habit of criticism, the habit of comradely polemic."

That learning, like the reform process as a whole, will be evolutionary. It will be part of a sea change, which neither Mikhail Gorbachev nor anyone else can wholly design or fathom. Television and the transparency of frontiers will be factors in the transformation, along with other elements, but there can be no sure measure of their pace or progression. Those treading water cannot readily detect the point at which the tide begins to shift.

The Soviet Union as a political culture is subject to more than one current. It contains within itself an unresolved debate between the pull of Western and Asiatic influences—between the provincial and the worldly, the soil and the city, the rational and the spiritual. This culture of contradictions is moving toward and looks likely to coalesce into a new national character, but it will do so in its own time. There is, we Westerners must remember, no tradition of "social contract" in the Soviet experience, no habit of separated powers, no expectation that private pursuits can yield public benefits. The Soviet Union at the turn of the millennium is still a theocracy in search of an effective creed.

In international affairs, Gorbachev's reform standard became something called "the new political thinking." It represented a bowing to realism, particularly to the nuclear realities brought home by advanced missile delivery systems. "The character of present-day weaponry," he said to his first Soviet Party Congress in February 1986, "leaves no country with any hope of safeguarding itself solely with military and technical means, for example by building up a defense, even the most powerful. To ensure security is seen increasingly as a political problem. . . . Without being blind to social, political, and ideological differences, all have to master the science and art of restraint and circumspection on the international scene."

This overture, and others that followed it, though odd and suspicious-sounding to Western minds conditioned by decades of Soviet expansionism, were followed up by concrete instances of "restraint and circumspection." In rapid order, Gorbachev agreed with an American invitation to "zero out," or remove, all intermediate-range nuclear missiles from Europe, and signed an INF Treaty to that effect. He tabled a proposal for fifty percent cuts in long-range or strategic nuclear warheads, and took a stance in favor of preserving the full force of the ABM Treaty of 1972. Gorbachev proposed substantial conventional force cuts as well, and took the lead in December of 1988 by announcing a unilateral Soviet reduction of 500,000 troops, including tanks and assault forces. Most surprising of all, perhaps, Gorbachev took the wraps off of long-guarded security secrets, publishing a Soviet version of the European military balance for the first time, accepting intrusive internal inspections for INF and chemical weapons, and allowing routine NATO observations of Soviet military maneuvers.

Gorbachev went further. He began withdrawing from overextended Soviet positions in the Third World. Soviet troops came home from Afghanistan, on a schedule announced and kept by Gorbachev. Surrogate Cuban and Vietnamese forces were ticketed for withdrawal from Angola and Kampuchea (Cambodia), two other "running sores" of Soviet security exposure. In each of these locales, the United Nations was invited in to play a part as negotiator or facilitator. The United States, too, was informed or engaged in advance; throughout the period, indeed, U.S. and Soviet diplomats exhibited a mutual "restraint and circumspection" by consulting quietly about regional trouble spots in regular bilateral meetings. In these and in other, more formal settings, the Soviets exhibited a flexibility and a straightforwardness of dealing that was new to American veterans of U.S.-Soviet security negotiation.

The key conceptual underpinnings for this Soviet approach were the ideas of *strategic interdependence* and *reasonable defense sufficiency.* When a Soviet security initiative upsets an adversary, Gorbachev was saying, it can soon disturb the Soviet Union by provoking a counter-response. Years of painful experience lay behind that observation. Under the banners of "parity" or "equal security," Soviet leaders had long sought to gain an advantage over the West only to have it repeatedly slip away from them. The Eastern European buffer zone, seized for security reasons immediately after World War II, provoked the formation of NATO and a state of militarized tension along the whole of the Soviet western flank. The Soviet SS-20 missiles, deployed at a later day against West European military targets, summoned U.S. Pershing-2 and cruise missiles into Europe to be deployed against Soviet military targets. So it went, in the Third World as well; everywhere that the Soviets reached for unilateral advantage they suffered some form of setback, if only in relations with the West.

Traditional Marxist-Leninist ideology contributed to the problem by positing the existence of "two camps," Communist and Capitalist, only one of which could survive. This underscored the appearance of a Soviet global menace, and invited a stiffer measure of Western resistance. The two-camps tenet was thus not helpful to Soviet interests, and it could not realistically survive into a day of high-speed, accurate, intercontinental nuclear-weapons delivery systems. By the time of Gorbachev's accession, the Soviet policy of global confrontation and its ideological underpinning were ready to be seen as wasting assets.

There is a Siberian bear story that illustrates the point. When a bee-keeper in Siberia wants to protect his honey from the bears, he suspends a log from a rope just below the branch that holds the hive. The bear smells the honey and climbs the tree but encounters the log. When he pushes it out of the way, it swings back. This annoys him, so he gives it a hard push. Now the log swings back and hits the bear hard. By this point the bear is furious, so he stops climbing and deals the pesky log a tremendous blow, whereupon it comes back and really hurts him. All thought of the honey is now abandoned, and the bear battles the log until, inevitably, it defeats him. For some reason, Siberians say, the bear never tries to climb around the log.

Not so Mr. Gorbachev. As human beings, he and his leadership colleagues were capable of learning from experience. They also had the benefit, it must be said, of the Brezhnev military build-up that had been started in the 1970's. There was less of a need, after that build-up, for the bear to feel vulnerable, less of a need to battle the log. Security could be treated as more of a political problem. One could take into account the interests of others. Policy could aim for what we might call Reciprocal Security.

Gorbachev began on that basis a movement away from ideology and toward the politics of realism, or *realpolitik* as it was known in the 19th century. The Soviet Union was still a major power, and still had global interests, but it could be concerned today with what is cost-effective. Moscow could prepare for summits in China and Japan while withdrawing troops from Afghanistan, could propose co-hosting an Arab-Israeli settlement conference while restraining the size of its Middle East fleet. Soviet behavior overall could be more adroit, less menacing, and—in terms of global opinion—more effective.

The propaganda or manipulative aspects of Gorbachev's international initiatives, while undeniably present, did not belie their authenticity. The new political thinking, for the Soviets, harked back to Nikita Khrushchev as well as to Albert Einstein. Einstein said of the nuclear revolution that, "Now everything has changed except man's way of thinking," while Khrushchev started the change of Soviet thinking by ruling out, in the 1950's, the inevitability of nuclear war. That was in keeping with the whole, slow, steady, linear evolution away from the core beliefs of the Leninist Revolution that the Soviets have experienced since 1917. It is also in keeping with the new Soviet concern about the precariousness of nuclear systems, in the wake of the reactor disaster at Chernobyl in 1987. Such concerns have been taken up, now, by a new generation of Soviet leadership, centering around Mikhail Gorbachev, whose political perspectives have been forged since Josef Stalin and since World War II. The new circumstances and the new perspective together create the so-called new thinking.

Domestic priorities unquestionably have helped to account for the changes of policy. But there are also fresh cords of rational connectedness in international security thinking itself. The new arms-control posture of the Soviet Union, for example, is connected to an evolving battlefield strategy and to a resource allocation plan that combine to give it depth and sustainability. As these elements emerge, they should serve to strengthen the perceived authenticity of key notions like strategic interdependence and reasonable defense sufficiency.

This is not to say that the Soviets will be immune from all temptations to advantage-seeking in the old familiar way. They are likely to seek their own balance of opportunities in the Third World, and not to accept dictation on this score from the United States. The Soviets may also be inclined, less wisely, to look for ways of dividing the Western alliance; that would not be in their interest, any more than it would be in the interest of the United States to fragment what remains of the Warsaw Pact. Both sides have things still to learn about stable de-escalation.

One of the most important of these will be to distinguish between agreements that are worth seeking and those that are not. Before Gorbachev's accession it was often claimed by American politicians that "you can't trust the Russians," and it is evident that this concern must be overcome. There have in the past been some agreements, like parts of the Yalta and Helsinki accords, that the Soviets have not observed, just as there have been others, like the Nuclear Test Ban and Nonproliferation Treaties, with which the Soviets have fully complied. The difference, which needs to be underscored, is that the honored agreements have (1) served the parties' interests and (2) been enforceable. Those are the only kinds of agreements to which the two parties should in future subscribe.

The interests of the Soviet Union and of the United States coincide in that each power needs to avoid nuclear and financial disaster. Arms restraint is therefore a proper subject for mutual agreement. Human rights may, however, be less so. The Soviets have their own internal reasons for wishing to modernize their society, but it is not in order to become fully Westernized and not in obedience to outside pressures. Any provision on human rights that fails to recognize those limitations, or is not suitably reciprocal, is likely to fall short. That could cast doubt, again, on the whole enterprise of negotiated de-escalation.

There will be enough difficulties without that, on the enforceability side of arms-reduction agreements. Both sides could benefit from a lower level of armaments, but to arrive at that level without destabilization will require a high degree of confidence in each other's performance. (This would not have been true of reductions carried out in the immediate aftermath of World War II, but there have been 40 years of distrust since then.) The problem is that verification is getting increasingly difficult to carry out, as mobile missiles and dispersed conventional forces make monitoring by established methods inadequate. Unilateral force reductions, of the kind announced by Gorbachev at the UN in December 1988, do not escape this difficulty; if they are to be successful in persuading others to follow suit, they too must be verified.

An unpatrolled arms agreement could be worse for mutual confidence in Reciprocal Security than no agreement at all. Also unhelpful for this purpose would be the adoption of unrealizable goals. Gorbachev seems sometimes to have fallen prey to that temptation, as when he called, at Reykjavik and elsewhere, for the elimination of all nuclear weapons—something as physically impossible as the destruction of all human memory. The call gave him a momentary high ground in public opinion, but that sort of ground cannot long be held. Also in the same category, perhaps, was Gorbachev's December 1988 troop cutback, or more exactly those parts of it that were pushed through against the advice of his military high command. The ensuing resignation of Marshal Sergei Akhromeyev, on grounds of "health," was not too serious a loss by itself, although it threatened to cost arms control one of its ablest and most respected negotiators. What would be serious would be any consequent loss of internal or international confidence in the political coherence of the arms-control process itself.

Security policy, unlike social reform, succeeds or fails in what other nations make of it. When Mikhail Gorbachev denounces nuclear deterrence, as he has done, he strengthens the hand of those in America who promote the SDI "space shield" he opposes. Without meaning to, he repeats the mistake of Leonid Brezhnev, whose invasion of Afghanistan helped to stimulate the so-called "Reagan doctrine" of assistance to anti-Soviet guerrillas. Before that, the errors belonged to Josef Stalin and Vladimir Lenin, creating a history and an atmosphere that would progressively militarize American foreign policy and make it difficult for Americans to adjust to a new Soviet outlook. Reciprocal Security, from now on, will require attention on both sides to what has changed and to what remains in need of change.

2

Cycles and Stabilities in American Perception

American receptivity to Soviet change has been constricted and made wary by past experience. In the spring of 1987, after two Reagan-Gorbachev summit meetings had already been held, the senior Kremlinologist on the White House staff could warn in a speech that "the U.S.-Soviet relationship is fundamentally one of competition, a competition of values . . . and a competition of power . . . notwithstanding the appearance of the Gorbachev regime . . . or of 'new thinking' in Moscow. . . . If the Soviets have their way, by force or duplicity, people will lose their freedom, war or the threat of war will continue, and vital U.S. security concerns will be jeopardized."

That was a reflection of the original Cold War understanding, first formulated in 1950 after the Soviets had moved to exercise control over Eastern Europe. "The Soviet Union," said the Truman White House and State Department in a document called NSC-68, "is animated by a new fanatical faith, antithetical to ours, and seeks to impose its absolute authority over the rest of the world." That description, since declassified, has never been revised.

American policies toward the Soviet Union have changed from time to time in the intervening years, but in a cyclical way, as if unable to free themselves from this founding proposition. In 1963 President John Kennedy pronounced a goal of global interdependence, and follow-up connective measures were initiated, only to be drawn back when the Soviets invaded Czechoslovakia in 1968. The Nixon administration then took up its theme of détente and carried that through to the beginnings of an arms-control regime, only to have Watergate and Afghanistan and the election of Ronald Reagan pitch relations back once more to the level of 1950. In the first Reagan term, there was actual opposition both to arms control and to any form of constructive diplomacy—because, as Arms Control Director Eugene Rostow explained it to a caller, there was no room for that: "The Soviets are out to conquer the world."

Much of this cyclical preoccupation has had to do with American reluctance to accept the possibility of Soviet change, as if that country alone in the whole sweep of history were somehow exempt from evolution. Soviet leaders certainly have been slow to recognize the need for change, and slower still to espouse it, but their political culture like any other is obliged to adapt or die. The Soviet learning curve has been an expression of their historical experience, whose movement and direction must be gauged by Russian criteria. The parallel for them is probably not with Europe or with America but with 19th-century Japan—another feudal society reaching, later than others and from necessity, toward modernization.

Americans should be able to recognize that the main, objective forces now reshaping U.S. policy horizons—namely, the fragility of the nuclear balance, the rise of regional power centers, and the costs of global superintendence—impose their weight on the Soviet Union as well. Both nations are beset by serious budget imbalances, both face unmet domestic needs, and both could profit from a reduction of global tensions.

As some see it, however, there is a possibility that the Soviets might use such a pause to modernize and regain their strength. The renunciation of international ambitions could emerge, in this view, as a step toward a future Soviet resurgence as a world power, using advanced weapons systems, for example, developed in the interim. Any prudent American policy would have to take that possibility into account. A Soviet resurgence would not, however, be able to overcome the objective limits to world hegemony. And there is at least an equal probability that the Soviet Union which emerges from a moderating pause, 15 to 20 years from now, will hold more moderate ambitions. To try to preempt such an evolution seems, on any thoughtful reckoning, imprudent.

Blunt exercises of preemptive force, assuming they were feasible, would not be likely to dissuade the Soviets from pursuing whatever course they choose. The World War II siege of Stalingrad, and the legendary ability of Soviet citizens to pull their belts tighter against outside impositions, should remind us of that. As Secretary of State George Shultz told a New York audience in 1984, power must be connected to diplomacy or neither will get very far. Our allies in Western Europe and Japan have been much attracted to the seeming reasonableness of Soviet world conduct since Gorbachev's accession, and for America now to be merely blunt would risk alienating those alliances and thereby weakening our security.

In the Third World, where Washington has tended in times past to see a Soviet hand behind every disturbance, the course of Gorbachev's retrenchment since 1985 has made it plain to objective eyes that the causes of instability, in Central America and elsewhere, are mostly indigenous and have little to do with superpower maneuverings. Attempted American subversion measures, like the Reagan Doctrine, are—as even conservative opinion now sees them—unsuited to countering the new Soviet sophistication.

The upshot of these tempering insights is not that the U.S. should withdraw from the world, but simply from the illusion that the world is locked in an ideological contest. The fact is, as Alexis de Tocqueville pointed out 150 years ago, that it is not the divergence of ideologies but the convergence of ambitions that has arrayed the two superpowers against each other. "There are," de Tocqueville wrote in 1835, "two great nations in the world, which seem to tend toward the same end. . . . I allude to the Russians and the Americans. . . . Their starting point is different, and their courses are not the same; yet each of them seems to be marked out by the will of Heaven to sway the destinies of half the globe." It was as he said the similarity of the two goals—both powers "tending toward the same end"—that drew them along competing paths, and not their differences. At the time this was written, Karl Marx was just a teen-aged boy who had yet to find his way to the British Museum. What was gathering its forces to produce the rivalry was not philosophical but political: the clash of great-power ambitions.

A contest of great powers—Sparta against Athens, Rome

against Carthage, England against Spain—can resolve itself through victory or exhaustion or the intercession of outside factors. In our day it is the outside factors of nuclear peril, financial stress, and global unmanageability that are laying the ground for a great-power settlement. Those factors speak with cogency to policy makers who are willing to pay attention in either the Soviet Union or the United States.

U.S. policies are ripe for reconsideration because, although they have won the peace, they have done so at high levels of cost and risk. If those levels could now be prudently reduced, it would help to carry the peace into the next century. Whether and how far this can be done will depend on the state of the rivalry and on the degree of American influence within it.

In 1947 the equation seemed clear: The Soviet Union had unlimited ambitions and so the United States would have to mount an unlimited defense. When President Truman asked Congress for economic and military aid to Greece and Turkey, he accompanied the request with what became known as the Truman Doctrine. "It must be the policy of the United States," this said, "to support free peoples who are resisting attempted subjugation by armed minorities or by outside pressures." The pronouncement was immediately heartening to people who were on the front lines of the Cold War; veterans of the American Embassy in Moscow from those days remember how their spirits were lifted by Truman's declaration. Others, however, both then and since, have been more troubled.

Senator Robert Taft, the conservative leader of the day, was concerned that an unlimited commitment could lead to world war or to bankruptcy. Certainly it could lead to confusion and overextension: Who would qualify as "free peoples," and how would we know whether "armed minorities" were acting for or against freedom? Senator Arthur Vandenberg, the Foreign Relations committee chairman in 1947, swept such distinctions aside and told Truman that if he wanted Congressional support he would have to "scare the country to death" with his description of the communist challenge. That is what was done.

When President Truman went to Congress, he was surely moved by the real necessity to shore up Europe against the threat of domination by the Soviet Union. Captain Harry Truman of the U.S. Army Artillery would also have remembered, however, the way in which Americans after World War I insisted on the immediate dismantling and return of the American Expeditionary Force. Truman must therefore have felt his own compunction to paint the Soviet menace in broader terms than were strictly warranted—to speak a "truer truth," as Dean Acheson called it. Hence the overcommitment of the Truman Doctrine, the pledge to combat communism wherever it emerged, even if wholly indigenous and even if it presented no threat to the objective interests of the United States.

This led in time to American military engagements outside Europe, to Korea and Vietnam and thus to the eventual unraveling of American public support for the overdrawn elements of the Truman Doctrine. The divisive experience of Vietnam, with its casualties and demoralization, was soon followed up by a comparable Soviet experience in Afghanistan; reunions even rose up among veterans of the two wars. If the Soviets now are willing to draw a lesson in favor of retrenchment, there seems little reason for Americans to demur.

There are those in this country, however, who doubt that the Soviets can be left to themselves to do the right thing. Among persons of this persuasion are both "Promoters" and "Preventers"—those who would aid and those who would block the process of Soviet reform. While the two groups disagree fundamentally with each other about the value of *perestroika,* both take the view that America can and should intervene to affect its success.

In this they are both almost certainly wrong. The Preventers, people like former Assistant Defense Secretary Richard Perle, never seem quite able to explain just how the United States would put together the leverage needed to thwart Soviet reform. Nor do they pay much heed to the dangerously destabilizing impact on world peace of any successful disintegration of the Soviet Union— particularly one whose result could be laid at America's door. As the historian John Lewis Gaddis has written, "some of the most dangerous moments in world politics come when a Great Power perceives itself as beginning to decline . . . and is tempted into irresponsible action against its rival to redress the balance while it still has strength left to do so."

On the other side of the equation are the Promoters, many of whose names appeared on a 1987 task force convened by the Institute for East-West Security Studies. Its report took the view that "it is an American interest to encourage Mr. Gorbachev's reforms" and that "the West should therefore seek to strengthen his hand." The U.S., they said, should offer rewards, such as the removal of trade and credit discriminations, if and when the Soviets carry out their announced reforms. This is called "probing" or testing, by some, and its difficulties are considerable. A self-regarding person whose good faith is "probed" by another is at least marginally *less* likely to carry out what he had intended to do; the intrusion, by standard behavioral principles, displaces the conduct being examined. If by chance the Soviets should accept an outside inducement to reform, it could be a sign that the reform impulse on that point was weak. For reasons of this sort, American "help" for Soviet reforms seems unwise, even though—and to a good extent because—those reforms are likely to be in the American interest.

There have been mixed opinions about intervention in the public media, sometimes favoring and sometimes opposing both "Prevention" and "Promotion" schools of thought. A *New York Times* editorial of March 9, 1987 expressed what seems to be the better view. Although "there is no guarantee that a reformed Soviet Union will be more benign," the *Times* wrote, "Washington and its Western partners should not fear saying yes on the theory that what's best for the Soviet Union is automatically worse for the West." The paper added: "It is a mistake to exaggerate the impact of American support or opposition on Mr. Gorbachev's reforms. They will turn preeminently on internal Soviet circumstances."

Or, as Congressman Lee Hamilton of the Foreign Affairs Committee put it more succinctly in the *Christian Science Monitor* of June 29, 1988: "It is not up to us, nor is it within our power, to 'help' Gorbachev. He must face his own problems and find his own solutions."

America lacks the capacity, realistically, to help or to hinder Soviet reforms. On a practical level, and despite repeated claims to the contrary, Western credits and technology are not essential to the Soviet Union. U.S. leverage on the Soviet economy is constrained by the core strength and self-reliance of that economy, and also by the divisiveness—within the U.S. and the West—of attempted economic controls. A professed aim of the first Reagan term, to "spend the Soviets into bankruptcy," wound up exposing a financial vulnerability in the U.S. economy. The reciprocal idea, of American collaboration made contingent on Soviet reforms, runs up against its own reality limitations. It is like the story of the hijacker who put his pistol to a pilot's head and demanded to be taken to Detroit. "But sir," the pilot sputtered, "this plane is already going to Detroit." Leverage of that kind is not likely to be useful.

Change with stability, historically, has been promoted less by sectoral leverage than by the tempering of general relations, coupled with the inner confidence to pursue reforms. That is the lesson of the Jackson-Vanik amendment and of other efforts to stimulate internal change by external "linkage." The effort has repeatedly failed: Soviet Jewish emigration has gone up and down, for example, with the general condition of East-West relations and not with particular U.S. inducements. In the closing months of the Reagan administration, when the Soviets stopped jamming Western radio transmissions and liberalized the award of exit visas, chief U.S. human-rights negotiator Warren Zimmerman candidly advised the press that these moves were products more of the internal Moscow reform movement than of any Western pressures.

The Soviet political culture, it must be said again, is a law unto itself. The culture is changing, but by its own inner logic and not by any ineluctable process of Westernization. The logic constrains both leaders and led along a certain path, even when it is awkward or painful to take that path. Western barriers and bridges are largely beside the point, except as momentary distractions. They are distracting not just to the Soviets but also to a proper American understanding of our interests and opportunities. There is a need at last to shed the old habit of projecting our culture onto the Soviet Union, and of supposing that we have the power of making that culture emerge. This is a basic error, and it distorts our perspectives.

Mikhail Gorbachev told NBC anchorman Tom Brokaw before the 1987 Washington summit meeting that "you should not go into another man's monastery with your own charter." Elaborating, in his book *Perestroika* Gorbachev wrote:

> It is probably not easy for a foreign reader to understand many of our difficulties. It is only natural. Each people and each coun-

try have a life of their own, their own laws, their own hopes and misconceptions, and their own ideals. Such diversity is wonderful; it needs to be developed, rather than stifled. . . . In our complicated and troubled world it is impossible to measure everything by one's own yardstick.

America for its part has tried two kinds of yardsticks, beckoning and belaboring. It is possible to think of these as alternative measures of engagement, or outside pressure: constructive and destructive. A posture of Destructive Engagement is what was on view in the Reagan first term, while Constructive Engagement was the Nixon-Kissinger pursuit. Neither succeeded, and neither—on reflection—could ever have had much chance of succeeding.

Robert Oppenheimer, the chief developer of the atomic bomb, once described the relationship of the nuclear superpowers as that of "two scorpions in a bottle." So long as neither scorpion has room to turn aside, all that either can do is sting and be stung to death. In the U.S.-Soviet context it is vital that there be room for movement, that deterrence not be so menacing for example as to provoke a deadly first strike. This is what was wrong with the Reagan administration concepts of counterforce strategy and of winnable nuclear war, with its deployment of the MX missile and its sponsorship of "Star Wars," along with the other incidents of a coercive policy. Their cumulative contributions to Destructive Engagement, or threatened superiority, were bound to harden animosities. It was only after they were abandoned or downplayed, in the second Reagan term, that improvements in the relationship and in the security balance could begin to take place.

The alternative posture—Constructive Engagement—was never adequately described by the term "détente," which in diplomatic parlance means the relaxation of tensions or a turning away from confrontation. The Nixon-Kissinger idea was to continue confrontation while surrounding it with a web of cooperation in scientific and business and other realms, so as to soften if not eliminate destructive propensities. It was virtually a policy of "entente," though never explained that way. Over time, the hope was, mutual trust would develop sufficiently to transform the relationship into a friendly one.

This did not happen, in part because too small a slice of the American voting public was engaged in the effort but mainly because cooperation is the product of good relations and not a sufficient basis for them. Virtually all of the Nixon-era agreements for U.S.-Soviet cooperation—on pollution control, health research, space missions, and the like—lapsed or were terminated when the political climate changed. That is because common behavior can be no more combining than the common interest that underlies it. There was, realistically, no over-riding common interest when it came to these more peripheral fields—certainly none that could survive the shoot-down of a Korean airliner or the invasion of Afghanistan. Candor compels recognition that, if the Soviet Union were not a military giant, we would pay little cooperative attention to it—and it has not been shown to be useful to pretend otherwise.

Politically, our two nations are more incongruent than congruent. That fact dooms Engagement of any kind, whether Constructive or Destructive. The two societies are just too different. There is a congruence on the root issue of survival; that much seems clear, even though it is sometimes disputed. But to encumber that mutual interest with an expectation or demand that the Soviets behave in accordance with our political wishes—on such matters as human rights, or Third World diplomacy—is to burden survival with an extraneous and unsustainable weight. The Soviets will and must act in accordance with their national character and history and interest as they see it, just as we must and do. Neither stick nor carrot, coercion nor collaboration, is going to change that basic truth. To build American security on any other expectation seems quite unwise.

Ordinary human experience tells us as individuals that if we insist on an office rival or a balky relative doing as we want, the only thing we will actually have done is to hand that person the power to determine our peace of mind. Far from exercising control, we will have handed it over. We will have positioned ourselves to jump when the other person sneezes—even though it may be clear that we are not at risk of catching cold. The only way to escape from such dependency is to *detach*. That may seem difficult sometimes, but it is done, and it is manageable. What is true in this regard for human relations on the individual level ought also to be broadly true for the relations of whole peoples.

There is a further related note. Adversaries come to resemble their enemies. America has been transfixed by preoccupation with one enemy or another for nearly fifty years—first with the Nazis, then the Communists. If we count the Depression and the special efforts it summoned forth, it is now more than sixty years since Americans last behaved in easy accordance with their own national character; and the state of American liberties frequently shows it. Yielding to an alien culture the power to determine our security creates a set of tensions that can only diminish *real security*, which is definable as the freedom from disruptive intrusion into personal or communal integrity. No one could persuasively claim that the United States has enjoyed much of that kind of security in recent years.

The internal disturbance we have experienced, our adaptation to insecurity, has bred periodically a mimicry of the disruptive behavior traits of our proclaimed adversary—even down to reflexive, tit-for-tat actions undertaken because the Soviet Union has done them or might do them, without any close regard to how such actions harm or benefit our national interests. How often have we been told that we must build such-and-such a weapon, or incur such-and-such an expense, with the only reason being to "counter" a parallel activity of the Soviets? There are, of course, routine matters that need to be dealt with on the basis of exact reciprocity, such as the construction of embassy buildings in the two capitals. Beyond that, however, reflexive parallelism shows up all too often in asymmetrical circumstances, where Soviet acceptance of a U.S. preference is desirable but not essential. The curtailment of travel privileges for American visitors in the USSR has led for example to like limitations on Soviet travel and speaking rights within the USA. As that case illustrates, tit-for-tat responses may displace American values and even procure a victory for Soviet values within our country.

A "Pavlov's dog" relation to the Soviet Union, where we salivate at their will, is neither dignified nor free. The neural jerk of reflexive mimicry, if extended broadly across our polity, would amount to a kind of national defeat, or loss of independence, every bit as diminishing in its way as an invasion or takeover of our society. Of course if there were no choice, if we had to jump to a Soviet tune no matter what, we would probably do so in good heart, like the defenders at the Alamo. But we are far from being without other choices.

The chief alternative is that set out long ago by Walter Lippmann, in a series of articles published the year the Truman Doctrine came out. Lippmann endorsed what he called "the Marshall line" of policy, for General George Marshall, the author of the Marshall Plan for Europe and of the non-intervention policy in China. Wrote Lippmann:

> The Marshall line in China is not an application of the Truman Doctrine, but of an older American doctrine that we must not become entangled all over the world in disputes that we alone cannot settle. . . . [Likewise the] Marshall Plan for Europe . . . was that only a European plan for Europe could save Europe. . . . The difference is fundamental.

For, as Lippmann summed up, "the line of the Marshall policy . . . [is] to give up the attempt to control events which we do not have the power, the influence, the means, and the knowledge to control."

The alternative to Engagement, put simply, is Detachment—from the things that we need not, or cannot, control. In traditional diplomatic terms, the posture suggested is one of Constructive Detachment, a reversion to that "older American doctrine" first set out by General George Washington in his Farewell Address. It is a policy not of isolation but of effectiveness, one that allows the nation to pursue its essential interests while eliminating distractions.

A policy of Constructive Detachment in today's world would enable the United States (1) to pursue its own vital interests, (2) to inform itself about comparable Soviet interests, and (3) to engage the Soviets where, and only where, those interests intersect. There is a difference for this purpose between interests and values. Americans have many reasons to disagree with, and to dislike, Soviet values; the reverse may be true for them. But relations between states with differing values have traditionally been made possible by resting them on a congruence of interests. That is how America has found it possible to maintain stable relations with states like South Korea and Chile, despite anti-democratic practices. The same should be true for the USSR, all the more so because of its great-power standing.

The second element of the proposed policy—informing ourselves about Soviet interests—is important and frequently overlooked. For Constructive Detachment goes hand in hand with understanding. It was the counsel of Talleyrand, the great French diplomatist, that for every hour of negotiation with a rival, ten minutes should be devoted to seeing how things look from inside his skin. It is not always easy to penetrate the Soviet skin, that "riddle wrapped in a mystery, inside an enigma," as Churchill called it in Stalin's day. But *glasnost* has begun to unwrap the enigma, and scholars can now describe with considerable accuracy the essentials of the Soviet political culture.

The roots of the Soviet experience are different from our own. They include the spiritualism of Eastern Orthodoxy, with its sense of "Mother Russia," or national destiny; a set of open borders that have attracted multiple invasions and occupations; and, along with that, a deep-seated sense of inadequacy toward the West. Soviet diplomacy, which can be brash and tough and secretive, derives from the fear-inspired practices of the medieval Byzantine court. Feelings of inferiority and of spiritual mission, taken together, can make up a volatile mix. It is important not to shake but to understand them.

Human rights, for example, could benefit from a thoughtful comparative analysis of values and practices on both sides. The Soviet tradition stresses communal values, downplays individual rights, and winds up promoting freedom to do something: hold a job, have a house, get medical attention. The American culture by contrast stresses individual rights, downplays communal values, and ends up championing freedom *from* something: press censorship, religious dictation, arbitrary arrest. The two formulations are not wholly at odds, but enough so that insistence on identity is a bootless enterprise. Time spent understanding each other's differences would be time better spent.

There are other bootless enterprises, which might equally be discarded. One is the idea, frequently put forward, that a web of economic relations by itself can take the animosity out of U.S.-Soviet relations. A senior British civil servant, experienced in the trade field and sympathetic to expanded economic relations with the Soviet Union, put this notion in perspective recently by observing that England in modern times has "traded with absolutely everyone and gone to war with absolutely everyone." There are many good reasons for enlarging trade and investment with the Soviet Union, but this is not one of them.

Another device that deserves to be abandoned is the use of

security negotiations to promote internal Soviet conduct that we might find congenial. There is a long history of this, going back nearly 60 years, and all of it has failed. In the Litvinov letters of 1933 (religious toleration), again at Yalta in 1945 (democratic self-government), in Washington with the 1974 Jackson-Vanik amendment (Jewish emigration), and finally at Helsinki in 1975 (freedom of press and petition)—on each of those occasions the United States has sought to extract assurances of political behavior from the Soviet Union that (a) it was not in that country's perceived self-interest to honor, and that (b) our country lacked the means to enforce. The "linkage," or confusion, of security with internal matters in this fashion has been neither advantageous nor effective. Secretary of State George Shultz eventually drew the appropriate conclusion and brought such linkage to a close. The two countries now still talk about human rights, but in a channel separate from security negotiations and free from mutual interference.

Where interests intersect, it is appropriate to engage. But the fact that some form of agreement can be written does not prove that there is an intersection. There have been several fruitless efforts to design "codes of conduct" as instruments of superpower restraint. President Nixon signed two such codes with the Soviets in his détente period, each with sweeping provisions and neither with any effect. A code of conduct, like these, that reaches for more than it grasps, can cause more harm than good by breeding suspicions of bad faith or noncompliance. Far more effective, to date, has been the quiet conduct of nonbinding diplomatic and military consultations aimed at discovering each other's interests and intentions.

Constructive Detachment, then, embraces the pursuit of *necessary* engagements, defined as those that directly affect and can benefit vital U.S. interests. We need for this purpose to distinguish between Soviet conduct that endangers and that which merely offends our interests. The denial by Moscow of human rights, as we Americans would define them; its political involvement in Third World countries; its championing by propaganda of what we would consider alien ideology—all these can be offensive to us because they dramatize the division between the two cultures and because we are effectively powerless to prevent them. They are not, however, threatening to our security; and the fact that we lack power over them is reason to detach.

The intersecting vital interests of the United States and the Soviet Union are few and simple. They are to avert nuclear devastation, and military hostilities that could trigger such devastation, while also avoiding financial collapse. That is essentially all. It is remarkable in this connection how little the two powers have between them that could serve as a cause of war—no disputed border, no competition for the same resources, no rivalry for the allegiance of a pivotal power that might change the security balance. It is also striking, and of equal importance, how little the two powers really need to agree upon. Across almost all of their relations, they can safely afford to leave their differences unsettled.

America cannot disengage from the Soviet Union, however, or find independent safety, on the issues of nuclear arms or European armies. The first is clear and the second should be no less so. Twice in this century American forces have been drawn into war by European hostilities. A World War III generated by any sudden breakdown in European security arrangements would probably be fatal to this country, and also to the Soviet Union. The two great powers therefore have a clear, continuing, joint interest in East-West European force stability during the extensive and intricate process of theater arms reduction that lies ahead. There can be no room in this process for unilateral burden-shirking or advantage-seeking, no matter how tempting either may be. Fears and concerns will have to be allowed to subside, over a considerable and complex period of adjustment, with all the patience and forbearance this implies.

The techniques of security engagement appropriate to this purpose will be both bilateral and alliance-wide. They will include arms control, trouble-spot consultation, and deterrence guided by considerations of Reciprocal Security—by a sensitivity, that is, to the impact on each country of force dispositions adopted by the other. "Star Wars" for example may appeal to a popular yearning for impregnability, but when its practical effect is seen as being to stimulate Soviet preparations for a nuclear first strike, the conclusion to be drawn is that it degrades American security. This is the teaching of the Siberian bear, which applies to both sides.

To understand each other's security perceptions, both nations will need to practice an active diplomacy backed up by an informed, objective intelligence. Official efforts along these lines can be reinforced by private travel and study, as well as by the conduct of ordinary business transactions. The insights that traders and scholars and artists bring back can serve as a valuable check on official perceptions in both countries, and ought for this reason to be insulated as much as possible from politics.

Beyond that, the United States and the Soviet Union can each detach from efforts to control the other, and reap the considerable benefits that ensue. This is not a contingent opportunity: It is available to either country, regardless of what the other does. Americans can save money, energy, and aggravation by letting the Soviets incur their own outward defeats, as they have done, in locales like Angola and Ethiopia and Kampuchea. We can let the Soviets dabble in Iranian politics, if they wish, secure in the lesson of recent years that whoever grasps that nettle will be less composed afterward than before. The more likely outcome of Constructive Detachment, however, is that the Soviets will continue their course of external retrenchment, in order to focus their attention on internal reforms. They too will find it useful to detach.

There is no aim or need in any of this to make the USSR an ally of the United States. "The history of diplomacy," as Walter Lippmann wrote in his 1947 series, "is the history of relations among rival powers, which did not enjoy political intimacy, and did not respond to appeals to common purposes." Such rivals can get along without being alike. Neither do they need to see each other as implacable enemies. To the contrary, it should become much easier to deal with the vital issues of nuclear and conventional arms once the clutter of political feelings is cleared away.

The financial interests of both countries would also be served, of course, by a reduction of resources devoted to nonessential ends. This is a matter of considerable importance to America's standing in regions like the Pacific Rim, whose countries have let it be known that they are concerned about the strength of the financial scaffolding behind our security posture. Economic solidity is widely perceived as being essential to political strength, and without some rigorous self-disciplining efforts both so-called superpowers could come to look like paper tigers.

In terms of the direct U.S.-Soviet rivalry, a prudent refinement of America's security posture would allow the United States to meet skill with skill at a lower level of engagement. During the Iran-Iraq war, America dispatched so many naval vessels to the Persian Gulf that they constituted a virtual occupying force; yet it was Soviet diplomacy, backed by a comparative handful of ships, that tended to carry the day. In politics as in art, less can quite frequently be more.

Non-military competition may be left to flourish without concern. A healthy rivalry would in fact be good for the United States. It could awaken us to our interests and opportunities in places where we currently take them for granted. Singapore, for example, has for some time been publicly pilloried by American publishers and politicians as a den of copyright "thieves," with little apparent concern for the vital security crossroads that Singapore commands. A little Soviet nibbling at our vulnerabilities in such quarters should help to restore a more balanced perspective.

Constructive Detachment would free America to pursue its own independent agenda in the world. Freedom and security both ultimately depend on our being able to set our own priorities, separate and apart from Soviet behavior. Americans have a positive face of their own to show to the world on each of the points of emotional friction with the USSR—human rights, Third World development, and ideology. It is time to get back to doing so.

The United States has cause to feel confident of its competitive capabilities in such a rivalry, if it lives up to its own principles. That is because concepts that are central to the American value system—consent of the governed, liberty of conscience, open markets—are widely prized; they have an instrumental value for all modernizing societies. There is reason indeed to suppose that history may be running with the American idiom of ease and freedom and openness, if we will just go with the tide and not try to force it.

For that to happen will require America to rid itself of the excess security preoccupations that have led it to be false to its own traditions. Cold War legislation like the McCarran-Walter Act, under which the United States has excluded "aliens" like Graham Greene and Pierre Trudeau because of their "past, current or expected beliefs, statements, and associations," have depreciated the First Amendment and diminished America's standing in our own eyes and the world's. Constructive Detachment can help to eliminate such liabilities.

Once that happens, America should be able to strengthen its magnetic influence on the tide of internal reforms all over the world—including the Soviet Union—by the power not of demand but of example. George F. Kennan's pivotal contribution on this point, his 1947 article on "The Sources of Soviet Conduct," portrayed America's influence on the USSR and elsewhere as a function of:

> . . . the degree to which the United States can create among the peoples of the world generally the impression of a country which knows what it wants, which is coping successfully with the problems of its internal life and with the responsibilities of a world power, and which has a spiritual vitality capable of holding its own among the major ideological currents of the time.

That still describes the pending challenge.

A successful American foreign policy must be responsive to the character of the American people, without whose support any policy will founder. Yet the course chosen must also be one that can serve the nation's long-range interest, of which the public may at any given time have only a limited understanding. Policy toward the Soviet Union has had difficulty holding its course against the fluctuating nature of American public opinion—impatient, generous, moralistic, self-critical, patriotic, uncompromising, and intolerant of ambiguity as that opinion has been since this nation emerged from isolation a few short decades ago. There needs now to be a more systematic educational effort. As John Steinbruner has written, "the United States is unlikely either to initiate its own changes in policy or react appropriately to Soviet diplomacy until there is a better developed, more widespread conceptualization of the need to do so."

We must begin with the values and psychology of a buoyant people, conditioned by history and good fortune to look for prompt and decisive results from their country's entry onto the world stage. World War I, we remember, was promoted as a "war to end wars" and to expand democracy. That optimism was drawn short after World War II by the frustrations of a protracted and unsettling Cold War. Now that the Soviets have opened up the possibility of ending that War, ways must be found of reconciling American impatience with the time-consuming business of an actual settlement.

Politicians in both countries may find it tempting, as they have in the past, to bypass public opinion or to manipulate it for their own ends. Impatience and intolerance of ambiguity are qualities that can be stirred. There are leaders, for example, like former president Richard Nixon, who have favored stimulating danger if need be so that Americans will not drop their guard all at once. Artificial stratagems can be heard also from the other side, such as Mikhail Gorbachev's suggestion that the two countries resume their World War II alliance. Neither euphoria nor suspicion of these sorts will establish the solid opinion base on which a stable relationship can be founded.

That is one of the lessons of the Reagan presidency. When President Reagan went to Moscow in 1988 and declared his close friendship with General Secretary Gorbachev, this represented not just the end of a particular policy cycle but also the continuation of its underlying premise. The U.S. approach to the Soviet Union remained, after this episode—as it had been for fifty years—bipolar and naive. We could still deal with the Soviets on the basis *either* of fear ("evil empire") *or* of hope (Red Square embrace), but not—up to that point—on any realistic combination of the two.

That is what remains to be changed; and in this, the American people may be out ahead of their leaders. The most searching opinion surveys on the subject, conducted by the Public Agenda Foundation, show that Americans want tension reduction but are also wary of Soviet advantage-seeking. They entertain, in other words, *both* hope and fear. Theirs is a movement of opinion into ambiguity rather than away from it, and suggests a readiness to support a realistic policy.

That invitation must be taken up by American policy makers, if they wish to bring about a soundly based change. Past shifts of policy have failed in good measure for lack of public explanation and engagement. President Nixon, for example, though he spoke often of "détente" and of a "structure of peace," never managed to explain to the electorate just why those policies should be expected to work. The Nixon-Kissinger diplomatic exploits, while striking, were so narrowly controlled within the White House that they could gain no lasting support among politicians or the public. The fruits of the 1972 Moscow Summit withered on the vine for want of a supporting consensus in the country at large. When Nixon lost office, his policies soon followed. The Soviets, who had agreed to keep the negotiating channels closed, discovered to their chagrin that their "private line" with the White House had no politically deliverable America on the other end. They are unlikely to want to repeat that experience.

A comparable misstep occurred just a year later, in the discussions leading up to the Helsinki Accords of 1975. Their so-called "Basket One" confirmation of post-war European boundaries was, standing alone, in the security interest of the United States. That is because Stalin's seizure of Eastern Europe had created a source of future instability for the Soviet Union, and therefore for all its Western rivals. Helsinki's renunciation of forced change in the territorial status quo was accordingly in the interest of stability and peace, and marked an important progression toward the future healing of the division of Europe: The radical Eastern transformations of late 1989, and the Soviet decision to accept them, would likely have been impossible without Basket One. All this must have been reasonably clear at least in outline to the Helsinki negotiators, who nevertheless in the end lost confidence in the American people. They judged that to cover themselves against criticism they would have to come up with some form of "compensation" for Basket One. The result, Basket Three, purported to transplant American human-rights practices onto the Soviet political system. That was not realistic. Such practices had never been part of the Russian political culture, under the Tsars or otherwise, as must have been plain to anyone who had ever read Pushkin or Dostoevsky. What was created, therefore, was a needless apology for a real security achievement (Basket One), and a new source of friction (Basket Three) to impede further security achievements.

There are ways, fortunately, to get past such misconceptions, and to bring the public constructively into the foreign-policy process, without forsaking the consistency or confidentiality of that process. One way could be by use of a Blue Ribbon Commission, backed by the President and composed of prominent political generalists, commissioned to search for a sustainable new consensus on U.S.-Soviet relations. Perhaps half of such a body's appropriation might be earmarked for public discussion of the commission's report, at the end of which the President might submit to Congress for its review and adoption a brief statement of the principles that should guide future policy. This would allow the Truman Doctrine consensus of 1947 to be brought up to date and reformulated.

For too many of the years since 1947 it has been the practice among national-security "insiders" to disparage the policy contributions of the press, the public, and the Congress, as if high policy were somehow too precious to share with the country it is meant to serve. The occasions on which political backing is sought, usually for budget or treaty approval, are too narrow and sporadic to capture the full nature of American security concerns. These encompass the whole ongoing rivalry between two large, diverse, changing, and incongruent systems. The American public, attracted by change but uncertain what to make of it, must be made to feel comfortable about the soundness of our basic approach to that rivalry. To generate that assurance, nothing can substitute for wide-open public discussion.

This book is an effort to promote that discussion. It aims in particular to aid public understanding of the limits of U.S.-Soviet commonality, and of the two countries' ability to persuade each other. It seeks to demonstrate that we cannot, and need not, change our separate societies into images of each other. America and Russia have a narrower field of common concern, one that can be made more manageable by excluding the unnecessary.

The essential elements of this approach, once more, are Constructive Detachment from what annoys us and Reciprocal Security for what endangers us. These coincide with declared Soviet aims ("New Thinking," "Reasonable Sufficiency") and are straightforward enough to commend themselves to American opinion. In diagrammatic terms, the elements look like this:

U.S.-SOVIET RELATIONS

General Disengagement:
CONSTRUCTIVE DETACHMENT

Security Engagement:
RECIPROCAL SECURITY
(Soviet "New Thinking")

Authentic Self-Expression:
Values, Traditions, Aspirations

Prudent Self-Defense:
Non-Provocative Force
(Soviet "Sufficiency")

Improved Understanding:
Diplomacy, Intelligence,
Trade, Education, Exchanges

It will be useful to bear this diagram in mind as we examine in Parts Two and Three the Soviet side of the balance, looking at the course of their reforms both internal and external. In a concluding section we will consider concrete proposals for an American security agenda that can connect to what is solid and durable in Soviet policy, and that fills out the schematic diagram.

PART TWO

Internal Affairs

3

The Need for Reform
of Soviet Internal Policies

The authenticity of the reform impulse in Gorbachev's Russia has been broadly accepted by all segments of Western opinion. This is important because the character of reform, and its future prospects, both depend upon a recognition of the basic need for change.

Gorbachev called the economy he inherited a "pre-crisis" economy. The Stalinist system was no longer working: Growth rates were flat, innovation weak, and internationally the Soviet Union had fallen to third place as measured by Gross National Product. So it was not really surprising that in February 1985 the Party Politburo should have turned to a known reformer for its next General Secretary; or that, a year later, at his first Party Congress, Mikhail Gorbachev should assign lead priority to revitalization of the economy: "The most crucial task of the whole Party and the whole country," he declared, "is to overcome the unfavorable tendencies in economic development . . . in the shortest possible time."

Those "unfavorable tendencies" had produced a series of economic disasters. In agriculture, the forced collectivization of private farms by Josef Stalin in the 1930's had put more than 98 percent of arable Soviet land into giant and inefficient collective operations in which the peasants worked as hired laborers. The wastefulness of this arrangement was dramatized by the fact that the remaining 2 percent of the land, which was divided into small private plots, produced some 30 percent of the country's food. Nearly half of the country's large collective farms operated either at a loss or on the margin, requiring annual subsidies of $32 billion. Perhaps a third of every Soviet grain harvest was wasted for lack of roads, storage, and transportation facilities, and never reached the consumer. Although the Soviet Union as a result imported vast amounts of expensive grain along with meat, sugar, and butter to feed its people, it was a struggle for the average citizen to keep the family larder stocked.

Factory output too was distorted by central determination of prices and production targets. Energy usage per unit of output was three times higher in the Soviet Union than in the average Western economy. Consumers had to make do with low-quality goods and services, long lines, and an absence of product innovation. On the job, morale was poor as manifested by weak productivity, absenteeism, and widespread drunkenness. Expectations of improvement had declined, and workers' children could no longer look forward to getting a higher education or better jobs than their parents.

The Soviet press reported the far-ranging effects of economic failure. *Izvestia* estimated in the 1980's that 120 million people, or 43 percent of the population, were struggling to make ends meet. The publication *Nedelia* reported that 150 million Soviets could not obtain a quality refrigerator or a washing machine. These shortages affected pensioners and young couples alike, along with millions of ordinary industrial and farm workers. Even two-wage families, becoming the norm in the USSR as in the United States, were described as having to make do without good clothes.

Housing was a particular sore point. While rent levels were kept low by a Soviet subsidy, few if any apartments were available. By the late 1980's, the waiting list for housing units in Soviet cities had reached five years, even for the privileged: The son of one senior Party official was reported in Western newspapers to be unable to join his new bride for want of a Moscow apartment.

The serious effect of these deficiencies on internal morale was heightened by their equally serious implications for Soviet world standing. Without a quickening of its agricultural and industrial pulse, the USSR might sink to the status of a second-rate power.

A wry joke to be heard in senior Soviet circles at this time was that the Soviet Union was descending to the level of a "Sierra Leone with rockets." This was intolerable for a self-proclaimed, science-based society. Particularly as the advanced industrial societies of the West were entering into the so-called Information Age, where productivity is an offshoot of data access and sharing, the tightly centralized control over economic transactions that had characterized Soviet society since before the Russian Revolution could not measure up.

Theoretical science and mathematics had always been a strong point for the USSR, but their application was much less so. To a considerable extent, the barrier was one of attitude. The best Soviet researchers were to be found in academic institutes, isolated from manufacturing plants, and their view of Western-style competitive research was that it was wasteful. Only 3 percent of *kandidat* researchers in the Soviet Union served in industry, as compared to 24 percent of scientific Ph.D.'s in the United States.

In the 1950's and 1960's, as the Soviets entered the Space Age with satellites and vehicles, their leaders and people could feel for a time that they were competitive players in the high-technology game and perhaps were even gaining on other countries. By the 1980's it was clear, however, that the West had been advancing more rapidly, so that while the Soviets were continuing to register gains, the gap between the two growth curves was widening. The Soviet Union in other words was falling progressively farther behind.

Soviet research strategies, particularly in the military, have registered successes with known challenges like the H-Bomb and space launches, but they have not been effective at looking over the horizon or at achieving full competitive equality. Soviet rockets are impressive but they use mostly liquid fuel instead of the more stable solid fuels, while the Soviet space program leads in levels of activity but lags in sophistication. The Soviet Union has not been a global competitor on such major technological fronts as superconductivity, the fifth-generation computer or communications transmission networks. Despite extensive efforts since the late 1960's, the Soviets have not been able to mass-produce or to absorb into industry a world-class personal computer.

The biggest competitive drawback for the USSR has been the absence of an independent, competitive, industrial sector, which in the West has served as the seedbed for high technology. Technology imports cannot cure this deficiency, and could perpetuate it by building in a dependence on foreign imports. Gorbachev insisted in a speech at the space complex in Kazakhstan in May 1987 that the Soviet Union must take pride in its own technology and scorn reliance on imports. As his advisers would have told him, even covert acquisitions of foreign technology miss out on spare parts and operating know-how; while reverse engineering of imported equipment can teach one at most about yesterday's technology. To recover momentum, and begin reducing the East-West technology gap, Gorbachev would have to restructure and revitalize the whole scientific enterprise in the Soviet Union.

Its deficiencies were part of a more general economic decline that Gorbachev had inherited. The Soviet budget deficit was running at about 11 percent of Gross National Product, roughly twice the rate of the more publicized American deficit. Defense spending, according to the best available estimates, consumed some 15 to 20 percent of GNP, as compared to 6.5 percent for the United States and 3.3 percent for the average West European economy. These disadvantages stemmed from a number of systemic causes, which Western economists identified as follows:

1. A long overemphasis on growth, as opposed to efficiency, and on security expenditures to the neglect of domestic infrastructure, along with the substitution of consumer price subsidies for the stimulus of needed innovation.
2. The convergence of economic, social, and political dilemmas for which there was no painless response. Letting Eastern European economies go free to seek their natural partners in the West, for example, would relieve a substantial burden on the Soviet economy, but at the cost of increased anxieties about security.
3. A declining rate of growth of the Soviet population, ruling out the traditional solution of using more labor to offset reduced rates of productivity. The one significant demographic increase, among Muslims in Central Asia, raised its own problems for social planners.
4. The nature of the system itself: Soviet society had many strengths, but its ingrained acceptance of authority, with

resulting passivity and inertia, cut the wrong way for a situation that demanded initiative and change.

There were, as this last point suggested, surviving strengths and stability in the Soviet economic system. Not all was a wasteland by any means. Economic security in the Soviet Union was widespread, involuntary unemployment was virtually unknown, and price levels had remained steady for a long time. How to keep that stability in place, while fostering growth and innovation, was bound to be a perplexing dilemma. Gorbachev would have to find a way, for example, of containing the enormous pent-up inflationary force of the 300 billion rubles estimated to be held in Soviet savings accounts, plus another 100 billion or so tucked away in mattresses. His success as a reformer would be measured by the degree to which he could manage to reconcile the conflicting impulses of stability and change, initiative and restraint.

The generally downcast state of Soviet civic morale by the winter of 1985 made it imperative that some start be made toward revitalization. There was economic stability but, along with it, a visible slowdown; also, a constriction of expectations and of social mobility; an impending loss of the Russian ethnic majority within the Soviet Union; widespread acts of drunkenness and misbehavior, coupled with low workplace productivity; and a decline of pride in Soviet accomplishments, whether in science or on the world stage.

Behind these factors lay the general passivity and inertia that had long characterized social attitudes in the USSR, not just under Communism but before that under the Tsars. There was a lingering medieval cast to Russian society, nurtured since time immemorial by a succession of strong national leaders, and left untouched by the humanizing sweep of the European Renaissance and Reformation. The Western idea of a "social compact," of society as something anterior to the state and giving it its legitimacy, had never reached Kiev or Leningrad or Moscow—never, at least, until now.

Josef Stalin's one-man rule had taken advantage of this disposition to impose a personal, almost oriental, despotism on the society. Nikita Khrushchev's great contribution in 1956 was to break this reign of terror and to replace it with oligarchic power-sharing within the ruling party. His successor Leonid Brezhnev in turn restored the privileges of officialdom and the penalties of dissidence, but without reinstating one-man rule. In December 1984, after Brezhnev and shortly before Gorbachev, a dozen leading American specialists on the Soviet Union summed up the resulting state of civic attitudes as follows:

There were, they thought, three main classes of Soviet internal unrest: (1) nationalistic and religious dissatisfaction with Communist control, believed to be widespread but not—apart from the author Alexander Solzhenitsyn—vocal or explicit or otherwise apparent on the surface; (2) liberal, democratic, intellectual dissent on the model of Andrei Sakharov—highly visible, but engaging a very small percentage of the population; and (3) the concern of the general citizenry to obtain rights and liberties that could be guaranteed in practice and not just on paper. None of these hopes or desires was then being given much scope.

Sakharov was a figure who had become a thorn in the government's side even before he won his Nobel Peace Prize in 1975. Twenty-five years before that, he had come to world notice as a principal developer of the Soviet hydrogen bomb. In 1968, he published an essay titled "Thoughts on Progress, Coexistence, and Intellectual Freedom," arguing for expansion of individual liberties in the Soviet Union and for cooperation between East and West. After the Helsinki Accords of 1975 Sakharov took up the fight for widening of Soviet liberties, and in 1979 he protested publicly against the Soviet invasion of Afghanistan. That led to his arrest in January 1980 on a Moscow street, and his banishment to Gorki, a city 250 miles away that was closed to foreigners. There he remained as a standing reproach, in Western eyes, to the Soviet political system.

A more instructive case in some ways was that of the 1987 Nobel Literature Prize winner, Joseph Brodsky. Brodsky was an émigré poet whose engagement was to the Russian language, not the state. A convicted "parasite" whose crime in 1964 was that he was too detached from the social struggle, Brodsky spent five years on a state labor farm for his posture of literary diffidence. He afterward said without irony that he enjoyed and profited from the solitude. When offered a chance after his release to emigrate to Israel, Brodsky declined on the ground that he felt no more affiliation there than elsewhere. Finally in 1972 he was forced onto a plane and sent to Vienna, where he was met by an American publisher who arranged for a home and a job. In the 15 years from that point to the awarding of the Nobel prize, none of Brodsky's Russian poetry had been published in the Soviet Union—until, just before the award, the journal *Novy Mir* offered to do so.

That offer was significant, as was Brodsky's reported response: "About that, I will not celebrate too much." Brodsky did not wish to be used by the Soviet authorities, or to enter into any sort of political transaction with them. In this he was quite unlike Andrei Sakharov, and more like the renegade ant that the young King Arthur was turned into, by the wizard Merlin, in T. H. White's *The Once and Future King.* That ant arrived in the colony and came across a large sign that read: "EVERYTHING NOT FORBIDDEN IS RE- QUIRED." Arthur, like Brodsky, declined the summons.

Many Soviets would not have done so. The regimented society that Brodsky left, and Gorbachev inherited, was an outgrowth of ingrained political attitudes that disparaged individual initiative and prized communal discipline. The idea of "democracy" was not wholly alien to Brezhnev's Russia, but it was enveloped by tradi- tion in a counteractive wrapping. "Democratic centralism" was the prevailing creed, with the emphasis heavily on the centralism. As the Columbia University political scientist Seweryn Bailer put it in the early Gorbachev period, even a democratically chosen Soviet government would be likely to be centrally directed, with a profes- sional bureaucracy in charge of things and selected by the leader- ship.

The political system inherited by Mikhail Gorbachev, from which he himself emerged, was one that focused all power in an authoritarian, self-perpetuating, and monastic Communist Party. That power in turn was lodged primarily in the Politburo and Secretariat of the Party's Central Committee. All of the important decisions—on the economy, on national security, on social af- fairs—were made in these narrow precincts and then imple- mented through a nominally separate government directed by a Council of Ministers. The legislative arm of that government, the Supreme Soviet, met briefly twice a year and rubber-stamped its approval of the measures put before it. The Presidium of the Su- preme Soviet represented the government between sessions, and its elected leader was called "President," but neither held any real authority.

The overlap between government and Party offices was considerable, in two senses. First, the senior office holders were often the same: The Politburo—as a kind of executive council for both Party and government—typically included the chairman and perhaps the deputy chairman of the Council of Ministers, the foreign and defense ministers, and the head of the KGB (state security). Second, there was duplication of functions as between the Party Secretariat and the Council of Ministers: The Foreign Ministry's organizational structure would be largely replicated, for example, in the International Department of the Secretariat.

Within the Party, the lines of authority ran to the Central Committee from a Communist Party Congress, which was ostensibly the supreme and legitimating organ. It consisted of delegates elected by local and regional Party committees around the country. Ordinarily, however, it convened only once every five years and its agenda was set by the central Party office. It served, therefore, more as a resonator than an originator of Party policy.

The Party Congress did elect the Central Committee, which met as a rule in plenary session at least every six months. The Central Committee was made up of some 400 members, as compared with the smaller Secretariat (about 10 members) and Politburo (12 or so members) that it formally elected. The Politburo in turn chose its General Secretary, who at the time of Gorbachev's selection was the single most powerful figure within the collective leadership. He had the power of initiative in personnel selection and policy formation, subject to the acquiescence and cooperation of the leadership structure as a whole. There were no term-of-office limitations on the General Secretary or on other Party leaders.

These arrangements made for Party control but also for inefficiency and the stifling of initiative. There was no feedback, or accountability, in domestic policy matters. The Party was able to communicate its intentions downward, but it had difficulty learning how well those intentions were received or how fully they were carried out by local officials.

When Gorbachev began devising his economic and social reforms, he soon encountered these limitations. The implementation of his reforms was blocked by mid-level managers and Party people who, in some cases, genuinely doubted the value of the measures, while they also feared the loss of their authority. The system did not allow Gorbachev to determine or deal usefully with the exact nature of their apprehensions. He was left to complain at large about the faceless bureaucracy, which was not calculated to win its support or to make Gorbachev look like a commanding leader.

There were reasons enough to be concerned about the unresponsiveness of entrenched authority in the government and Party. The managers of bureaus and offices and economic administrations throughout the country had acquired the status of a *nomenklatura*—"listed insiders"—who could claim special privileges in housing, chauffeured automobiles, access to Western consumer goods, and the like. It was a factor tending to divide the servants from the served, and to set the former apart from the public. Officials who were cosseted in this way could not be expected to lead the charge for broad-scale displacements of the status quo.

Another impediment to social and economic improvement lay in the Soviet legal system, which was both arbitrary and manipulable; it fed the prerogatives of the *nomenklatura* and discouraged the initiative of ordinary Soviets. Partly, there was no effective instrument for law enforcement within the government: Decrees or regulations drawn up at one level could be rewritten or ignored at another, by officials who probably thought themselves better able to determine what would work. This allowed a way to defeat both reforms and their accountability; it would have to be cleared up in some manner before any effective restructuring could take place.

The problem was also one of excessive, and again undisciplined, law enforcement *outside* the government, against people like Andrei Sakharov who were trying to improve their society. A great deal of unchecked prosecutorial and police discretion was vested in the authorities, through broadly worded Criminal Code prohibitions of social criticism and of "hooliganism"; under these laws, journalists and other perceived troublemakers could be swiftly restrained and intimidated. There was in the law no right to defense counsel before a judicial investigation was concluded, no right to bail or other release during the nine months this inquiry might take, no right to a jury, and no right even to an unbiased court. The Soviet judicial system was notorious for its "telephone justice," by which Party officials felt free to tell judges how to rule.

Plainly this was not an environment that could encourage

private initiative or daring. There were in the Soviet law at this time no enforceable rights of expression, or conscience, or privacy. Nor were there individual rights of property or any comparable bases for a "social compact" between citizens and their government. The industrious ant of King Arthur's fantasy would have seen no need for such a thing. All it would have expected from the law was what, historically, had been provided in the Soviet Union: Party control over the state; state control over the economy; and "parental" guidance for the people.

That had been enough, perhaps, in the pre-decline USSR. But by the mid-1980's it was evident that authority alone would not be able to rescue the Soviets from their near-crisis condition. There would need to be initiative, and challenge, and competition; and all these non-antlike attributes would have to have their way cleared for them by purposive political reform.

There was at the time, however, no separate legislature by which to check the Party or government; no autonomous press or judiciary to hold either of them to account; no federal sharing of powers with regional or local governments; and no competing political parties to put the ruling Communists to their mettle. What there was, mainly, was a governing monolith that operated more as a barrier to structural reform than as a channel for it. There would have to be some institutional change.

But there would also have to be some elements of continuity. The Soviet monolith for all its limitations had produced internal peace and stability, as well as external power and prestige. As with economic reform, so also with social and governmental change, the new policies could not run all one way. There would have to be a mixture of volatile and sometimes antithetical elements; the chemistry might be exacting. A reform administration, such as Gorbachev was invited in February 1985 to establish, would need to make measured choices and be willing to return to them from time to time as required.

4

The Character of Reform

Gorbachev and his colleagues applied themselves to the task of internal reform by stages. First they took small, relatively conservative steps aimed at making the existing system work. When these fell short, progressively larger bites were taken at the problem—not by any overall design but experimentally, to find a solution. Some initiatives caught on, others were less successful. The new feature with Gorbachev was that he was prepared to keep trying, to abandon or reshape his own ideas when they missed fire, to pull back and await a better occasion. He was also ready to move ahead when conditions allowed. This made for a string of remarkable accomplishments in his first five years, and laid the foundation for further progress in the years to come—even though many of the practical difficulties he had inherited, in agriculture and industry, technology and consumer goods, were left unimproved by 1990 over what they had been in 1985.

Gorbachev came to the leadership from several years as Minister of Agriculture, where he had developed a technique of "contract" agriculture, by which small groups in a collective farm could contract to produce certain yields, the incentive being that they were allowed to keep and market the surplus. That was expanded, after 1985, to a system of family contracts for the short-term leasing of land and equipment from a collective farm. This was not

privatization on the Chinese model, it did not allow for employment of workers from outside the farm or family, and it did not
do much to expand agricultural production. There was, really, no
large-scale market to sell to apart from the collective farms themselves.

In industry, Gorbachev began with exhortation and calls to
discipline, aimed at squeezing the "human factor" to push more
productivity out of existing arrangements. This yielded little improvement, so Gorbachev introduced the idea of structural
change, proposing to shift resources and rewards away from inefficient sectors and workers and toward more efficient ones. At the
27th Party Congress, his first, Gorbachev described the task of
industrial reform as one of shifting from more to better use of
resources, from quantity to quality of output, from "extensive" to
"intensive" development of the economy. To achieve this objective
would require some decentralization of authority from ministers
and mandarins to enterprises, their managers, and workers. In
1986, however, his first full year as General Secretary, Gorbachev
simply put these ideas on the table without specifying how they
were to be achieved.

In the social realm, again, Gorbachev attacked the problem of
low morale at first by a regime of discipline, cracking down on
shirkers and alcohol abusers. His anti-alcohol campaign was me-
thodologically a mistake, repeating the fallacy of Prohibition in
the United States. The restriction of sales bred resentment and
resourcefulness in equal measure. In 1987, the whole of Cuban
sugar imports disappeared into private Soviet distilleries. After an
estimated 10,000 deaths had resulted from "bathtub vodka," the
restrictions were relaxed to the extent of allowing uncontrolled
sales of wine and beer. Soviet medical authorities began at this
time to express serious interest in the Western experience with
noncoercive addiction-correcting techniques.

1987 was also the year in which Gorbachev turned more generally to the relaxation of social controls as an instrument of
morale improvement: A few days before that year began, he put
in a telephone call to Andrei Sakharov's Gorki apartment and
invited him to return to Moscow to do "patriotic work." Sakharov,
the patron figure of Soviet dissidence, at once accepted the invitation and returned to the Academy of Sciences; from there he
emerged periodically in succeeding months to bestow public

praise or blame on Gorbachev's policies and performance. At one stroke, the most visible outcast from official society had become a highly visible participant in its reform. This made an immediate and favorable impression on his younger fellow scientists, and on the Soviet intelligentsia generally, who began from that moment to believe there was a real prospect of revitalization.

Other noteworthy dissidents were also released from confinement during this period, including Yuri Orlov and Anatoly (later Natan) Shcharansky, who wanted to leave the country and whose departure was more beneficial to Soviet morale and prestige than their retention had been. Even though some of these persons took up campaigns of vilification against the Soviet regime, the bad press this occasioned was less severe than what had been produced by their imprisonment. Gorbachev was beginning to see the true cost of a pound of flesh.

A sampling of stories from the Soviet and Western press during 1987 gives an idea of what liberalization looked like in its first full year:

- Workers in a bus factory who went out on strike were saved from criminal prosecution when the investigative *Moscow News* reported that the plant had been refusing to buy needed new equipment. In the end the plant manager was fired and the automobile ministry authorized a fresh investment.
- The film *Repentance* explored the crimes of Stalin before packed audiences, after a ban on its showing was lifted. A play by Mikhail Shatrov, *The Brest Peace,* dealing with the Soviet Union's 1917 withdrawal from the First World War, was cleared for presentation after 25 years; it showed Lenin debating on equal terms with Trotsky and Bukharin, both "non-persons" in official Soviet history.
- *Doctor Zhivago,* by Boris Pasternak, was brought down off the shelf of prohibited works two decades after his Nobel Prize. A comprehensive showing was held at the Pushkin Museum of the expressive folk paintings of Marc Chagall, the first ever provided in his native land.
- Mikhail Gorbachev told *Pravda:* "There should be no forgotten names or blank pages in history or in literature." On the 70th anniversary of the October Revolution, he condemned

Stalin's crimes as Khrushchev had done, but this time in public; and he took the first steps toward the political and legal rehabilitation of Bukharin.

- A welter of informal membership groups sprang up to champion social reform, among them Press Club Glasnost (human rights), Delta (the environment), the Perestroika Club (the economy), and the Federation of Socialist Clubs (an umbrella group). Communist Party auspices were provided for their meetings, and a commission was set up to assign them some kind of official status.

To match these indications of a political new beginning, Gorbachev moved promptly in his first year in office to start changing the faces of the leadership around him. He saw to the creation of a favorable working majority in the Politburo, appointed five out of the then seven non-voting members of that body, and named six out of the seven non-Politburo members of the Secretariat. In the estimation of Oxford University specialist Archie Brown, "no Soviet leader had presided [in his first year] over such sweeping changes in the composition of the highest Party and state organs as Mikhail Gorbachev." A year later, in 1987, the Joint Economic Committee of the U.S. Congress calculated that Gorbachev had by then replaced about 40 of the 90 heads of ministries and state committees. It said he had created "an air of momentum and expectation."

But this did not carry very far into the Central Committee, a majority of whose members remained independent of Gorbachev, or into the deep substructure of local and regional Party officials who sponsored and sustained those members. Everywhere, outside of Moscow and a few major cities, the secretaries of the Party organs and their thousands of underlings owed, in Seweryn Bialer's reckoning, "neither bonds of personal loyalty to the General Secretary nor a deep commitment to his reforms." They were resistant to those reforms and to their own replacement.

Gorbachev began to work at that, but incrementally, as was becoming his practice, finding a less controversial starting point for his more controversial objectives. In a speech to a January 1987 Central Committee plenum on personnel restructuring, he proposed that workers choose their managers and that Party committees elect their leaders—by secret ballot, from slates of multiple candidates. He also proposed in a preliminary way the competitive election of local legislatures, as a step toward democratization of governmental bodies. The aim of all this, he said, would be to inject accountability, or what he called "control from below," into the operations of economic and Party and state units throughout the country.

Although not widely noticed in the West at the time, this January 1987 speech was, as Andrei Sakharov termed it, "an extraordinarily important" one. It kept that character even after the Central Committee had watered down Gorbachev's specific proposals, calling in general terms for public "expression of attitudes" and "participation" in the selection of leaders. The door was now open.

That same month, a Komsomol (Young Communist League) chapter in Alma Ata, Kazakhstan chose its secretary from among a slate of three candidates. In Dnepropetrovsk, in March, the two candidates proposed for department head of a mining enterprise by the local Party bureau were rejected by workers, who nominated and elected a third candidate by secret ballot. And in Moscow, after the leadership slate of the local Filmmakers' Union was thrown out by the rank and file, more than half of the national directorate was replaced by younger writers and directors, who pledged themselves to resist censorship and to put art ahead of politics in their work.

In June 1987, elections for local legislatures, or soviets, were held in selected districts around the country, offering a choice of multiple candidates and a secret ballot. A few Party secretary posts were also put up for competitive election by local leaders sympathetic to the course of reform. At the same time, Soviet employees became broadly free to choose their managers in "enterprises, factories, workshops, departments, sections, farms, and teams," to use Gorbachev's inclusive phrase.

There was some question about the utility of such elections. Seweryn Bialer wrote, persuasively, that plant democracy was not efficient and Party efficiency was not democratic; Gorbachev was "inverting" democracy and putting elections in at the wrong end. But the new Soviet leader had his own tactical reasons for doing so. As later appeared, he was preparing the ground by stages for higher-level elections; and, at the local or plant level, he had interests other than immediate efficiency in mind. "A house can be put in order," Gorbachev said at the January 1987 plenum, "only by a person who feels he owns the house." That sounded a symbolic more than a practical note, and would have to be appraised on that basis.

A course of "trickle-up" democracy could be slow, however, and the need for senior leadership changes—or, more precisely, for the picture of policy dynamism these would convey—could become acute. On September 30, 1988, a Central Committee meeting was held in Moscow at very short notice. Andrei Gromyko was ushered out of his ceremonial presidency and Mikhail Gorbachev was ushered in. Yegor Ligachev and Viktor Chebrikov, two important conservative leaders on the Politburo, were rotated out of their sensitive assignments in charge of Ideology and State Security. Vadim Medvedev, a Gorbachev protégé, was given the Ideology brief and Alexander Yakovlev, a close Gorbachev ally, was put in charge of Foreign Policy. Ligachev and Chebrikov assumed new responsibilities for Agricultural and Legal Policy, respectively, while a new figure, Georgi Razumovsky, took charge of Party Building and Personnel Policy. There were other shifts, but these were the major ones.

Their sudden accomplishment was a sign that Gorbachev had taken charge of the Party hierarchy; beyond that, estimations differed. Robert Legvold of the Harriman Institute said the meeting was notable chiefly for not having dealt Gorbachev a setback. From the perspective of the Soviet political establishment, this assessment seemed justified. The chief obstruction to *perestroika* was coming not from the top of the structure but from the mid-level and local managers and functionaries. Rolling a few heads at the top, by itself, would not do much to lift up the dragging feet at the bottom.

The most significant appointment in this regard was probably that of Razumovsky to head the personnel policy commission. Gorbachev had let it be known that as many as a third of all regional Party organizations, along with half of the Central Committee bureaucracy, might be targeted for elimination. This meant, if such reductions were carried out, that the "barons" of the Party would have fewer resources with which to intrude into day-to-day economic and social activity. On April 25, 1989, at another special meeting, the Central Committee received the engineered resignations of a fourth of its own membership, Brezhnev-era holdovers known as "dead souls." Now the barons themselves were changing, and the new ones brought in—people like Eugene Velikhov and Valentin Falin—were politically aligned with Gorbachev. Responsibility for decisions would be pushed by these changes from Party toward government, from center toward periphery, from official toward private, and from collegial toward individual shoulders. That in the main was Gorbachev's political objective.

A Central Committee plenum in June 1987 gave approval to a set of far-reaching economic "theses," designed to grapple for the first time with the structural shortcomings of the Soviet economy. Gorbachev identified these with scathing particularity in his opening speech, and pressed the Central Committee to endorse new legislation for state enterprises and private cooperatives. What emerged from the plenum was a basic policy shift.

There was to be more independence for the large state enterprises, which were to be free to negotiate with each other and thereby to move away from the command environment in which they had grown, toward a regime, primarily, of contract. The enterprises were to become "self-financing" out of their own earnings, and to turn for outside capital to repayable bank credits rather than to government handouts as in the past.

There was also to be a diminution of the layers of bureaucratic supervision, so as to make them more strategic and less intrusive. Producer goods such as flour and steel and machine parts were to be traded at wholesale among the state enterprises, rather than allocated centrally as had been the case. There were also to be changes in price levels and price-setting mechanisms, with most prices set in negotiated transactions and only a few—for critical commodities like fuels and raw materials—continuing to be fixed by central authorities.

Also, private enterprise was to be sanctioned to a certain degree, for after-work "moonlighters" or authorized cooperatives. As this idea developed, it grew to encompass the hiring and firing of outside workers (previously regarded as "exploitation"), the buildup and reinvestment of enterprise capital, and the formation of joint ventures with state-owned firms. Mainly the idea was to set a competitive standard for lethargic state companies, in light industry and consumer goods like restaurants and repair shops.

The cooperative idea spread, in time, to farming. In July of 1988, a new law authorized collective farms to rent out their land and livestock and equipment to private farmers for periods up to 50 years. That, it was hoped, would help turn around the growing shortage of food on the consumer's table, and would also cut the large operating losses being run up by inefficient collective farms.

The guiding objective in all this was to move toward incentives and opportunities, and away from obligations and penalties, as a way of achieving distributional efficiencies and levels of quality that the Soviet system had not until then been achieving. Tatyana Zaslavskaya, an economic sociologist who came out of Siberia (Novosibirsk) to become a close policy advisor to Gorbachev, described the reforms as a package that would define "the rights, obligations, and responsibilities of the economy's basic component." She said it would constitute "the genetic code for all our economic legislation."

The 1986–88 reform package by itself, however, represented less of a code than it did a concept of how to proceed from bureaucracy to initiative, from command to contract. The parts did not all fit together. Some moved in conflicting directions, others were internally incoherent or incomplete. What the Gorbachev leadership produced at this period was a call to policy combat, with two crucial steps in the battle plan still unfinished: (1) a fleshing out or explanation of the basic strategy, and (2) its implementation in practice. Both would be difficult to complete, although each received a boost from the spadework of these years.

Strategically, it is important to observe that the Soviet reform architects were not aiming for full-blown, Western-style market competition or even for the Hungarian or Chinese variants of "market socialism." They did not really know what these models entailed, having never been exposed to the central ideas of economic value or allocation as taught and practiced in other countries. In the Soviet economic culture, markets have been seen as messy and chaotic. So, in moving "from socialist competition to economic competition" as Gorbachev put it, market forces would be given room but not dominance. Their key Western attributes—pricing freedom, ease of entry, freedom to fail, and access to capital—were absent, in any systematic sense, from the Soviet plan.

What Gorbachev was seeking instead was a revitalization of the traditional Socialist system drawn, this time, by a new engine to be put together as things went along. What exactly this engine would use for traction—some parts pushing and others pulling— was left to be worked out by experience and opportunity.

Higher motivation and morale, Gorbachev hoped, would supply a good part of the fuel. The technological and literary intelligentsia had by then been captured for *perestroika*, through the release of Andrei Sakharov and other liberalizing measures. What was to follow was a systematizing of social reforms under the general heading of *glasnost*.

Glasnost signified the public airing, or ventilation, of significant matters for a public-policy purpose. The root of the word lay in "glas," meaning "voice" in Church Slavonic. It did not mean a freeing up of discourse for its own sake, nor freedom of expression in the Western sense. In the hands of the Soviet leadership, *glasnost* meant "voiceness" for a purpose, and that purpose was to galvanize society for service of the state.

Alexander Yakovlev, the Politburo member and ally of Gorbachev who at one point directed the propaganda department of the Central Committee, made this explicit when he told the Soviet media under his charge that they should seek out controversy and report with accuracy so as to create support for *perestroika*. Gorbachev himself directed the press to feature "heroes of restructuring" in their coverage. Viktor Afanasyev, the editor of *Pravda*, said that for him there was no conflict between *glasnost* and propaganda: "We are a Party newspaper." Although stories began appearing that had never been seen before—crime, corruption, scandal, condemnation—they were the product not of any general freedom but of a directed license. The "voiceness" was didactic.

This was illustrated in the new regime's handling of Soviet history, which was ventilated as never before but still for political purposes, not as an exercise in dispassionate scholarship. Gorbachev's 70th anniversary exoneration of Bukharin, for example, rehabilitated the theoretician of Lenin's New Economic Policy at just the time that Gorbachev was promoting his own version of a similar economic renewal. His continuing silence about Leon Trotsky, an advocate of worldwide communist revolution, was in keeping with Gorbachev's efforts to reduce tensions with the West. Both were purposive treatments of history—as was also, for that matter, the release of the Shatrov play *The Brest Peace*, which showed Lenin arguing against Trotsky (and on the side of Gorbachev) that the Soviet state needed peace as a "breathing space" for its development.

The purpose of *glasnost,* and of social liberalization in general, was to revitalize a moribund state. It was to modernize the culture, the Soviet way of mind, by drawing out in a controlled way the latent creativity of the people. *Glasnost* offered a means of overcoming entrenched social and political barriers to *perestroika,* by shaking up the apparatus of officialdom and enlisting energies outside the established structure. It was played out for this purpose across the whole gamut of what Americans would call civil liberties—of person, discourse, assembly, worship, and travel. The enlargement of these liberties by the Soviet government, and their continuing curtailment in certain respects, are both instructive.

By mid-1987, the number of prisoners of conscience in jail in the Soviet Union was already less than in several authoritarian countries aligned with the United States. Further releases followed, and new arrests declined, as did the practice of interning dissidents in psychiatric hospitals. Gorbachev wanted such people at large, for the contributions they could make and for the stimulus their freedom would provide to other thinking people. Andrei Sakharov's comment was: "Objectively, something real is happening. . . . I myself have decided that the situation has changed."

Sakharov also made note of the changes in press freedom under Gorbachev, saying that the articles then being published looked like those for which people had been jailed in the 1970's. Unofficial journals, produced by released dissidents and others, began appearing. Soviet television started casting its eyes on the shortcomings of officialdom, in shows like *Twelfth Floor* and *Spotlight on Perestroika,* which were not only searching but smart with a new and arresting tempo and style. *Vremya,* the evening television news, a show seen across all eleven Soviet time zones, became accurate and persuasive; listenership for the BBC and the Voice of America dropped correspondingly for the first time in decades, without any Soviet jamming. Muscovites began lining up at their newspaper kiosks for the daily and periodical press, with its salty new diet of revelations, in the outspoken *Moscow News* and in *Ogonyok,* as well as in other journals.

Full freedom of the print or electronic press, to criticize any aspect of the ruling government or Party, was not introduced. The announced policy was that Soviet correspondents were free to question announced policy, but that did not happen to any degree. Instead there was a draft Press Law, which undertook to divide the press into "official" and "unofficial" segments. In theory that would open up the latter to journalistic freedom. But, as drafted, the law would hold all reporters penally accountable for their errors. The controller of journalistic license would remain the government— which, for the moment, chose to see press latitude as being in the public interest.

Another liberty whose scope was enlarged was that of assembly, of meetings and demonstrations. Small unofficial discussion groups were both encouraged and protected by the policy of *glasnost,* in part to stir up stodgy organizations like Komsomol, the Communist youth league, which was losing membership and interest. Larger voluntary organizations, like the neo-Stalinist *Pamyat* and the anti-Stalinist *Memorial,* were tolerated but not visibly encouraged. The smaller groups met in August 1987 and drew up a set of social goals which the authorities to some extent supported: an end to censorship, access to official archives, and the freedom to stage demonstrations. News conferences and small demonstrations were in fact permitted by the KGB in 1987–88, at least in places where the Western press could observe them, so long as they did not provoke disturbances. A group of Crimean Tatars was even allowed to stage a "homelands" protest right next to the Kremlin walls—a high-water mark from which toleration thereafter receded.

Nationalities protests were in general not favored. They were an awkward reminder that the Soviet Union is a non-homogeneous society, a mosaic of some 120 distinguishable nationalities, whose cultural and political harmony remains unaccomplished. *Glasnost* without limits might let loose a discontent among these groups that would be difficult to manage. That was one boundary to the right of assembly. Another was the articulation of political goals by the new, informal groups, which might if allowed pose a challenge to the political monopoly of the Communist Party. The August 1987 Federation demand for the right to nominate dissident candidates, and to publish their platforms in the established press, was ignored by its Party sponsors. The proper use of assembly, in their eyes, was to promote social engagement and not political pluralism.

On the religious front, Gorbachev's aim was not promotion but toleration. He offered legislation to confer on church congregations the rights and powers of legal entities, withheld since Lenin's 1918 decree, "On the Separation of Church and State." Dissident priests, like Gleb Yakunin, an outspoken Orthodox cleric, were released from confinement and reinstated in parishes. *Moscow News* and the *Literary Gazette* carried articles defending the rights of churches and believers. Baptisms were freed from the requirement of prior notice to the government, and they multiplied. The teaching of Hebrew was authorized, along with the establishment of a Moscow Center for Jewish Studies. Bibles became easier to secure. In 1988, to celebrate the Russian Orthodox millennium, Gorbachev received its hierarchy in his Kremlin office and authorized the transfer of the Patriarch's headquarters from Zagorsk, 60 miles away, to the newly restored Danilov Monastery in the capital city.

This did not erase the provision in the Soviet constitution declaring atheism to be the official state belief. Gorbachev summed up his policy in 1988 as follows: "We do not conceal our attitude to the religious outlook as being non-materialistic and unscientific. But there is no reason for a disrespectful attitude to the spiritual-mindedness of the believer, still less for applying any administrative pressure to assert materialistic views." The truth was that Gorbachev needed the energies and the sustenance of Russia's 100 million professed believers, more than five times the listed membership of the Soviet Communist Party. Once before, during the terrible World War II sieges of Stalingrad and Leningrad, the Party had rallied the nation with appeals to the memory of the great patriarchs of history. Now again, more subtly, the same kind of appeal was taking place.

Religious believers were among those who had difficulty securing the last of our examined liberties: the freedom to travel. Most publicized among those detained were the Jewish *refuseniks,* people whose very applications to emigrate doomed them not only to denial of a visa but to the loss of domestic jobs and status. In 1974 the U.S. Congress tried to affect this situation by passing a law, the Jackson-Vanik amendment, that conditioned the normalization of U.S.-Soviet trade on a relaxation of Soviet travel restrictions. The numbers allowed to travel went up for a time, to 51,000 in 1979, but then declined steeply to only a few hundred a year by

1986. Gorbachev turned the figures around, pushing the authorized departures up to 8,000 in 1987 and 19,000 in 1988; by the end of 1989, the annual exit figures exceeded 60,000, well above the levels achieved a decade earlier.

The reason for this relaxation was not so much to benefit those who left as to gain the allegiance of the many more who would remain. The Vice President of the World Jewish Congress, Rabbi Alexander Schindler of New York, put the issue in perspective by stating that in 1985 some 200,000 Jewish applications for exit visas were on file in Moscow. As to these, he said, it was appropriate to insist: "Let my people go." For the two million Jews who would choose to remain in the Soviet Union, and whose natural increase would replace the ones that had departed, the demand should be: "Let my people stay . . . with full encouragement of the Jewish tradition." This was the line that Gorbachev himself adopted, against the resistance of Soviet officials who traditionally saw departure as an act of hostility, or unpatriotism, against the state. Foreign Minister Eduard Shevardnadze had to warn the Soviet consular service, explicitly, in November 1988 that the time had come to stop treating émigrés like "class enemies." That same year, for the first time, past emigrants were given entry visas for short return visits to their homeland.

The two main purposes of *glasnost*, then, as exhibited in the treatment of these various liberties, were to stimulate creative energies and to overcome bureaucratic obstacles. When either of these purposes would be served by the exercise of a particular liberty, the practice under Gorbachev was to allow it. Thus the release of prisoners of conscience, assuming they remained in the Soviet Union, would make available to that society the independent critical faculties of a significant class of people. Likewise the allowance of an investigative press would goad the bureaucracy and provide a forum for fresh thinking. The association of like-minded people, in voluntary organizations, could create new "energy centers" for reform and restructuring of the state. These three liberties, therefore—of the person, of expression, and of association—tended to be favored by the supervisors of *glasnost*. They looked with somewhat less favor on the freedoms of religion and of travel, which might unleash loyalties other than to the state.

This, again, was a sign of the "official" character of *glasnost*, which was purposive rather than permissive. As it had throughout

Russian history, the state dispensed opportunities for its own benefit, which was seen as the highest good in a managed society. But that was not necessarily the end of the story. *Glasnost* and its feedback could serve over time to inform Soviet leaders about what they needed to do—carrying beyond what they may have first intended—to make *perestroika* work. It might lead, in this way, in the direction of a genuinely expanded individual autonomy, not for ideological reasons but because that is what makes a modern economy function. There could be no assurance that this would happen, and there were serious obstacles in the way; but what could be said with some assurance was that cultural determinism ("what has always been must be") was no surer a guide to the future than economic determinism. *Glasnost* had started something that might transcend its origins.

Demokratizatsiya, for its part, could both draw from and contribute to this process. There was much creative ferment around the major political event of Gorbachev's early years, which was the 1988 Communist Party Conference. Conceived as a way of circumventing or replacing the old guard in the government and Party, it failed of that immediate purpose but generated enough attention and energy to begin reordering the basic instruments of governance in the Soviet Union.

There may have been only a minority of pro-reform stalwarts among the 5,000 delegates who came to Moscow in late June of 1988, but Gorbachev saw to it that the ratio was higher among the 50 recognized—and nationally televised—speakers. In the words used by the *New York Times* to describe what then happened: "The Conference shattered the stifling customs of the political system, making candor, pointed debate, and even public confrontation between Party leaders acceptable." Delegates called for the resignation or criminal prosecution of other delegates; one roared for the death of people who insist on useless paperwork. Gorbachev said in his concluding speech that "the Palace of Congresses has not seen such a meeting before, and we have not seen anything of this kind for almost six decades."

The openness of expression was not confined to the meeting hall. Almost a third of *Moscow News* was given over that spring to public contributions, in wide columns titled: "What I'd say from the Rostrum of the 19th Party Conference." Authorized street rallies were held to promote reform, with speeches by Sakharov and other pro-Gorbachev intellectuals. Television projected the sense of vitality back out to the country at large. An elderly woman in Yaroslavl, whose brother had disappeared under Stalin, said the new freedom was "a miracle, a true miracle." The editor of that city's newspaper chimed in, "People are chained to the television and the radio. The interest is enormous and passionate."

Among the rank-and-file delegates in the hall, the sense of involvement was tangible and momentous. One delegate from the Caucasus, Khashbikar Bokov, said he would tell his grandchildren he had taken part in a "revolution." In his words, "this was not programmed, this was not the old way. This was democracy."

And so it was, to a considerable degree. Unlike the customary Party Congress and Central Committee plenums, the leadership proposals this time were published in advance and distributed for discussion among six separate committees with rank-and-file membership. There the proposals generated discussion, amendments, and some divided votes. When the final resolutions reached the floor, they provoked further divisions. The floor debates were reported in the press and the minutes were committed to publication. All in all, the procedure was one that would not have seemed unfamiliar to the Philadelphia delegates at the American Constitutional Convention 200 years before.

The floor discussion of the final resolutions was described in the Soviet press as "unusually stormy and prolonged." New amendments and even new resolutions were introduced at this point, and many were brought to a vote. Roald Sagdeyev, a member of the Supreme Soviet and a senior adviser to Gorbachev, took the initiative to oppose the automatic nomination of Party secretaries to the chairmanship of local and regional legislatures—a Gorbachev idea. Sagdeyev's motion was brought to a vote and attracted 209 supporters out of the 5,000; although a small number, the experience of open opposition marked a clear step away from the vertically imposed lockstep uniformity of the past.

As for the products of the Party Conference, the political and legal changes it approved were designed to press the bureaucracy to do what the leadership wanted, and to begin to subject the leadership itself to accountability to the nation. In particular, it undertook to revise and strengthen the operations of the central government and of the nation's legal system.

The new national government endorsed by the Conference

reposed its executive authority in an elected "president," or chairman of the Presidium of the Supreme Soviet, until then a ceremonial office. This chairman would decide key issues of foreign policy, defense, and national security, nominate senior executive officials, and propose domestic policy and legislation. He would be elected (and could be recalled) by a new parliament, the Congress of People's Deputies. The expectation was that Mikhail Gorbachev, along with Party secretaries at other levels, would be nominated without opposition to serve as chairman of his presidium. He would then serve for a maximum of two five-year terms, as would anyone in an executive post elected, appointed, or confirmed by a legislature.

The new Congress of People's Deputies would also select from its number a smaller, bicameral, Supreme Soviet to sit in extended session. That body's members, serving staggered terms, would exercise supervisory authority over executive officials and enterprise managers, none of whom would themselves be eligible to serve in the Supreme Soviet. The deputies would be released from their regular work during sessions and continue to draw their ordinary pay.

Among the duties assigned to the Supreme Soviet were the confirmation of ministers and military commanders, the formation of the Defense Council, the election of the Supreme Court, the adoption and revision of national laws, and the repeal or modification of unconstitutional legislation.

The election of both the Supreme Soviet and its chairman would be by the Congress of People's Deputies. Its 2,250 members were to be elected in groups of 750 each, one group on a population basis (like the U.S. House of Representatives), one on a jurisdictional basis (like the U.S. Senate), and one through the internal voting of recognized organizations like the Communist Party, Komsomol, and the Soviet Academy of Sciences. There would be a single, five-year term for all legislators, who would have their election expenses and media access provided by the state.

The Constitutional amendments and new election law enacting these several changes were pushed through to adoption by the end of 1988, and the first elections for the national Congress were conducted the following spring. Their results were revealing, in terms of both continuity and change.

Ninety percent of the seats in the new Congress were taken by

Party stalwarts, either elected from within organizations (as was, for example, Mikhail Gorbachev) or accepted by the voters (especially in the rural areas.) But the 10 percent who were defeated, in the urban and suburban areas, included many prominent leaders and—remarkably—a number of people who had run unopposed. Under the new election law, it was possible by majority vote to strike names off a ballot, and in places like Kiev and Leningrad and Lvov and Moscow the voters did so again and again.

Significantly for the Communist Party, 35 of its regional secretaries, and many of its local leaders—including all five of the top Party functionaries in Leningrad—were rejected. Among those defeated was Yuri Solovyev, a candidate (non-voting) member of the Politburo who had been offered to the voters rather than slated for election within the Party as he might have been. In the Baltic states, where candidates endorsed by "popular fronts" won a majority of the available seats, the roll of the defeated included the prime minister of Latvia and both the president and prime minister of Lithuania.

The message overall was favorable to reform. The successful insurgents all campaigned in favor of Gorbachev's program, as did most establishment victors. Gorbachev thereby gained an instrument beyond the Party barons by which to bring about change. The defeated barons lost standing and became vulnerable to losing Party office. Assuming that future elections would continue to reconcile stability with change, the prospects for overall reform were enhanced by this exercise in partial democracy.

There was still a question to be faced: Would the legislative decisions taken by the newly democratized machinery of government stick, or would they be warped and frustrated by Party administrators? This was a stated concern of the 1988 Party Conference, Gorbachev telling the delegates they must "rule out any possibility of power being usurped or abused." The Conference responded by adopting provisions to strengthen the judiciary, protect individual rights, and enhance legal regularity.

The Soviet judiciary was given ten-year elective terms, along with new powers to curtail prosecutorial discretion, and greater trial publicity. It was committed to "unswerving observance of the presumption of innocence" of criminal defendants—a presumption already on the books, but undercut by the practice of holding accused persons incommunicado for up to nine months. The Conference undertook, in principle, to redress that imbalance.

The Party Conference also proposed legal and Constitutional changes to expand individual rights and liberties, including opportunities "to take part in government, to express one's views on any issue, and to enjoy freedom of conscience." It followed Gorbachev's lead in professing solicitude for "the citizen's personal dignity, the inviolability of his home, and the privacy of his correspondence and conversations." Legislation was promised to follow.

The Conference's direct contribution to civil liberties took the form of new provisions for review and revision of unconstitutional action. There had never in Soviet history been any effective provision for such review. Now, Article 125 of the amended Constitution, proposed by the Conference and approved in November 1988, set up a Constitutional Oversight Committee within the Congress of People's Deputies—to review legislative and executive acts at both the national and republican level, to recommend their repeal when inconsistent with the Constitution, and to suspend their execution while such recommendations were being considered by the originating body. Among the Constitutional standards provided for this judgment was a new, implicit "supremacy clause," making national law superior to republican law, legislative acts superior to executive action, and the decisions of the more popularly elected Congress of People's Deputies superior to those of the indirectly chosen Supreme Soviet. It might be years, if ever, before the political realities would catch up with this legal opportunity, but Article 125 would be in place and waiting.

Another step forward, which was very much so regarded by the Soviet leadership, was adoption by the Party Conference of the principle: "Everything is permitted which is not prohibited by law." That phrase was repeated on at least three prominent occasions in the Conference proceedings. Partly it served as an homage to George Orwell, and a rejection of Josef Stalin, stilling the public's fear of an arbitrary knock on the door in the middle of the night. Partly too it was a denial of the claimed right of current officials to disregard or rewrite reform legislation. Whatever balance might be struck in the future by such laws, as between freedom and order, would have to be respected by people in the field. That is what the formulation proclaimed.

In the eyes of legal scholars in both Russia and the West, this marked an evolution of the Soviet system in the direction of a law-state, or *Rechtsstaat* as it was known in 19th century Prussia. The Conference announced the "formation of a socialist law-based state," bringing with it "the enhancement of the authority of the law and of strict compliance therewith on the part of all Party and state organs, social organizations, collectives, and citizens." The state would still predominate, but predictably, and in keeping with its own declarations. For Mikhail Gorbachev, who must have studied the concept of *Rechtsstaat* at Moscow Law School, this would be a way of moving Soviet law beyond the confines of random and undisciplined coercion.

But coercive limits on *perestroika* would not be abandoned, nor would Soviet communism under Gorbachev give way to a regime of freedom. There was, assertedly, to be only one authorized political party with the power to nominate candidates for election. A suggestion for self-nomination of candidates, put forth in the letters column of *Moscow News,* was disregarded. Roald Sagdeyev, when he was twitted on this point by a visiting American in the spring of 1988, was emphatic on the persistence of one-party government. The informal groups and the popular fronts lobbied for electoral recognition in their own right, but they failed to get it. Gorbachev told NBC television, before the Washington summit meeting of December 1987, that "I see no need for any other party, and I think that is the view of our society." In 1989, after the Congress elections, Gorbachev allowed the formation of a pro-reform caucus within that body but denied it its own independent staff and funding. He then opposed, successfully for a time, a reform movement to abolish Article 6—the constitutional guarantee of a Communist Party monopoly. Gorbachev urged the need for a united vanguard party to carry the country through its turbulent reform period, a consideration to which he and other established leaders seemed likely to continue to adhere.

Other reforms also on the agenda, potentially, could be said to include these further citizen suggestions from *Moscow News:*

- to publicize central Party meetings
- to disclose the Party budget
- to create non-Party advisory bodies

- to take away the KGB's domestic authority, and
- to abolish internal visa systems.

Further, qualitative changes might also be added, to strengthen reforms already adopted. One such would be to raise the prestige of the judiciary, which legal experts considered to be dead last among lawyers' career preferences.

Overall, the governmental reforms adopted at Gorbachev's urging were aimed at improving the system, not transforming it. The goal for these reforms and for Russian society in general was diversity, not pluralism; populism, not democracy; reform, not republicanism. The aim was to strengthen the leadership by legitimizing it sufficiently to draw out fresh energies from the people.

There remained real restraints on the exercise of such energies—some even added after the Party Conference. Independent organs of political opinion were no longer shut down automatically as they once had been, but they were obliged to operate without assured access to printing presses or photocopiers and, sometimes, with rationed allotments of newsprint. Dissident demonstrators were no longer automatically jailed, but their access to banquet halls and center-city locations was limited by the police, who were freshly empowered (after the nationality protests of 1988–89) to imprison people making "public insults" against the USSR.

The potential for excessive or abusive police discretion remained, by such means, considerable. Nor was this an aberration. The 1988 Party Conference resolutions made it plain that liberty for Soviet citizens did not mean license. *Glasnost* was not to be used, in the words of a Conference resolution, "to harm the interests of the state or society." Rights in this society were still correlative with duties: "Socialist democracy is incompatible with both willfulness and lack of responsibility." Andrei Sakharov could complain, as he did, about the restrictions growing out of this conception, but Sakharov was not in charge and his views did not prevail.

The carrot did not invariably win out over the stick in Soviet economic restructuring, either. Incentives alone were not trusted to produce the results sought by the authorities. So, while the scientific and technical community was being wooed to contribute its best efforts to the nation, another wing of the government was imposing coercive, and reputedly much disliked, state quality inspections on innovative production.

The contradictions carried farther. The scope of contract transactions between state enterprises, on which so much hope was officially reposed, was undercut by the retained power of ministries to issue *goszakazy,* or directives, commanding the allocation of particular products to designated recipients at fixed prices and quantities. This authority (which did not exist, for example, in the Hungarian reform system) was conceived to protect a limited class of priority claims on production, but in practice was broadened to reinstate a regime of commands in place of contracts. The directives took the place of obligatory plan targets, and survived several pledges by Gorbachev to curtail them.

Cooperative shops and services were similarly restrained by a network of local and national taxes and regulations. To begin with, their licensing and price control was left to local officials, who normally had little enthusiasm for private ventures. Then, when a number of the variously estimated 20,000 to 30,000 cooperatives caught on and started raising prices and earning profits, the national authorities stepped in to limit prices and to withdraw certain zones of activity—such as health care, publishing, and film production—from competition. At one point they threatened to impose steeply progressive taxes, though at this the usually supine old legislature sat up and called a halt.

A Western response to perceived price gouging would probably have been to introduce more competition, but this was not the Soviet way. Their custom was to cure misdirection with new direction. So, on Moscow television in March of 1987, the first deputy head of something called the Apparatus Department, one Miliukov, came on the air to warn that the law would "punish" even state enterprises for "baseless increases" in price. It would have seemed more effective, to a Westerner, for the authorities to cure price excesses by freeing up domestic and perhaps foreign entry into the market; but market freedom was seen by the Soviets as messy and uncontrolled, and it did not happen.

The arrangements required to introduce effective competition would not, in all fairness, have been easy to bring about. Banking and credit facilities, for one thing, were seriously underdeveloped in the USSR. The key concept in the Soviet reform plan was "self-financing," which was taken to mean that each sector must generate its own growth capital out of earnings. There was no reliable, independent source of funding to iron out the disparities this could produce. The fledgling computer sector, for example, which needed to grow, would not have the earnings to do so, whereas the large energy sector, which needed less growth capital, would have no place to put its earnings. The effects on pricing would almost certainly be perverse, as ministries moved to push up computer prices, slowing demand and growth, while they pushed down energy prices, with the opposite effects. The proper workings of a capital market, as this indicated, were not understood by Soviet authorities.

Specialization of enterprises was another capitalist idea not readily adopted in the Soviet Union. Industrial plants tended to regard themselves as autonomous units, generating their own auxiliary products and services to meet internal requirements rather than buying these on the open market. They might manufacture nails for inside repair work, for example, rather than sending to the Soviet equivalent of Sears. This could be highly inefficient, and could stifle new entry of efficient ventures. The new long-term lessees of collective farms would similarly have had a better chance of success if there had been some place other than those collectives from which to buy seed and to which to sell produce.

Effective competition was not really the aim of such early reforms as the Law on State Enterprises. Wholesale contract transactions between large and sluggish firms, even if they took place, were bound to be slow and sluggish. Gorbachev proposed no Soviet-style Sherman Act to stir up competition, and indeed his June 1987 plenum speech encouraged mergers and amalgamations of smaller industrial units. If competition were somehow to take hold, it would produce winners and losers, and that would mean plant closings and job layoffs for inefficient producers. This was a fact that Gorbachev recognized but did not deal with. Inefficiencies therefore continued.

The same was true of consumer price subsidies, which distorted the economy but whose removal was bound to cause severe morale difficulties. The Politburo moved slowly on this front, remembering the riots that had taken place in Poland when food prices were raised in 1981. This left a serious problem for Gorbachev, because wrong prices send wrong signals to profit seekers, who typically respond by developing wrong products—which may discredit reform, and lead to its abandonment. No quick or easy solution was perceived for this dilemma.

What was required to spur the Soviet economy was, ultimately, a price mechanism that could respond to supply and demand, and allocate resources, independently of official decisions. The Gorbachev reform program identified no clear conceptual or practical path to that goal. The specter of transitional unemployment and inflation was a daunting one. The Chinese, who had earlier adopted price reform, were obliged to abandon it in late 1988 when retail prices in the major Chinese cities jumped by 30 percent. The Soviets shortly thereafter decided to defer their own consideration of price reform for the time being.

Abel Aganbegyan, Gorbachev's early economic adviser, accepted this decision but was dismayed by it. Americans who saw Aganbegyan, on a speaking tour of the United States in the winter of 1989, saw a worried and discouraged man. The Soviets were avoiding extremes, keeping policy lines open, but failing to resolve any of the tough issues of entry and pricing, finance and competition, that alone could produce the success of economic *perestroika*. These issues could not be tackled without an overt plan, but even outside specialists could think of none that would work without pain—and pain at a higher intensity level than the Soviet system seemed ready to support.

At stake in all this, eventually, was the resiliency and direction of *perestroika*. Gorbachev may have been speaking in radical terms about the redefinition of socialism, but he was acting in guarded terms that would just keep his platform afloat. Whether, how soon, and how far the broader promise might be realized would depend on the push and pull of forces within the culture as a whole.

5

Internal Sources of Resistance and Support

The Gorbachev reform program had to struggle against resistance not just from self-perpetuating bureaucrats—the frequent object of his reproofs—but from values and preferences that they and the society at large shared in common. *Glasnost* had an appeal but the thirst for direction was more deep-seated. The entrepreneurial spirit, to which Gorbachev was reaching, had been flattened by the Stalin and Brezhnev years, and any resurgence would have to surmount very large transitional difficulties. For strong support, Gorbachev could count only on the intelligentsia and the young and on some of his own, Khrushchev-era generation. Beyond that he would have to look to what some observers were calling a new "civil society"—a better-educated, more urban populace then emerging to support and perhaps to sustain a transformation of the Soviet way of mind. At the outset its emergence caused fresh difficulties, in the form of unruly social and nationality groups pursuing agendas for which the nation at large was not prepared. Over time, however, and with the aid of more transparent information practices, the new attitudes could spread and coalesce into substantial support for Soviet reform.

To begin with, among ministries and managers, there were conflicting imperatives. Regulators were supposed under *perestroika* to concern themselves only with broad objectives, leaving the choice of means and day-to-day achievements to the collective farms or factories or other state enterprises. The regulators knew, however, that they would also be held responsible for the ultimate output of these enterprises, which created an incentive to intervene into details. It must have seemed easier, to many, to ignore the supposed diffusion of authority and to continue managing in the old way. Reform decrees could be "lost" or forgotten, their freedoms granted or withheld. Farm managers could manage resources so as to keep a leash on their lessees. All this, inevitably, was done.

Resistance was displayed at both top and bottom. Gorbachev's farm-leasing program was stalled by prolonged opposition in the Politburo and Central Committee. Cooperatives were taxed or regulated prohibitively by local officials, acting out their disapproval of private profit-making. Everywhere the managers played the game of "positive inertia," adopting Gorbachev's vocabulary of reform to cover their continuation of the practices they had been following for the previous twenty years.

It was not just official privileges they were defending, but also and more deeply the sense of communal values traditional to Russian and Soviet cultures. Yegor Ligachev, the head of the conservative faction in the reform Politburo, spoke for many when he cautioned against the break-up of collective farms or other institutions of state socialism, saying in one speech, "We are after all a society of social justice." The petty capitalists, or kulaks, that Stalin had exterminated had been also and before that the objects of Chekhov's disdain. Neighbors today still resented the unequal prosperity of neighbors, and in some cases trashed or burned the property of any who profited from *perestroika*. The general view about cooperative owners was that they were "thieves, profiteers, speculators." Even Gorbachev sometimes turned on these people; he accused them of engaging in "open money grubbing," and proposed a steep tax to limit their profits.

Similarly regressive attitudes were carried over into social reform. Letters to the editors of Soviet newspapers in 1987 reflected a sizeable segment of opinion that opposed any relaxation of police restrictions on disruptive behavior. The dominant preference of much of the population remained centered on the quality of disciplined leadership. It was this more than his program of reforms that commended Gorbachev to his people. A jointly designed Soviet-French opinion survey, conducted in October of 1987, showed that Moscow residents rated Gorbachev high in historical importance (31 percent), but only marginally ahead of Stalin (25 percent) and well behind Lenin (64 percent).

Discipline as a quality is not so much contradictory to *glasnost* as it is complementary. The idea of candor-for-a-purpose, or *glasnost,* carries with it the notions of order, stability, responsibility. It differs centrally in this respect from the American tradition of free·expression, which the American commentator Marvin Kalb once described as being politically "irresponsible." In the Soviet political culture, freedom has its uses but not in isolation from responsibility. Balance and order are the key.

So, competition among enterprises or ideas has a value, but not—among Gorbachev's compatriots—to the derogation of consensus. Initiative for them must find its place in the framework of discipline, freedom in that of equality, the individual in that of the community. Debates and disputation are all to the good, but when people get to the voting booth they tend to ask themselves, "Has it got approval at the top?" The traditionalists who wrote to *Pravda* said they would just as soon have the authorities make a decision in the old way and tell them what it was.

The role of the military in all of this was instructive. There was no question of a coup, the Soviet Union was not a South American country and its army had no independent political standing; but in a society so preoccupied with security, the adequacy of military preparations is always a political issue. As one aspect of *perestroika* the armed forces were obliged to accept a loss of priority in their current claim on the budget, receiving in return the promise of a strengthened industrial base for future high-technology instruments. If that expectation were to be frustrated or delayed, as some Western economists believed it would be, the reform agenda might be in trouble. There was a further factor to be considered, which was the declining status of the Soviet military as a profession. In the Gorbachev regime no military member was named to the Politburo, two chiefs of staff and a defense minister resigned or were dismissed over matters of policy, the corps of senior marshals was allowed to dwindle toward zero, and armies and armed ventures were recalled from around the globe. This was inspiring internationally but less so internally, where peace must contend to some degree against prestige.

From the perspective, then, of the patriotic citizen or the Party loyalist, the beleaguered worker or the harried consumer, there were doubts and deficits associated with reform. Farmers, whose sense of enterprise was appealed to, might find that they preferred the steady wages and protection from risk provided by collective farms. Some farmers would remember that the last private program, initiated by Lenin in the 1920's, had ended with forced collectivization and harsh repression by Stalin. That was the experience that had turned Soviet farmers from entrepreneurs into assembly-line workers, and had driven the initiative largely out of them. In polls taken during 1988–89, a large majority of Soviet farmers said they were confused by leasing, unsure of their access to fertilizers and tools, and content for the present to stick with the collective system.

Industrial workers were also fearful of the changes they were being invited to make. Prices as they saw them were heading up, and work guarantees down. It was not just potential layoffs and shutdowns at inefficient plants that concerned them, but also the morale-impairing lesser actions of reduced wages, longer hours, higher prices, and diminished privileges. Polls taken in the spring of 1987 in Moscow and Kazakhstan showed that the closer one got to blue-collar workers, the weaker was the expectation of beneficial change from economic reform and the stronger was the fear of harm.

If farmers and workers were daunted by *perestroika,* consumers were left largely unmoved by the promise of some future economic improvement. On budgetary grounds Gorbachev initially resisted advice to bring in foreign goods as an incentive for consumer support, but in 1989 he authorized an "emergency fund" of foreign currencies to import European and Japanese shoes, boots, razor blades, cassette tapes, soap powder, and other quality items. Whether this would generate an effective constituency for reform was problematic. The "fund" was small and temporary. An all-out housing program, capable of lowering the apartment waiting period from five years to two, would be more dramatic and more lasting, although it too would take resources away from the modernization of Soviet plant and equipment.

There were transitional difficulties to be faced as well, on the consumer side. The withdrawal of price subsidies from food and housing and other articles, which was needed to cure resource misallocations, was not something that could be carried out without turbulence. The Polish disturbances of the 1980's provided fresh reminders of that fact. Nor could pricing freedom—which reformers saw as essential to economic revitalization—be achieved without releasing huge inflationary pressures from the pent-up demand, and savings, of Soviet consumers. The mere prospect of price decontrol ignited a late-1980's run on the shops and a resulting accentuation of consumer-goods shortages. Gorbachev moved for that reason in 1989 to put off pricing reform until sometime in the 1991–96 period. His action looked prudent when compared to the Chinese reform program, which was obliged at this time to retreat from price decontrol, having stimulated an inflation rate of more than 30 percent in the major cities.

Despite these serious economic constraints and limitations, the social-policy side of *perestroika* made headway. It appealed to intellectuals as a class by its opening up of creative expression. This was significant because of the leverage historically exercised by the intelligentsia, as the minority that moves the masses—not least in the Russian Revolution of 1917. But there were limits to the likely effectiveness of this class. It provided, in the words of the economist Joseph Berliner, "a constituency of conviction rather than of personal interest." Its ranks were also thin, and were not being broadened: There was a rote quality to much Soviet classroom instruction, and little opportunity for independent scholarship below the level of the senior research institutes. Education for thinking, as opposed to career preparation, was in short supply.

The support of the thinkers was, in addition, fragile. Many had bet on Khrushchev's promises of reform and had found themselves out in the cold. The signs of permanence, of a governing consensus in favor of change, were stronger this time, but there were tremors all the same. *Glasnost* as they were often reminded did not exist for its own sake, but to build a stronger state. Gorbachev warned specifically in July of 1987 against any movements that tried to go "beyond socialism."

The limits were illustrated by the Boris Yeltsin affair of October–November 1987. Yeltsin was a popular official who had been brought in by Gorbachev from Sverdlovsk to serve as Moscow Party chief. He swept out inefficient ward leaders, arrested corrupt store directors, bullied unreliable bus operators, and opened up the city to speeches and demonstrations. His swaggering style played well until he brought it into the closed proceedings of the Central Committee. There, on October 21, 1987, he attacked the slowness of *perestroika,* claiming it had given "virtually nothing to the people," and theatrically tendered his resignation. Gorbachev, who had asked that this complaint be deferred until after the preparations for the 70th anniversary of the Revolution, accepted the offer. Yeltsin was out as Moscow chief and as a candidate member of the Politburo.

It did not seem to matter to the intellectuals that this dismissal was probably justified, and would have been repeated in a similar Western setting. It looked to them like a reversal. The Central Committee proceedings were, by custom, kept secret, while Yeltsin's reputation for championing the downtrodden was public. By the time all the facts could be aired, some months later, Yeltsin had become an emblem of embattlement. His election to the Congress of People's Deputies, in March of 1989, was by a heady 90 percent of the at-large Moscow vote; the intellectuals supported him, as they told Western friends, not for who he was but for what he stood against.

What that was showed up once again in the Nina Andreyeva letter of March 13, 1988. This letter, ghost-edited (it was thought) by the conservative Politburo leader Yegor Ligachev, was published in *Sovetskaya Rossiya* while Gorbachev was out of the country. It was a bill of complaints against the alleged "excesses" of anti-Stalinism, recalling the positive achievements of the Stalin era—industrialization, mobilization, the defeat of Hitler. Sacrifice, it maintained, along with hard work and the common interest, were not to be thought inferior to self-expression or material satisfaction. The letter attained instant prominence when *Tass,* the official news agency, advised provincial newspapers to reprint it. There matters lay, unrebutted, for three long weeks while people wondered whether this was the end of reform. At length there was a *Pravda* editorial, ghost-written (it was believed) by Gorbachev's ally Alexander Yakovlev, reaffirming the anti-Stalin line; but again the faithful had been shaken.

Pro- and anti-reform alignments of a generational sort were reflected to some degree in this incident. The Gorbachev generation, having come of age politically under Khrushchev, favored the continuation and completion of his anti-Stalin campaign. Those of the preceding and following generations, men and women of Stalin's and Brezhnev's day, tended to favor the more traditional Andreyeva line. Gorbachev could place his long-term hope on the young people of the late 1980's, students and others who were forming their political consciousness, as he had done, in an era of reform. But whether the intervening layer of people—those in their 30's and early 40's—would want to continue or suspend reform was something not yet known.

There were geographic as well as generational divergences in the pattern of support for reform. Concepts of private enterprise and of social initiative were better received in the Caucasus (Armenia, Georgia) and the Baltics (Latvia, Lithuania, Estonia) than in the larger republics of Russia and the Ukraine. Cooperatives, for example, flourished in the outlying regions to a degree not experienced in the center, where traditional values of social "leveling" held sway. But Russia and the Ukraine were the political centers of gravity in the Union, and without their engagement the future of *perestroika* would remain in doubt.

Further sources of support were emerging at this time to strengthen the prospects of reform through changes in the Soviet way of mind, its values, and its attitudes. The new Soviet leader was himself a product of such forces, of a social environment that had been changing and growing more sophisticated throughout his life. Tatyana Zaslavskaya, Gorbachev's sociological adviser, described the changes in a now-famous "confidential" report from Novosibirsk in 1983, suggesting that Moscow could no longer expect to run the Soviet Union by centralized administrative control. The population was too advanced for that, she wrote, and its interests and views would have to be consulted.

There were perhaps four underlying, late-20th century trends in Soviet society that accounted for this development. The first was a weakening of the traditional "peasant" mentality, with its impulse toward conformity, as more and more of the population came to settle in or near major cities. The second was the emergence of a more educated and independent urban personality—of a new, professional "middle class," with tastes and expectations beyond the rudimentary—that was accustomed to making life decisions on its own. The third was the development of greater complexity in social interactions, beyond the capacity of bureaucracy or Party discipline to control. The fourth, finally, was a muted "information explosion" that was invading previously sheltered official transactions and making greater public accountability, or *glasnost*, a fact of life even before it was declared as policy.

The early stirrings of this "civil society," as some observers called it, sparked hopes of a bottom-up movement that could join forces with the top-down Gorbachev revolution to overcome social inertia with new energy and resources. At some point, if this joinder were maintained, it could lead to an authentically expanded diversity and freedom. What had begun as "instrumental" reform, in Seweryn Bialer's phrase, might by these means acquire a life and momentum of its own. Human rights and liberties, and enthusiasm for reform, could thereby grow from within.

To begin with, however, the new society erupted with uneven geographic force inside the Soviet Union. Those regions that were most amenable to reform, like the Baltics, took *perestroika* as a signal to promote their own autonomy. They were quick to authorize private services, which Gorbachev welcomed, and they looked for other ways to serve as a benchmark for the rest of the country. The question was how far such vitality could be allowed to carry without destabilizing the state.

Glasnost had an initially disturbing effect on Soviet cohesion, casting doubt as it did on the history and legitimacy of the multinational state. Internal nationalism provided an alternative focus of loyalties, particularly for the many peoples and regions—Moslems, Moldavians, others—that had been taken into the state with little effort at assimilation. For such people the hallmarks of regional language, culture, and religion took on an accentuated importance as a result of *glasnost*. These characteristics expressed their separate and surviving identities, as Georgians or Armenians, Ukrainians or Balts.

Religion was a particular sore point, as Stalin and Khrushchev had destroyed all but 7,000 (out of some 75,000) churches, temples, and mosques, many of which had once served as centers of ethnic as well as spiritual expression. Professed believers were excluded from membership in the Communist Party, and hence from most higher education or opportunity. Worship was driven underground, particularly in the Ukraine, whose Catholic Church was officially broken up and merged into the Russian Orthodox Church in 1946. (The Western Ukraine, where this church once flourished, was historically a font of anti-Russian nationalism, and it adjoined Roman Catholic Poland.) But the Ukrainian church persisted, as the largest underground congregation in the Soviet Union—3 million adherents, going to Orthodox services on Sunday but using their own boarded-up buildings for baptism, marriage, and other sacraments. *Glasnost* drew these practices into the light, as it did also the distinctive Orthodoxy of such regions as Armenia and Georgia.

A sense of resurgent nationalism could arise in the Russian republic as well. Russian churches and culture had been smothered under the Soviet mantle, on top of which many sacrifices had been exacted for the benefit of non-Russian minorities. Now those minorities were growing into a majority, and still the Russian standard of living was lower than that in any other Soviet region. This fact was resented, and the resentment took expression among other ways in the neo-Stalinist organization called *Pamyat*—fittingly, "Memory."

In the main, however, both politically and culturally, Russians imposed on their neighbors. Higher education and business and government were all conducted, at a national level, in the Russian language. The upper ranks of the KGB and the military, including those posted in regional centers, were generally Russian. Russians disproportionately dominated the central government: As of late 1989, there was only one non-Russian (and non-Slav) among the voting members of the Politburo. And Mikhail Gorbachev, a Russian, disparaged nationalist expression: He told the Central Committee, at its January 1987 plenum, that a leading objective of political reform must be to "save the rising generation from the demoralizing effects of nationalism."

That aim was in for some difficult times. When Gorbachev removed the local Kazakh Party chief in 1986 and replaced him with a Russian, the people of Kazakhstan took to the streets in tumultuous disorder. Another and longer-lasting disturbance broke out in Armenia in 1988, as the result of a territorial dispute between the Christian Armenians and their Turkic Moslem neighbors of Azerbaijan. Gorbachev was unable to settle that issue peaceably and, after hostilities erupted he was obliged to send in forces and establish martial law. Likewise in Georgia in 1989, an ethnic minority within that republic was able to fan the flames of nationality to the point where Soviet troops reacted and innocent onlookers were killed.

In the Baltic republics to the West, the outbursts of nationalism were neither violent nor inter-ethnic. They were mainly polite, civilized, and legal in character. They were also anti-Russian and deeply earnest. First Estonia and then Latvia gave birth to broad-based "popular fronts" to pursue separatist objectives. In Lithuania the short name of the front was *Sajudis.* On the August 1988 anniversary of the Hitler-Stalin pact consigning the Baltics to Soviet control, there were huge rallies in all three republics. The long-banished national flags re-emerged. Pieces of destroyed national monuments were dug up from family gardens and reassembled. On November 16, the Supreme Soviet of Estonia went so far as to declare its "sovereignty" in all domains except defense and foreign policy. Moscow rejected this assertion, as it did—a year later—the threatened assertion of Lithuanian independence. Neither side yielded, and there matters were left, uneasily, to sit. It was a serious challenge to central authority.

Conceivably that challenge could be turned to Soviet advantage, by letting one or more of the Baltic states serve as a kind of "Hong Kong" outpost for external Soviet commerce. A territory opened to trade and investment from the West, under its own economic legislation, could employ a loose political connection to pass its foreign-exchange earnings back into the main economy. (In the spring of 1989 the Soviets announced consideration of special economic zones for this purpose, but not for the Baltics and still under Soviet rather than local law.) The concern was how much Baltic sovereignty could be allowed without provoking other, destabilizing demands for similar freedom from other republics.

There were limits on the extent of autonomy those other republics might be able to manage. An Armenia cut loose from the Soviet Union would find itself at the mercy of antagonistic surrounding peoples. A Kazakhstan would have to look about for reliable trading partners. There were competing separatist minorities within some republics, like Georgia. The Ukrainian regions of east and west differed markedly from each other in culture and religion. And so it went, from one territory to the next: To confer any sort of independence on such locations would be to open them up to inner and outer strife.

A regional or republican sense of nationality is also not necessarily at war with a sense of Soviet nationality. The two can coexist, along with the other affinities— educational, social, and professional—that are becoming more significant for many Soviets than their cultural or ethnic ties. The emerging "civil society" has in fact emphasized self-expression along sectoral lines, creating some initial further difficulties for the reform regime.

The informal interest groups that Gorbachev championed had an array of sectoral reasons for coming into being. They pressed new demands and expectations upon government, for environmental improvement and free speech and other causes. Gorbachev looked on them as a constituency for change, and hoped their outspokenness could be managed to serve his ends. But just as some nationality leaders sought real measures of autonomy, so some informal groups asked for genuine political power. The August 1987 manifesto of the Federation of Socialist Clubs demanded the right to nominate candidates for election and to publish their platforms in the established press.

Such requests could be declined, as these were, but not without cost. If the voluntary groups were kept away from elections, and denied the opportunity to advance their own causes and candidates, much of the participative energy for which Gorbachev was reaching might be withheld from, or conceivably turned against, the process of reform. If on the other hand the groups were given too explicit a role, the result could be the formation of focused political organizations capable one day of challenging the lead role of the Communist Party.

For Gorbachev that was unacceptable. He told NBC's Tom Brokaw in a televised interview before the December 1987 summit meeting that he saw no need for any other party. The informal groups would have to "comprehend their place . . . and incorporate their creative potential" within the historic one-party system, as a "mechanism . . . of criticism and self-criticism"; so said the Party Conference Resolution on Reform of the Political System, in the summer of 1988. The Soviet Union would not at the time follow the example of Hungary or of Poland, who were then making plans to usher rival parties into their national election systems.

The Soviet solution was to authorize nominations by "mass social organizations," defined as groups with legal status and with all-Union jurisdiction. The informal groups typically had neither.

It was open to them to endorse candidates, which the mass-member Baltic popular fronts did to powerful effect in the March 1989 elections; but the smaller and more splintered groups had no such sway. Still, these ambitious new societies—with grand names like Democratic Union and All-Union Club—did help to persuade voters to strike the names of candidates they opposed. With this negative but notable success, they inscribed themselves on the political map.

Gorbachev's efforts to lift his nation from its condition as a passive society had to contend with pervasive information restrictions—along with the cynicism they had bred, and the turmoil their removal might cause. The challenge for him, once again, was to promote creativity without disarray.

Information systems in the Soviet Union, as elsewhere, can be divided into two classes: the mass media, such as television, which operate outward from a central point of origin; and the dispersed media, like telephones, which do not. Governments that aim to control the flow of information in their societies, as Russian and Soviet governments have traditionally done, tend to regard the mass media as an opportunity for control and the dispersed media as a threat to it.

In the Soviet information society that Gorbachev inherited, 92 percent of the population could receive television channel One, and 75 percent could get channel Two, but only 23 percent of urban households and 7 percent of rural households had any telephone service. Television program listings, similarly, were widely accessible while telephone directories were scarce. The question of interest was what, if any, changes in this pattern might be ushered in by the confluence of *glasnost* with the newer information technologies.

The data showed that the older, established channels of dispersed communication—the mails and the telephone—experienced an immediate jump in usage after *glasnost* was proclaimed, rising 30 to 40 percent in 1987 over previous levels. If that pattern were to carry over into the more modern media like computer and facsimile transmission, it could be significant. But, as the American specialist Seymour Goodman observed:

> Soviet authorities remained very cautious with regard to the
> widespread introduction of any of the information technologies
> that have serious potential for being used to increase exposure
> to information from foreign sources, that may be willingly used
> for dissident activities, or that increase the volume of private
> two-way communications.

The new technologies were being introduced, but at a pace and in
a manner that—on the available evidence—seemed unlikely to
threaten any social or political uprising.

To achieve a full-scale, decentralized, information economy,
it is necessary to be able to install the technology (hardware, soft-
ware, systems design) and the distribution system (telecommuni-
cations) that can get the information around. The Soviets had
problems on both of these fronts, and an even deeper problem
with a third requirement, which is absorption capacity, or user
demand. The newer applications of computer technology, such as
for computer-assisted manufacturing, found no demand in Soviet
plants or offices. They were perceived as disruptions to the work
force, threats to plant autonomy, and challenges to the jobs of
middle management. The costs of computer introduction, with its
learning-curve reductions in productivity, loomed large.

There was a substantial demand for personal computers, but
it came from a limited and manageable class of people. The scientific and technical intelligentsia, spearheaded by the Soviet Academy of Sciences, was enthusiastic about PCs for professional use,
as "knowledge extenders." The same group also supported a program of computer literacy in the schools. The plan was to link a
dozen or so student workstations to a teacher who would control
the printing and storage units, the whole constituting an instruc-
tional "laboratory." There were supposed to be 30,000 such labora-
tories in existence by 1990, and 120,000 by the turn of the century.

But the socially transforming potential of all this dispersed
computer power—assuming it was achieved—along with that of
perhaps 200,000 PCs in the professional research community,
looked puny in comparison to the reach of the mass media, with
its saturation of up to 90 percent of the Soviet population. Soviet
authorities under Gorbachev showed no sign of worrying about
computer-led subversion. They recognized that the kinds of access
restrictions they had fastened onto photocopying might be more

difficult as a technical matter to apply to personal computers. But, given presently foreseeable applications and users, the destabilization by computer power of central control over the society was not a serious concern.

Nor was intensification of such control. Modern KGB computers might be used to make surveillance of suspected citizens more efficient, but not more pervasive. The introduction of "Big Brother" telescreens to monitor individual behavior was improbable for technical and financial, and also for political, reasons: it would provoke a resistance from the educated classes out of all proportion to its benefits. The future of computer applications lay in decentralization.

Yet there were limits to the reach of decentralization. Assuming all technical and economic barriers to the mass introduction of personal computers were somehow overcome, and that radical dissidents could gain access to the computers, the uncontrolled messages that might issue would still be limited to fleeting electronic transmissions. Hard copy—a durable, shareable record—would remain under the control of Soviet officials, who would regulate access as always to printers and interface devices.

Copying machines might make a greater contribution to information dispersion, if restraints on their access and use were ever relaxed, as was periodically suggested. Adding 100,000 telephones, along with useable directories, could also make a substantial difference by facilitating the exchange of ideas among dissidents and with foreign visitors. But neither of these things was actively proposed.

One instrument of potential decentralization that was introduced, and that overcame Soviet efforts at its control, was the videocassette. Cassettes first came across the border in a trickle, then a rush, and then ignited a demand that outstripped all available supply. The Soviets responded, preemptively, by turning out their own videotapes—of movie classics, and health and "how-to" programs—but these did not begin to meet the need. Still, however, the market for cassettes was more "yuppie" than it was dissident, engaging the tastes of the rising managerial elite; and the costs and the relative scarcity of video recorders were such as to keep things that way.

Matters were otherwise with the mass media, particularly broadcast television, which became under Gorbachev the first truly mass medium in Soviet history. It was the chief instrument for promotion of *perestroika.* Television carried particular impact in the USSR, where the level of newspaper reading and comprehension was lower than in the West. The broadcasting system, which with satellite retransmission now spanned all eleven time zones, could reach audiences of up to 150 million for such broadcasts as *Vremya,* the evening news. The whole "look" of Soviet television—its tempo, graphics, and performance—was overhauled after 1985 to attract the mass audience and to hold its attention.

In part the goal of this change was defensive, to preempt Western sources of information, which came in through the BBC and Voice of America and other means even when there was jamming. The Soviets especially after the Chernobyl nuclear-plant disaster became anxious to report significant occurrences first, or at least to mount a rapid response. Their need for strengthened internal credibility led to a remarkable parade of Western figures on Soviet television—Phil Donahue, Generals Edward Rowney and David Jones, Secretary of State George Shultz, Prime Minister Margaret Thatcher—who took the occasion to deliver uncensored challenges to Soviet policy on human rights, Afghanistan, nuclear armaments, and other subjects. The Soviet screen was transformed.

A second and more affirmative goal of television *glasnost* was to overcome internal alienation and passivity, to generate public support for change, and to hold Soviet officials accountable for their part in making it happen. This was displayed on such nightly programs as *Spotlight on Perestroika,* a searching review of bureaucratic errors and omissions. Another program, called *Twelfth Floor,* brought officials of Komsomol and of government bureaucracies out on camera to be questioned by young people about their actions and policies. It was Soviet television, as well, that first encouraged the formation of voluntary interest groups. Television, unlike anything else, became an instrument of controlled controversy.

This did not always sit comfortably with all elements of Soviet society. In letters to *Pravda* and other organs, traditionalists complained that they did not like all the debate and disputation; they wished the authorities would make a decision in the old way and tell them what it was. Others saw in the change of television programming a sinister Western conspiracy to promote anti-Soviet sedition. (*Pravda* responded drily to this that "there are others who hold this opinion.") The cultural resistance this suggested was not something staged by Party conservatives, but a reflection of attitudes that were genuinely held, along with others, in the society at large.

The limits to risk-taking such resistance could induce were not defined in any Party directive; they tended to be self-imposed by media organs conscious of past history. In the aftermath of the Yeltsin affair, journalists could be observed to be taking their lead from the multilingual *Moscow News,* a bellwether of permitted frankness. The TV revolution itself was probably not a recallable experiment. Television in the Soviet Union was no longer predictable or boring; it engaged a huge public, or sets of publics, in ways never before experienced and very difficult to annul. It was a building-block element in the new civil society.

6

Political Management and Measurement of Change

Gorbachev's reforms prevailed to the extent that they did against built-in constraints and opposition because, in large measure, of his remarkable skills as a politician. He saw himself as a proposer who could not always or immediately dispose, but who could keep looking for ways of improving the odds in his favor. Gorbachev was adroit, he knew how to move a consensus, and he was ready to engage in tactical advances or retreats as the occasion required. He was frequently disappointed but seldom defeated: The battle did not end with any single skirmish. It was enough sometimes to keep the momentum going, to look for incremental gains even though their ultimate yield might remain uncertain. Something else could always come along to help them bear fruit.

There was more than a little resemblance in all this to the inspired pragmatism of Franklin D. Roosevelt, another reformer who had reached across ideological divisions in the 1930's to shore up and ultimately preserve a faltering system. Roosevelt used to fix the U.S. gold price each morning while still in bed, according to his biographer Arthur Schlesinger, Jr. One student of his behavior was Gorbachev's eventual ally Alexander Yakovlev, who read about the New Deal at Columbia University as an exchange student in the 1950's, and who may have drawn on its lessons when later designing a Soviet plan of action. In the Soviet Union of the mid-

1980's, as in the America of 50 years earlier, the contours of effective reform were uncertain—*perestroika* meaning different things to different people, just as the New Deal once had. But socialism was not to be abandoned by its reformers, any more than capitalism had been in the United States.

Gorbachev was not going to "sell out" to Western-style capitalism: His conservative opposition, as well as his own political orientation, would see to that. Yegor Ligachev, the conservative leader who was handed the agriculture portfolio in the September 1988 Politburo shuffle, insisted in speech after speech that policy decisions must follow "socialist goals and objectives"; farm leasing was adopted subject to that reservation. In the social policy field as well, Ligachev regularly cautioned against undue reform haste or zeal, and he was not alone. Many shared his concern that the questioning of Soviet history and the abandonment of traditional restraints might, if carried too far, promote a kind of nihilism that would threaten the stability of the society. Gorbachev listened to these concerns and he strengthened his leadership by drawing on them.

This was shown, once again, by the Yeltsin affair of October-November 1987. Yeltsin was a Gorbachev appointee and a natural foil to Ligachev, but he overstepped his bounds when he insisted on speaking critically of the opposition at a Central Committee meeting. Yeltsin specifically attacked Ligachev and the Party Secretariat for failing to give Gorbachev their support. The rebuttal to this came from Gorbachev himself, who defended the pace and the politics of change. This served to highlight a key difference between him and Nikita Khrushchev, who had failed in the 1960's to attend to the maintenance of political consensus and whose tenure was accordingly cut short by the Party regulars. The Yeltsin dismissal, while open to more than one interpretation, augured favorably overall for the persistence of reform.

Such was in fact the tone of Gorbachev's subsequent comments on the affair. Speaking on NBC television before his December 1987 summit meeting with President Reagan, Gorbachev said:

> We will follow the path of *perestroika* firmly and consistently, we will follow the path of democratization firmly and consistently, but we will not jump over phases. We will wage our

struggle without allowing any adventurism and at the same time resolutely combating conservatism.

Gorbachev was aiming for the progressive middle way. In government, he favored what *Pravda* called "an organic combination of democracy and discipline," with some emphasis on the discipline. In social policy, as the 1988 Party Conference put it, he wanted "rights and liberties" for the people, but only such as were "inseparably connected with their civic duties." Order, duty, and direction were the keys, to which democracy and freedom could serve as an accompaniment.

This sense of prudence or balance was not simply personal to Gorbachev but was demanded by the society he was confronting. "Jumping over phases" would have been destabilizing to that society, after its experience of Stalin. The film *Repentance* captured this precariousness by showing the different impacts on the tyrant's son and grandson of learning the full horrors of that regime. The grandson turned on the son, his father, to accuse him of responsibility, and the latter found himself as helpless with his explanations as he once had been to prevent the horrors. This middle generation—those slightly older than Gorbachev—deserved some understanding, and it obtained it from Gorbachev.

On the other side, of course, Gorbachev could not just sit still. The downcast morale of the general public demanded some forward movement. The road ahead, however, was not at all clear. The basic concepts of economic value and allocation were not understood among Soviet leaders, and the foreign economists who did understand them were hard put to say what combination of steps, in what sequence, might draw the Soviet economy out of its morass. The image brought to mind was that of a coal miner, dropped at night into an unfamiliar mine shaft and obliged to find his way to the surface with no headlamp and no map. There were bound to be some bumps and errors along the way.

Gorbachev himself may not have had any clear idea of how far he would have to go with economic reform to make it succeed. In a sense this may have been just as well, to keep him and his senior colleagues from losing heart. So long as the Soviet leadership held firm to its non-negotiable goal of high-quality, efficient production, the likelihood was that economic reform would persist, despite all the turbulence it might encounter along the way. Trial and error might not be the smoothest way of achieving reform, but it was one way and in time it could meet success.

The criteria for judging economic success or failure, at the enterprise as well as the national level, would have to change to conform to the new Soviet objectives. At the enterprise level, the percentage of business covered by contracts would need to replace the degree of satisfaction of centrally determined output targets. At the national level, growth as a standard would have increasingly to be supplanted by improvements in the quality and efficiency of production.

Gorbachev's first five-year plan (1986–1991), drafted in the earliest stages of his administration, did not provide a reliable guide to what could be expected to happen. Little progress was made during its term toward the stated goals of replacing capital stock, raising investment, or institutionalizing quality controls. Those aims, it appeared, had been more conceptual than practical.

The questions to be asked for the ensuing years were: (1) Was real change taking place; and (2) were quality and efficiency improving? Gross National Product figures were too crude to capture these indications, and the Soviet income data were notoriously unreliable. Measurements in the coming period would therefore have to be more anecdotal than statistical; but useful evidence could be obtained through reports of such things as television sets that did not explode and apartments that were ready on schedule. The Soviets were also beginning in the late 1980's to make wider use of consumer surveys, which should help assessment.

A high-quality scenario for the 1990's, in which shoddy work and useless output were diminished, could therefore be marked by a considerable *reduction* in GNP as traditionally measured. This would signify not failure but success for the Gorbachev reform program. Thereafter, if and when efficiency gains cut in, overall growth might begin to move upward. But in the near term, a picture of slow or even no growth would be more consistent with successful reform.

On the social front, where a great deal had been happening in both qualitative and quantitative terms, it was easier to measure new output—of films, plays, books, broadcasts, and commentaries—than it was to determine their impact. The "Soviet way of mind" and its turnings were elusive, and of fundamental importance. One striking thing about the Soviet Union at this time was that it had no reliable, institutional pulse-taking or feedback mechanism by which to gauge the effects on public opinion of *glasnost* and its progeny. This magnified the risks and limited the flexibility of the reform regime.

Mobilization by mass media is inevitably a gamble. If it does not yield appreciable results within a reasonable time, the effort can forfeit credibility and attention; more, it can breed renewed alienation and passivity. So it was necessary to find some way of monitoring effects. In 1988, at length, Gorbachev's adviser Tatyana Zaslavskaya was given charge of a new All-Union Center for the Study of Public Opinion, and authorized to survey public attitudes on social and economic change. If candid answers could be obtained—an uncertain matter, in a society emerging from submissiveness—they could affect the character of broadcast programming and of Soviet information practices in general.

Zaslavskaya had been a leading critic of statistical inadequacies in the Soviet Union. She argued that reliable and coherent data were essential to political accountability and effectiveness. Until her advent, there was no Soviet center for opinion research, no established statistical modeling system, and not very much in the way of experience or practice that could be converted into either. This was potentially a serious deficiency, because of the volatility of what was at play—the forces of modernization against those of traditional culture. It was this mixture that had exploded in the late 1970's in the face of the Shah of Iran. Mikhail Gorbachev and the reform group he headed could not safely afford to let their own modernization program run unsurveyed.

Assessments would have to extend to the computer side as well. If dissidents were not to be the beneficiaries of advanced information services, Soviet "yuppies"—the next managerial class—might be. As in the West, computerization could lead to the rise of a two-level society, with an information elite and an information underclass. If (to avoid this) decision data were broadly shared among ruling circles and with concerned publics, pressure could grow for faster and possibly less far-sighted decisions—as some believed was already happening in Western business corporations. If on the other hand the data were not widely distributed, decisions might fall increasingly into the hands of an inaccessible elite. What was at stake in this area was again important: the mix of command and accountability in a changing social and economic system. As with the mass media, the question seemed ripe for assessment in the framework of a conscious plan of national development.

That did not emerge, in the early Gorbachev years. The new Soviet leader approached the uncertainties of reform more as an artist than a mathematician. There were, he may have judged, limits to the value of any benchmarks that might be chosen, and doubts about the wisdom of stirring up debates over their selection. Better perhaps in some cases to press ahead and hope for the best. What was being aimed at, overall, was a sea change in Soviet attitudes and perspectives. That is not something to be closely controlled or measured.

In the shifting sea, not all of Gorbachev's reforms will make it to shore but many will and some already have. The television revolution, and elections with real choice, are two systemic changes that can probably not be recalled. Other initiatives, still in the launching phase, may fail or fall short. But insofar as their fate depends on Gorbachev's skill and authority, these have themselves been strengthened by some of the early reforms. The creation of a working national legislature, for example, with popular participation, gives Gorbachev an instrument other than the Party hierarchy through which he can move reforms that get bogged down. His own election as Chairman of the Supreme Soviet gives him a tenured authority to enhance, and perhaps eventually to supplant, his leadership as General Secretary of the Communist Party. This may have been his objective all along.

Gorbachev has not by these means become entirely immune to a Khrushchev-style removal from power. The question his displacers would have to ask, however, is where else they could effectively turn. There are alternatives to reform, but most are discredited or inadequate. The Soviet leadership could turn to more discipline, tougher supervision, or the churning of personnel. It could discard the carrot and retry the stick. But it plainly does not want to, and in this the senior political figures stand united with Gorbachev.

If the whole reform leadership were to be replaced, it would have to be by something like *Pamyat*, the bastion of patriotic conservatism with a potentially broad appeal. *Pamyat* as a movement, however, is too riven by nationality frictions, including anti-Semitism, to constitute an effective governing force. A reversion to

Stalinist practices is unlikely, moreover, as even the old guard recognizes that this would court internal failure and external decline. The old guard itself, if it resumed power, would be obliged to continue with some kind of reform.

If, therefore, Gorbachev were to die in office or to be removed, the likelihood is that his policies would remain broadly in force. They might not be pursued as vigorously or with such skill; there are not many Gorbachevs in any system. But his revolution is not a personal one. Gorbachev is not some Peter the Great who has come out of the whirlwind to make dramatic changes that will recede into history when the whirlwind subsides. The new leader is more a product of his times, selected by peers and supported by a society that requires reform. The dynamics of *perestroika,* for this reason, seem largely irreversible. They have emerged from sources too deep to permit their suppression. Gorbachev is a shaper of history but also a creature of it, and the reforms are an outgrowth of this conjunction.

7

The Pace and Prospects
of Soviet Reform

The Gorbachev reforms of the 1980's took effect too slowly but were also introduced too suddenly: That was the impression an outside observer might have gleaned from the grumblings on offer in Moscow and other places. Inevitably, there was truth to both observations. It would take time to reorient the Soviet way of mind, and the effort to do so was bound to be disruptive. Gorbachev was not stampeded into action by the slowness of results, but he did tend sometimes to set ambitious goals and timetables. This risked a loss of confidence, both at home and abroad, when his mobilization efforts fell short; but it had the useful effect, from Gorbachev's perspective, of preempting counter-reactions. Words can do service as deeds when they change the agenda and reorder the debate.

In the Soviet Union the quality of the debate was at first shrill from lack of practice, but under Gorbachev it improved. The incremental gains registered by *perestroika*—toward market dynamism, electoral choice, and open discussion—began attracting adherents and developing a potential for fuller realization. Ultimately the confluence of a reform agenda with a more modern society could achieve far-reaching changes, beyond the present imaginings of either reformers or reformed. But this would take time. The goal, at the outset, was to begin to shift the society's cast of mind.

One practical necessity was to stimulate small centers of innovation and creativity such as are found at MIT, Cal Tech, and other university centers in the United States. What was required from the Soviet Union's scientific establishment was a readiness not only to meet and to resolve specific, identified problems but to anticipate the next generation of challenges. This was not a state of mind that could be imposed successfully from the top down, but it could be induced by example and encouragement.

One example not encouraged was that provided in the late 1980's by Poland and Hungary. Both of these Eastern bloc countries espoused free-market policies and multiparty elections, which even with limitations went beyond anything the Soviets were ready to adopt. Adam Michnik, the spokesman for Poland's now-legalized Solidarity Union, said: "If we make it we will surely become the model for Russia." In practice they became the model for reform upheavals in East Germany, Czechoslovakia, Bulgaria, and Rumania, but not—immediately at least—in the Soviet Union. Gorbachev would not jump over the sequential steps of an orderly progression.

Yet there were occasions when he could and did set far-reaching goals for the Soviet Union, and accompany them with short timetables of doubtful realism. This was puzzling to those Western observers who were otherwise prepared to applaud Gorbachev as a pragmatist. Was he in fact a practical leader, or just some kind of new doctrinaire pushing for goals without regard to their attainability?

Gorbachev sometimes announced unattainable objectives, he sometimes claimed to have reached them when he had not, and he sometimes was obliged to postpone scheduled achievements that could not be attained. His June 1987 Central Committee speech and the accompanying "basic theses" fixed on 1991 as the year by which significant economic changes were supposed to be in place and producing results. This imposed what the University of Virginia economist Gertrude Schroeder called "a staggering set of tasks on the central bureaucracy and on the producing units," at a time when they were struggling to carry out the then-current requirements of the 1986 five-year plan. The pace was plainly unrealistic. In Abel Aganbegyan's view Soviet economic reform was like "the regeneration of vineyards," complicated by the need to "renew virtually all our vines at the same time." True and lasting improvements in the Soviet economy were unlikely to emerge until the end of the century, when the leading American authority Ed Hewett believed it would be enough if the *momentum* was going in the right direction and was firmly based.

At the UN General Assembly in 1988, Gorbachev laid claim to a degree of social reform, "based on the rule of law," that had not yet been achieved. "Work on a series of new laws has been completed or is nearing completion," he said, referring "in particular to laws on the freedom of conscience, *glasnost,* public associations and organizations and many others." In fact the key laws—on press freedom, the rights of a criminal defendant, and the status of voluntary organizations—were at that time hung up in adversarial drafting exercises, from which they were not yet ready to emerge. Gorbachev was not quite falsifying his report, but he was coloring it.

The Soviet leadership did move promptly—too promptly for some—to translate the 1988 Party Conference resolutions into action. Gorbachev applauded those resolutions in his closing speech, and warned: "If we delay in implementing them . . . much could go for nothing." He secured the Conference's immediate approval, without committee consideration, of decisions calling for: (1) Party elections in the fall of 1988; (2) Constitutional amendments and election law changes by the end of 1988; and (3) national elections in the spring of 1989. The amendments were published in the press for "nationwide discussion," limited however to one month. This provoked strenuous complaints, from the intellectuals in particular. Andrei Sakharov protested that such sweeping reallocations of power, without time for reflection, were "tantamount to a coup d'état." Historian Leonid Botkin agreed, saying that "we have been waiting a thousand years for democracy in this country. Why can't we wait another three months?" In the event, there were numerous comments, and some 40 revisions were adopted; but the most difficult questions—of federal relations, and of political pluralism—had to be postponed for separate later consideration.

Various explanations could be offered for this rush to record achievements, each of which may contain some validity. The Soviet Union has been described by historians as a "mobilization society," meaning one that requires strong exhortation and bright banners to get it moving. Stalin collectivized the peasantry and stiffened the defenders of Leningrad, in part by such means, and Khrushchev used exhortation to tear down the forests of Kazakhstan. Gorbachev may similarly have believed that it was only by establishing ambitious early objectives that he could generate the reform momentum needed, and attainable, by the end of the century. If so, that would tend to refurbish his credentials as a realist. On the other hand, the newly emerging Soviet civil society on which reforms must rely may no longer be so susceptible to mobilization campaigns as were earlier generations of Soviet citizens. Exhortation without timely fulfillment could become, for this generation, an act of estrangement.

Why risk that? For Gorbachev there were mileposts of accountability to be considered. He had consumers and the military to keep in mind, both of which had been asked to defer their immediate claims on the economy in the expectation of greater rewards to come. The next Party Congress, initially, was scheduled for 1991, and if the glow of reform were to fade this could be a time for some leadership challenge to emerge.

Beyond such specific hazards, there was in the late 1980's a sense of national crisis which demanded a spirit of urgency to confront it. The Reformation and Counter-Reformation had once taken a century or more to play out. In the late 20th century there was not time for such a pace. The skeins of travel and publicity connect the citizens of today to their fellows, and societies to the world, with an immediacy unknown in the Middle Ages. There is a force of expectation, a rush to improvement, that presses insistently on the hand of the reformer. Gorbachev held out against this pressure when he could, and moved in front of it when he could not.

There was more to be considered. By laying claim on occasion to more than he could manage, Gorbachev might hope to preempt competing agendas. This was something that, paradoxically, his periodic successes made more necessary. In the March 1989 elections, the Communist Party leaders who were defeated became immediate antagonists of reform. They could point to economic and nationality disturbances, among other things, as failures of the Gorbachev regime, and argue that the old way for all its failings was better. To avoid being branded as a losing heretic, it could have seemed necessary for Gorbachev to maintain that success was near at hand.

Nor was he lacking in the skills or support needed to sustain that posture. At each of the key political occurrences of his first five years, at meetings of the Party and the Central Committee, Gorbachev showed himself to be an artful player; he made perceptible gains at each. He displayed among other things a sense of the practical that was keener and more supple than that of his predecessors. Eugene Primakov, a Gorbachev appointee as director of the Institute for World Economy, said in a 1987 interview that "we are no longer setting fixed deadlines for ourselves." Gorbachev himself had been chosen quite deliberately by his peers as a reformer—a fact that distinguished him from Khrushchev, who was chosen more to erase the past than to invent a future. Gorbachev was given high-level, concerted political support for far-reaching change, a mandate that no one since Lenin had effectively enjoyed.

Consensual reform of this sort can be more effective than dictated change, but it also takes more of an effort at persuasion. It calls for diplomacy as well as strength, and the willingness to seek a common course. Soviet political and social debates, at this period, were much in need of such direction. Appeals to the millennium, or against ultimate evil, may have a galvanizing force but when overdone they can fracture, rather than forge, a needed consensus. Sergei Grigoryants, the publisher of *Glasnost,* showed that reformers could be as guilty as anyone of this failing, when he argued that unless certain particular archives were preserved, "there is no hope that we will avoid another stage of Stalinism."

Such assertions were altogether too shrill, too self-righteous, to admit debate. The Andreyeva letter of March 13, 1988, edited perhaps by Yegor Ligachev, was a comparably dogmatic assertion of conservative opinion, with no invitation to debate. Its rebuttal, in *Pravda,* at least took the form of an editorial embracing differences of view, and inviting more letters to the editor.

Debate in due season became more sophisticated and more common under Gorbachev. If the economy remained resistant to effective reform, at least the key terms—money supply, budget deficits, property rights—entered into the public domain, where they had rarely if ever appeared before. On the political side, plays like *The Brest Peace* began promoting an acceptance of the legitimacy of debate. Soviet leaders, it could now be seen, had not always agreed among themselves, in Lenin's day or since.

A debate that can stimulate reform, the Soviets were learning, is one that does not insist too dogmatically on the correctness of anyone's position. Gorbachev's view of this matter could almost have been taken from a statement once made by the American Supreme Court Justice Oliver Wendell Holmes, Jr.:

> All rights tend to declare themselves absolute to their logical extreme. Yet all in fact are limited by the neighborhood of principles of policy which are other than those on which the particular right is founded, and which become strong enough to hold their own when a certain point is reached.

Gorbachev, a Marxist and therefore a Hegelian, would probably have added that one needs a compelling antithesis to dislodge a settled thesis, and to move society toward a durable new synthesis. This could be true, as well.

Rhetoric, in his hands, at all events, led to deeds, and also was one: a rallying cry that could lift the agenda beyond the immediately attainable. And Gorbachev's rhetoric did not have to carry the whole momentum of reform. There were also reform achievements, which if somewhat less extensive than proclaimed nonetheless created an impetus of their own for further change.

The establishment of business cooperatives, for example, though hindered by taxes and regulations, instilled a new taste for alternative goods and services that could spark demand for wider competition. The feedback arising from that demand, through the channels of *glasnost*, might tell the Soviet leaders what they needed to do—carrying beyond what they may have first intended—to make *perestroika* a success. It could in this way serve to guide economic restructuring toward a true market mechanism, with progressively decentralized decision-making.

The instrumentalities and practices of *glasnost* themselves, while falling short of a Western-style free press or information society, opened up new vistas for the nation's intelligentsia and reposed new confidence in them. So, although Andrei Sakharov might complain that Gorbachev's 70th-anniversary speech was too soft-spoken about Stalin's purges and foreign-policy blunders, the speech was soon followed up by a full-page *Pravda* criticism of the Hitler-Stalin pact as well as by Party authorization of a memorial statue to Stalin's victims. Likewise, the tediously exacting process of clearing Nikolai Bukharin's name, which looked at first suspiciously like a coverup, in the end allowed historians and other thinkers to take the outcome as a starting point. One could write after that "about the 1930's, the depression," said the previously silenced Roy Medvedev. "One can write about Brezhnev."

The new opportunities, when taken together, could also stimulate a fresh spirit of scientific inquiry and application. They could, over time, erode the habits of authoritarianism that had kept Soviet industry and technology in arrears. Already by 1989 there was a new vigor and purpose in the creaky Academy of Sciences, arising from the general ferment and more particularly from the elections in which Andrei Sakharov and Roald Sagdeyev were at first kept off the Academy slate for the People's Congress, and then pushed onto it by a majority of the electors.

The very act of voting, in that election and in others that would follow, created a demand for fair voting and therefore for voting reform. The practice of debate, in election campaigns and in legislatures, began to strengthen its quality and thereby to sharpen policy choices. Divisions of opinion within the Communist Party might eventually crystallize into proto-political parties, with alternative programs and emphases. Already after 1988 it was no longer a group of isolated dissidents that confronted the Party, but a collection of more or less disciplined and coherent popular fronts and voluntary groups. The Gorbachev reforms had spawned these for instrumental purposes, but like the sorcerer's apprentice they were exhibiting a life and momentum of their own.

The political anatomy of Estonia in 1989 gave some sense of the direction in which the nation as a whole might eventually be moving. There was first an Estonian National Independence Party, consisting of perhaps 200 members, many of them former prisoners of conscience. These were absolutists, uninterested in compromise and refusing even to take part in national elections. Then there was the Heritage Society, concerned primarily with promoting the Estonian flag. Next there were the Greens, whose desire to conserve what was native to Estonia included keeping Russian exploiters out. After that there was the mass-membership Popular Front, which included many Communist Party officials and members. To the "right" there was the Inter-National Movement, consisting of Russian and other non-Baltic people who found themselves in the odd position of arguing for political pluralism. Finally there was the established Communist Party, whose new Party Secretary made it a practice to consult regularly with the leaders of the other movements, particularly the Greens and the Popular Front. This was party politics of a kind that would not have been unfamiliar to New York or Chicago practitioners of the late 19th century.

Ultimately what would come of such changes would be the product of the Soviet reform agenda, intersecting with the new society it was helping to shape. Gorbachev by his works and pronouncements was sowing the seed, but the nutrients would come from the changing soil of the Soviet culture. The plant that eventually emerged would be one that neither Gorbachev nor the culture, nor any outside stimulus, could claim of itself to have grown.

8

Western versus Soviet Criteria for Success

There has been a tendency in some quarters to see the Gorbachev reformation as a victory for American values and to judge its progress by American or Western standards. Gorbachev has sometimes fed this tendency by his appropriation of Western terms, like "democracy." But there can be no such thing, in truth, as an Americanized USSR. The Soviet Union is a political culture with a history and an opportunity of its own, and it cannot be understood or measured apart from those points of reference.

A political culture, scholars tell us, is the sum of habits and values and expectations that shape a nation's institutions and modes of behavior. For the United States, that culture was once summed up by Justice Benjamin Cardozo of the Supreme Court as consisting of "ordered liberty"—of freedom, that is, with restraints appropriate to its flourishing. For Gorbachev's USSR, the counterpart phrase is something nearer to "democratized discipline"—order, that is, with ventilations suited to its effectiveness. The two systems are not the same, or even really comparable.

The Soviet value structure is derived from that society's feudal origins more than from its imported Marxist overlay. The preference for order over spontaneity, for discipline over initiative, for equality over freedom, and for community over the individual, are products of a millennium of history unpenetrated by the European

Renaissance or Reformation or Enlightenment. That history has avoided Westernization while still adopting such elements of modernity as have seemed conducive to the culture's needs and growth. The West as such—and the United States in particular— has not been a forcing agent in the Gorbachev reformation, and cannot become its tutor, though it may yet serve as a model if it keeps itself quiet. The moving force will be Soviet public morale, demanding of change and capable of sustaining it.

The economic reforms introduced by Gorbachev have not, for example, been Western in shape or content. This can be seen from a list of the dominant attributes of a market system as understood in the West: pricing freedom, ease of entry, freedom to fail, and capital markets. While room may be found in the Soviet reform plan for some part of each of these features, it will be limited and controlled. Western ideas of economic value and allocation did not even enter into Soviet scholarly circles until 1959, during the Khrushchev thaw, which was after Gorbachev and his senior advisers had completed their educations. The reforms that this group now favor will be market-assisted, not market-determined. Their economic changes will bump along toward improvement on the basis of Soviet experience and not of capitalist doctrine.

The practical need for better housing and a fuller larder is what will drive the search. At stake, eventually, may be some kind of a working redefinition of socialism. But economic reform is not a textbook enterprise. If it were, the effort would have been halted early on. *Perestroika* has persisted through drawbacks and disappointments that would have finished off a merely intellectual movement. All Gorbachev could sometimes do, at the beginning, was to bring in new people and point a new direction. It was enough to allow a start.

On the social-reform side, *glasnost* has ushered in a fresh-sounding debate about state and society. It presages the possible acceptance, one day, of the idea that individuals and societies exist not to serve the state but to be served by it. Nothing like that, however, is in prospect at the outset. The Western concept of a "social compact," of society as something anterior to the state and giving it its legitimacy, is at this point still basically alien to the Soviet way of mind.

There are some, like Andrei Sakharov, who take a liberal democratic view of Soviet possibilities, and who gain from *glasnost* the opportunity to air those views. But Sakharov is in a small minority. Much more in the cultural mainstream is a figure like the exiled author Alexander Solzhenitsyn, who takes a hostile view of Western social permissiveness. To him the Soviet failing is not authoritarianism but misapplication of the necessary authority. Disciplined leadership is for him more appealing than *glasnost.*

There is some utility in comparing Soviet human-rights traditions with those in the United States, if only to clarify the differing social frameworks from which each has emerged. In America the phrase "human rights" comes from the Declaration of Independence ("certain inalienable rights") and implies freedom from despotic government. In the USSR, the phrase means something closer to economic and social entitlements—the "right" to affordable housing and education and health care, all dispensed by the government. The Soviets consider themselves free in this context to criticize the human-rights record of the United States.

The difference shows up in the two constitutions. The U.S. Bill of Rights is phrased in terms of what the state may not do: "Congress shall make no law. . . ." It recognizes rights preceding the formation of the state, and superior to it; if the state violates those rights, the victim may have recourse at law. In the Soviet Constitution, by contrast, many of the same rights are recognized but only as commitments on the part of the government to identify and secure the appropriate benefits. The counterpart language reads: "In accordance with the interests of the people and for the purpose of strengthening and developing the socialist system, citizens of the USSR shall be guaranteed freedom of the press, of assembly, of meetings. . . ." If the government of the day fails to enact or enforce such guarantees, the citizens have no recourse.

Professor Harold Berman of the Harvard and Emory law schools, who has twice taught law at Moscow State University (where Gorbachev studied law), has proposed that the U.S. and USSR forego trading charges of noncompliance with each other's different conceptions of human rights. Each can argue if it wants to that the other's standards are inadequate. But compliance as such can be measured only in terms of the progress of each country inside its own historically developed framework of political institutions and values. There is need of an American yardstick for American rights, and of a Soviet yardstick for Soviet rights.

By that measure, *glasnost* is not an adoption of First Amendment freedoms, but it is an expansion of Soviet liberties. *Glasnost* is a directed license, a lever for change. It strengthens the state by opening up the society, within limits. The limits are intrinsic to its value; and while these may erode with usage, the state will not hasten to tear them away.

Americans ought probably to have known that this would be the case. In the 1970's, when the Brezhnev government of the day was stirring up Third World nations to censor international press freedom, the most effective counter-argument the West could come up with was not ideological but instrumental in character. It was that a developing country might choose to distrust Western-style democracy, but its rulers should still want to have independent channels of accountability so as to keep their development programs on track. That argument eventually prevailed—not only in the Third World but, after Gorbachev's accession, in the Soviet Union as well.

Instrumental liberalization has also been the moving force behind the historical revisionism experienced under Gorbachev. There has long been a divergence in the practice of history-writing as between Russia and America. For Americans, as children of the Enlightenment, history is thought to be truth-seeking, its guiding legend George Washington and the cherry tree. Watergate and other exceptions can arise, but these are perceived as anathema to be rooted out when found. On the Soviet side, history has more often been truth-molding. Former UN ambassador Jeane Kirkpatrick could argue, as she did, that "Soviet leaders have made the writing and rewriting of history one of their spoils of victory"— although this was almost certainly too broad a condemnation. Of Lenin's four healthy successors, two have been truth-manipulators but two have been truth-seekers, at least up to a point. Stalin was a radical falsifier of history, and Brezhnev a fiction-preserver, to sustain their legitimacy. Khrushchev and Gorbachev began letting enough truth into the public arena to topple those legitimacies, while upholding their own.

This was not a matter of obeisance to objective truth. Khrushchev used revisionism to buttress his partial reforms, removing despotism at its apex and restoring collective rule. It was not necessary for these purposes to turn the searchlight of history onto pre-1934 practices, and Khrushchev did not deal with this period in his 1956 "de-Stalinization" speech. Gorbachev in time did take on and denounce that history, because he needed for his own broader reform objectives to revalidate the pre-collectivization economy. Also, the memory of the Stalinist terror still hung like a pall in the late 1980's on the Soviet mentality—and its exorcism was needed to allow the movement of mind from coercion to opportunity, from stick to carrot, on which Gorbachev's reform program depended.

By Soviet standards, then, the overall changes of social atmosphere brought in by Gorbachev have been limited but significant. New truths admitted into the arena, new confidence reposed in the people, are vitalizing and quite possibly irreversible additions to the sum of social goods, no matter how circumscribed they may be. They look permanent and they may grow, always from Soviet cultural soil.

That cultural reminder is necessary also for the assessment of governmental reforms, whose proclaimed standard of "democratization" has so distinctly Western-sounding a tone. The fact here again is that the Soviet political changes of 1988–89 were not really Western in character. They installed a one-party government, chosen by indirect elections, with few checks or balances, and only limited legal accountability. The reforms were nonetheless significant, by Soviet standards, both immediately and potentially.

The contrasts with the American form of government should not, to begin with, be overdrawn. It is true that the popular voice in the selection of the Supreme Soviet and of its chairman was only indirect, through the Congress of People's Deputies, and that this choice—like the election of the Congress itself—was made without the benefit of debate between rival parties. But those who saw this as deficient, in an American sense, may have forgotten that it was James Madison, in *The Federalist,* who first defended indirect elections and the absence of party rivalry as not only consistent with democracy but perhaps its saving grace: "We may define a republic," Madison wrote, as "a government which derives all its powers directly or indirectly from the great body of the people. . . . On comparing the [American] Constitution planned by the convention with the standard here fixed, we perceive at once that it is conformable. . . . The Senate derives its powers indirectly from the people. The President is indirectly derived from the choice of the people" (No. 39). Madison argued further, in No. 10, that the whole Constitutional plan could be celebrated as an instrument to "break and control the violence of faction." John Jay joined the two arguments together, in No. 64, where he maintained that:

> This mode [of indirect elections] is superior to elections by the people in their collective capacity where the activity of party zeal, taking advantage of the supineness, the ignorance, and the hopes and fears of the unwary and interested, often place men in office by the votes of a small proportion of the electors.

The American practice has since been stretched and modified, of course, though not necessarily improved; but this was the view of the 18th-century Enlightenment, and the Gorbachev reforms measure up.

It must be swiftly added, however, that the American framers could count on specific, built-in checks and balances to curb abuses of elected authority—through Congressional impeachment or refusal of appropriations, through judicial review, and through the operations of an independent press. Such powers were all talked about to some degree by the 1988 revisers of the Soviet Constitution, but they were not meted out in anything like the American manner.

Under Article 120 of the amended USSR Constitution, for example, the chairman of the Supreme Soviet is made recallable from office, but only by the Congress of People's Deputies, which is to meet infrequently and to house an unwieldy number (2,250) of legislators. It seems quite doubtful that a Soviet-style "Watergate" would ever give rise to an impeachment in these circumstances.

To continue the comparison, the power to raise and appropriate funds is, by the U.S. Constitution, vested exclusively in the national legislature—the very provision at issue in the Iran-Contra affair of the 1980's, with its political repercussions. No comparable exclusivity is vested in the Soviet legislature by Article 113 of that amended Constitution, which charges the Supreme Soviet merely with overseeing "the *management* of the national economy . . . [and] the budget and finance system." So far as appears, it remains open to the Soviet Executive to raise and appropriate year-to-year funds by decree.

As for the judiciary, in America its independence is guaranteed by specific provisions in Article III of the U.S. Constitution, assuring life tenure to federal judges at undiminished pay. The revised Soviet Constitution proclaims in its Article 155 that Soviet judges will likewise be "independent and subordinate only to the law," but the practical bulwarks for that assertion are missing. Under Article 152, judges are to be elected for a term of ten years, with no guarantees as to salary, and are recallable by the soviet that elected them. In the case of the USSR Supreme Court, that will be the Supreme Soviet, a much smaller (542-member) and more active legislature whose deputies are at least as certain to be distressed with judicial judgments from time to time as are their counterparts in the 535-member U.S. Congress. The climate for judicial protection of individual liberties, therefore, and of unpopular defendants, does not look propitious.

There is in addition no First Amendment or Bill of Rights in the amended Soviet Constitution, hence no enforceable guarantee of an independent press. Gorbachev has found it instrumentally useful, for policy reasons, to promote forthrightness and self-criticism in the conduct of governmental operations. But on sensitive subjects like nationality disturbances, he has shown himself ready to curtail press coverage. Nothing in the revised Constitution will check that executive discretion. The new USSR Constitutional Oversight Committee, while it has the power to identify infringements of Constitutional guarantees and to refer them back for correction, cannot create guarantees where they do not exist; and there simply are no enforceable assurances of an independent press.

This is emblematic of a further and more pervasive difference between the constitutional systems of the United States and the Soviet Union. The Soviet reformers are aiming for a *Rechtsstaat,* or "law-state," which is something distinct from the Western idea of a "rule of law." A law-state is one that obeys its own legislation; and this, for the Soviet Union—with its history of arbitrary authority—is a goal of undeniable importance. A rule of law carries further, however, and submits the legislation itself to a higher standard of natural or constitutional law. Here is where the idea of a "social compact" enters in; for, as Alexander Hamilton put it in *The Federalist* (No. 78): "It is not to be supposed that the Constitution could intend to enable the representatives of the people to substitute their will to that of their constituents. . . . In other words, the Constitution ought to be preferred to the statute, the intention of the people to the intention of their agents." In the Soviet Union, however, the legal reforms of the late 1980's left the Communist Party and not the Constitution as the supreme guarantor of the people's will. Theirs remained at this point an oligarchical and not a democratic system.

There is no alternative, in the end, to using Soviet standards for the measurement of Soviet reforms. By those standards, what emerged from the new Constitution was a modified, law-limited, consultative autocracy in which the people's advice and participation were invited but did not control. Nothing achieved by that Constitution would displace, in particular, the two cardinal principles of Party control over policy and state control over the economy. The exercise of those controls might be modified over time, and with experience, but not by ideological choice. As Seweryn Bialer described it:

> The Western democratic model is not the birthright of every nation or society nor is it the natural state of all societies. The odds of a Western-style democracy developing in an immense, multi-national country that has never in its entire history known a single day of political democracy are very long.

The point is not so much that the Gorbachev changes were limited, but that they were introduced into a culture that was deeply and pervasively limiting. Alexis de Toqueville, the great historian of democracy, observed in his book *The Ancien Régime and the French Revolution* that the most harmful feature of the Bourbon state—its centralization—was unwittingly carried forward by its successor. The same could as readily be said of the Gorbachev revolution.

Yet Andrei Sakharov's recurrent complaint, during the 1988 deliberations over constitutional revision, that "democracy" was being incubated by "undemocratic means," seems wide of the mark. Not only was "democracy" in any full sense never the object of the reforms, but for Gorbachev to push any changes through the state and Party as he found them was bound to require a high degree of concentrated initiative. The real questions were when and how far that concentration might be relaxed.

Gorbachev was not the first General Secretary to reach for the additional title of head of the Supreme Soviet, but he was the first for whom this would mean an addition of power. The Presidium leader would henceforth be wielding the Executive authority in fact as well as in name, and without the collegial constrictions of a Politburo or a Council of Ministers. Some delegates to the Party Conference thought this was a good idea where Gorbachev himself was concerned, one of them saying, "I am for giving *this* General Secretary full presidential powers." Others had misgivings. Sakharov opposed the provisions that were adopted, arguing that they would vest the new national leader with a dangerous monopoly of authority. "Today it will be Gorbachev in power," he said, "tomorrow it can be anyone. As in the past we are relying on one man."

The Constitution as adopted made only a semantic nod to these objections, vesting the new Presidium leader with sweeping powers of domestic initiative and external authority, and withholding only the title of "president" (which Western press organs and politicians went on using anyway). Under Article 120 it was the "chairman" of the Supreme Soviet who would serve as "the highest official of the Soviet state," implying in theory at least that the various associate and deputy members of the Presidium might have some say in his decisions. But there was no legal assurance of this, and until some countervailing power centers develop—until, perhaps, the Council of Ministers acquires the offsetting stature it enjoys in France—Sakharov's concerns seem justified, even within the context of Soviet political culture.

It will ultimately be experience, however, and not the text, that controls. The Constitution itself, like the Election Law, remains amendable by a simple revisory vote of the national legislature. Nothing is firmly assured, and nothing forever precluded, by these laws. It is what will happen under the law, in keeping with social attitudes, that will set the course of future internal developments in the Soviet Union. This is what Gorbachev himself probably had in mind from the beginning—a process or system by which to draw out and stimulate changing attitudes. For, as the *Moscow News* legal correspondent suggested in a comment on the process:

> Democratic principles will flourish . . . only when society realizes we are all equal under the law. . . . We are always asking, "May I?" There are many reasons for this, including the long and

persistent humiliation of the individual before organizations, "bodies," or the "majority."

As Soviet citizens acquire the habit of being consulted, of having their government held to account, of seeing the laws applied as they are written—and as they observe that their society holds together under these changes—the taste for political participation should grow.

9

Implications and Opportunities for the U.S. and the West

The movement toward internal reform in the Soviet Union has presented the West with several substantial questions concerning its own response:

1. Would a successful reform of the USSR be in the interests of the West? The answer, though not free from debate, is probably yes.
2. Is entry of the USSR into the world community a good and likely thing? Again, probably yes, but it will be slow in coming.
3. Could the West, by its efforts, effectively prevent or produce a successful Soviet reform? The answer to this, despite a wealth of contrary disputation, is almost certainly no.
4. What then can be done to promote and protect Western interests? America and its allies can aim to be true to themselves and to their own essential interests in an orderly and stable world.

A reformed and chastened Soviet Union may be a stronger rival for world leadership, but its challenge is likely to take less volatile and dangerous forms. The only other alternative—a failed or fragmenting USSR, particularly one that is able to blame the

West for its disintegration—could be severely destabilizing. Non-military competition, while perhaps a challenge to the status quo, should on the whole be bracing for the world. It is what for decades the leaders of the West have invited the Soviet government to undertake.

The changes in that government could, for a time, concentrate undue power in the hands of a single person. There may be associated efficiency gains—a strengthened defense-policy planning staff, improved internal information flows—of benefit to the USSR and to its negotiating partners. But a chief executive who is freed from the necessity of securing consent from his Politburo or ministerial colleagues is a chief executive who can lose his sense of boundaries. Collegial authority, since the days of Khrushchev, has from a Western perspective been a prudent authority. Now that could change, to the potential detriment of stability.

Yet as popular participation broadens and legitimizes the internal authority of the Communist regime, it should help also to moderate Soviet conduct toward the outside world. As George F. Kennan wrote in 1947, the Soviet leaders have long been "absorbed with the struggle to secure and make absolute the power which they seized in November 1917. They have endeavored to secure it primarily against forces at home, within Soviet society itself. But they have also endeavored to secure it against the outside world." If, as a result of reform, legitimacy becomes less of a concern at home, it could also become less of a spur abroad.

President George Bush decided at all events in May of 1989 to invite "the integration of the Soviet Union into the community of nations." His statement, coming at the end of a four-month senior policy review within the new U.S. administration, suggested a general acceptance of the currents of change and a broadly benign interpretation of them.

The West does have a positive interest in encouraging international economic participation by the Soviet Union. Over time, such involvement can have a generally civilizing or tempering influence on the perceived self-interest, and therefore the behavior, of the USSR. There has in fact been a steady progression toward integration of the USSR into the global economy, as illustrated by Soviet adherence to world copyright and patent conventions in the early 1970's. The progression cannot, however, move faster than the capacity of the changing Soviet economy to absorb it. Integration will have to be the work of decades.

For the Soviets, full integration can only follow ruble convertibility which must await the lifting of internal price controls. Gorbachev's senior economic advisers, like Abel Aganbegyan, have favored the removal of these controls and the introduction of imports on a mass scale to promote price and quality competition. But the disruptive effects of such actions on the traditionally shielded Soviet economy have been seen by the leadership as prohibitive, or at least daunting.

The Soviet practice has been to look on open trade, and the global market, as unsettling and chaotic. This viewpoint is rooted in the historic insecurity of the Russian state and reflects an attitude of autarchy, or economic self-reliance. To navigate the path from autarchy to interdependence could be even more difficult for the Soviet Union in the late 20th century than it was for Japan in the late 19th. Not only was Meiji Japan geographically more secure, but the high-speed global money flows of the 1990's are much less amenable to control by any government. So, although the winds of world competition may ultimately be invigorating for the Soviet economy, in the short term it is difficult to admit them.

Gorbachev's reform program did call for some changes in Soviet international economic operations. New administrative structures were created and others were streamlined, bringing the Soviet Union in this respect up to about where their Eastern European partners had been in the 1960's. A new joint-venture law, allowing foreign firms to collaborate in the production of Soviet goods for export, was adopted. And the Soviets expressed interest in some form of affiliation with the International Monetary Fund (IMF) and the General Agreement on Tariffs and Trade (GATT).

Of these, the joint-venture law attracted the earliest and liveliest attention. It invited new and established foreign firms to gain a foothold as exporters and, potentially, as importers of goods on the world market. The law was complex and contradictory, however, so that even after liberalizing amendments the most interesting deals were those that were negotiated separately from its provisions. There were both practical and policy problems with implementation: how to repatriate inconvertible ruble earnings, and how even to achieve such earnings in the face of incompatible Soviet objectives. The Soviet goal was to expand the export and hard-currency earnings of home-made goods, whereas for the

Western businessman the attraction lay in building up sales of imported products to the huge and underdeveloped Soviet market. The official position on this conflict, according to business accounts, was that once there had been major sales of joint-venture goods in Western markets, the Soviets would open up a place in their own markets for these goods. But that was a chancy prospect, and only those outside enterprises that were willing to take a fairly long (10- to 20-year) view of their returns were likely to stay around.

In 1989 an "American Trade Consortium" of six U.S. firms reached a special agreement with Soviet trade authorities that appeared to solve one part of the problem. It allowed them to aggregate export and import earnings in such a way that even the import-only members of the consortium could be compensated out of the hard-currency export revenues of others. For the majority of outside companies that could not arrange such offsetting opportunities, however, the prospects remained tentative. The Monsanto Company, for example, was unable to identify a countertrade product to balance the sales of its weed-killer, "Roundup," in the Soviet Union. Its announced conclusion was that "joint ventures will not be a significant factor with the Soviet Union until the ruble is convertible and hard currency is not an issue."

That could be well off in the future. A convertible ruble in the current Soviet internal market would be highly vulnerable to invasion by marks or dollars or yen in search of low-priced goods. The Soviet authorities have not believed they could afford to let this happen, so they have put off price restructuring and are likely to do so again. Convertibility, as a result, will probably occur as an end product of domestic economic reform rather than as an element of it.

The Soviets also announced in 1989 that they were giving thought to the creation of "special economic zones," near Leningrad and Vladivostok, where wholly owned Western plants could earn a new, freely convertible currency. This showed a desire on their part to gain some vitalizing access to global enterprise, without incurring its disruptions. Judging from experience, the yield could be slow in coming.

*   *   *

The suggested Western objective, then, which President Bush called "the integration of the Soviet Union into the community of nations," is not something that the West by itself can bring about. It can "contain" the Soviet Union against that country's wishes, but cannot integrate it; that will require affirmative steps by the Soviets themselves. Nor can the U.S., or the West, oblige the Soviets to meet the various pre-conditions outlined in the Bush approach, such as: "Achieve a lasting political pluralism and respect for human rights." These are matters for the Soviets to address, as elements of their own culture and not on external demand.

Americans are still at this stage accustomed to seeking a leverage over other people's affairs that they do not really possess. Some contend that the Soviet Union needs a period of relaxed international tensions in order to get its internal house in order, and will be prepared to "pay" something for it; others assert that the Soviets cannot possibly achieve their restructuring objectives without access to Western credits and technology. Neither assertion, though earnestly pressed, is accurate.

Peaceful conditions would certainly aid economic revitalization in the USSR, but they are not a prerequisite for it. The Soviets can be expected to seek arms reduction and improved East-West relations on their own merits, not just to benefit the economy. If those relations for any reason turn sour, and the Soviet people come to feel themselves beleaguered, that would tend to shift the onus for economic shortcomings from the Soviet leadership to the West. The Soviet experience throughout the Cold War has been studded with occasions when the economy was weak but morale and political cohesion remained high. Western pressure or leverage could, like the World War II siege of Stalingrad, serve to draw the Soviet people closer to each other and to their government.

As for Western technology and credits, these again could assist Soviet development but are not essential to it. If all U.S. financing and technology were kept entirely out of the Soviet Union, the economist Ed Hewett told the Senate Intelligence Committee without contradiction, it would not injure *perestroika* or the Soviet defense system. Necessary imports could still be brought in from other sources, financed if necessary out of Soviet energy and arms exports. High technology will be taken from the West when it is useful and available, but for its own security reasons the Soviet Union will continue to avoid outright dependence on such imports. It is not, for this purpose, without capacities of its own. In the late 1980's, after the American space shuttle program had been shut down by the Challenger disaster, the Soviets offered their own launcher services on the world market at attractive prices, and also offered remote-sensing earth images of a higher resolution than anything then available elsewhere.

So it was not just bluster when Gorbachev told a meeting of American businessmen in Moscow in December 1985 that he wanted mutually beneficial two-way trade but could live without it: "Our two countries are economic giants, fully able to live and develop without any trade with each other whatever."

As a political matter, Western constraints on trade with the Soviet Union have often proved more damaging to the West than to their intended target. The grain embargo imposed by President Jimmy Carter in the wake of the Soviet invasion of Afghanistan had, for example, no impact on Soviet grain inventories, which were quickly filled up from other sources. It was deeply divisive within the United States, however, where grain producers permanently lost an important part of their market.

A similar effect was produced, in the early 1980's, by President Reagan's attempt to prevent Western exports of equipment for the natural gas pipelines then being built from Siberia to Western Europe. This may have delayed the completion of those lines for a time, and forced the diversion of some East bloc resources. But it also stirred the Soviets into developing their own productive capacities for the pipeline equipment, infuriated American machinery producers and their laid-off work forces, and created severe antagonisms between the U.S. government and its West European counterparts. No such adverse effects were experienced by the USSR.

The effort to "spend the Soviets into bankruptcy" through the arms race, as desired by some officials in the Reagan administration, was likewise unsuccessful. It strengthened Soviet cohesion and divided American opinion. Eventually, as became plain, it displayed the incapacity of the United States economy to absorb limitless increases in arms spending.

President Bush resolved to drop that aspect of his predecessor's policies. "The purpose of our military policy," he said in May 1989, "is not to pressure a weak Soviet economy, or to seek military superiority." This was an important step away from attempted leverage, and toward realism.

The same Bush speech, however, endorsed and employed one piece of economic leverage that, the evidence showed, had never worked. This was the so-called Jackson-Vanik amendment, attached by Congress in 1974 to the trade agreement reached at the Nixon-Brezhnev summit in 1972. It made the normalization of U.S. tariffs on Soviet products contingent upon an expansion of Jewish emigration from the Soviet Union. The effort conspicuously failed. Emigration went up in 1972–73 when the Soviets thought that would forestall the legislation, and again in 1977–79 when talk of repeal was in the air. Other than that it declined, and never more steeply than in the early Reagan years when the exercise of leverage was official policy. After 1985, once the new Soviet leadership had decided for its own reasons to relax social controls, the emigration figures went back up.

President Bush offered in 1989 to waive the provisions of Jackson-Vanik temporarily, as allowed by the terms of the law, "should the Soviet Union codify its emigration laws in accord with international standards and implement its new laws faithfully." A year-to-year waiver is not, however, likely to stimulate much in the way of new trade. Business planning horizons demand longer lead times than that. The waiver could not therefore generate much of an economic incentive, even if the Soviets were inclined to respond to such incentives, which both reason and experience showed they were not.

Outside probing or "testing" just does not work. The well-known Heisenberg principle, which says that the very act of probing distorts a response, is a distillation of human experience. The English statesman and historian Thomas Babington Macaulay spoke to this point in the House of Commons as early as 1845. Rising to oppose restrictions on the importation of Brazilian sugar grown with slave labor, Macaulay said:

> No independent nation will endure to be told by another nation, "We are more virtuous than you; we have sat in judgement on your institutions; we find them to be bad; and, as a punishment for your offenses, we condemn you to pay higher duties at our Customs House than we demand from the rest of the world."

The parallel with Jackson-Vanik could not be more exact.

That law has come to symbolize for the Soviet Union a confrontational and intrusive American stance, one to which they cannot as a self-regarding nation allow themselves to give way. It has become, for this reason, counterproductive. Gorbachev said flatly to a group of American publishers at the Washington Summit in 1988 that he could not submit to the law's provisions and would not be respected in Soviet political circles if he did.

The general state of U.S.-Soviet relations has had far more to do with the allowance of Soviet emigration than any particular U.S. law. There was liberalization by the Soviet government after détente (1972) and hardening after its collapse (1979). A group of a dozen leading American specialists on the Soviet Union, meeting in 1984, thought that U.S. and Western efforts to influence Soviet internal behavior had enjoyed some scattered success but not much. Firm, quiet assertions of American public opinion, from one leader to another, had been effective, as had private diplomacy by senior political figures interceding on humanitarian grounds in particular Soviet cases. Beyond that, the specialists believed, the relaxation of international tensions could do more for the loosening of internal controls than anything producible the other way around; and developments within the Soviet Union would be of governing importance.

President Jimmy Carter departed from these lessons of history, as had Senator Henry Jackson before him, for domestic political reasons having essentially nothing to do with U.S.-Soviet relations. By 1976, when Carter was elected, America had suffered the twin humiliations of Watergate and Vietnam, of disgrace and defeat. At Notre Dame University in early 1977, Carter began his administration with a pledge to promote universal respect for "protection of the individual from the arbitrary power of the state." The need, he said candidly, was for America "to regain the moral stature that we once had."

The problem is, however, that moral stature will not prevail against external resistance, and is not needed when that resistance wanes. Gorbachev announced at the UN General Assembly in December 1988 that, for his own reasons, all Soviet prisoners of conscience had been released and strict time limits had been placed on the "state-secret" reason for refusing emigration. A month later, at Vienna, the Soviets pledged themselves to further liberalization—not, the top U.S. negotiator told the press, as a result of any Western pressures but because it suited the Soviet internal reform agenda.

Thanks to that agenda, the Soviets under Gorbachev have decided they can withstand outside scrutiny and even rebut it. In early 1987 they stopped jamming BBC and Voice of America broadcasts. They also joined in sponsoring "Capitol to Capitol" live television exchanges between senior U.S. and Soviet officials, including one two-hour exchange in October 1987 on the subject of human rights. Soviet viewers, for whom this was a daytime program, were exposed to American charges of widespread human-rights violations—which, surveys showed, were not kindly received but were broadly watched anyway.

The Soviets took these occasions to criticize what they saw as Western shortcomings. In December 1987, on the eve of departure for his Washington Summit meeting with President Reagan, Gorbachev was asked on NBC television about human rights. He gave the term its usual Soviet reading and then charged the United States government with failure to satisfy the economic and social "rights"—to housing, employment, health care, and the like—of its citizens. The broadcast was shown in both the Soviet Union and the United States, and displayed a Soviet readiness to engage in open debate on the human-rights question.

In the same vein, the Soviets began in late 1986 to promote the idea of an international human-rights conference in Moscow, focusing on economic and social entitlements but open also to broader discussion. The idea was vigorously disputed at first, by Western governments and particularly by the United States, which thought that acceptance would confer an undeserved human-rights parity on the Soviet Union. The ensuing debate, which led in the end to acceptance of the conference, began for perhaps the first time to draw the competing ideas of state and society into concrete comparative focus.

That may prove generally useful. The idea of "humane" governmental practices, of a "humane" social system, is not something alien to Gorbachev's vocabulary. He specifically proposed, at his Washington Summit meeting with Congressional leaders in 1987, that a joint symposium be created to examine differing U.S.

and Soviet perspectives and performance on human rights. If
something like that could be structured in a non-contentious, non-
accusatory fashion, it might bring into focus what the two societies
have in common along with what sets them apart.

A shared code of internal conduct is unlikely to emerge from
this effort. There is no such code as yet in international law, despite what is sometimes claimed on the subject. The human-rights
covenants that the Soviets have accepted either embody their own
definitions of the rights, or are not legally binding, or both. The
Helsinki Final Act of 1975, for example, loosely called the Helsinki
"Accords," was not a treaty or a binding agreement but a plain
declaration of political intent. The text was signed by heads of state
and government, but it was forwarded to the UN Secretary General under the explicit admonition that "this Final Act is not eligible in whole or in part, for registration with the Secretariat under
Article 102 of the Charter of the United Nations, as would be the
case were it a matter of treaty or international agreement, under
the aforesaid Article."

Basket III of the Helsinki Act, containing the human-rights
provisions, is—with limited exceptions (international media, family contacts)—as broad and as general in its terms as the otherwise
divergent provisions of the U.S. and Soviet Constitutions; like
them, its content is left to be gathered out of varying political
conditions. The Final Act also contains an explicit savings clause
reserving authority over internal affairs to national jurisdictions,
in accordance with customary usage, and prohibiting outside enforcement by "military, political, economic or other coercion." In
practice, the only leverage left open for human-rights matters is to
argue about them in public or to entreat for them in private.

The U.S. has tried both approaches in the years following
1975, with more success in private than in public. Virtually any
American involved in U.S.-Soviet relations in the early Gorbachev
years has some satisfying story or another to tell about helping
Soviet emigrants get exit visas, through quietly persistent interces-
sions on their behalf. The Soviets have preferred to deal with these
cases as humanitarian appeals to their mercy, rather than as
human-rights demands on their justice. Public protests by interested private groups have occasionally caught their attention, but
these have also sometimes hardened Soviet resistance to concessions.

What has been most problematic is the recurrent, highly confrontational, official Helsinki review process, which Freedom House director Leonard Sussman once characterized as "bringing East bloc spokesmen to the dock, and charging them—citing names, cases, and institutional procedure—with violations of the Helsinki code of humane practice" as construed by the complainants. The process has undeniably provided a forum for accusation, and for the venting of human frustrations, but the cost-effectiveness of its prosecutorial approach to human-rights improvement is subject to serious question. Ordinary human experience suggests that reforms brought about by public embarrassment are likely to be short-lived and grudging, and the record of Helsinki follow-up has been consistent with that expectation.

Keeping up the morale of an imprisoned Sakharov or Shcharansky, as the process does, and showing the concern of Western political culture for their condition, can be an important task. But there is seldom any prospect of publicly persuading or even shaming Soviet delegations, all of whom have been amply schooled in defensiveness. It has proved worthwhile to hold separate, informal discussions with senior Soviet delegates, away from the noise and publicity, to impress on them in private the genuine dismay aroused in American citizens by Soviet internal repression. But this can be done just as well, and is done, in other diplomatic settings.

It is difficult to make progress, on human rights or on the other important issues with which human rights may get entangled, in a prosecutorial posture. As Senate Foreign Relations Committee Chairman Claiborne Pell put it to his Kremlin hosts during a Moscow visit in the 1980's:

> American attitudes and beliefs are such that Soviet aspirations for improved relations are likely to be frustrated in the absence of improvements in Soviet human rights policy. But the realities of Soviet politics are such that these human rights improvements are most likely to occur—over the short and long term— in an atmosphere of improved relations.

Something in this structure of offsetting conditionalities had to break loose—as it did, finally, when Gorbachev began improving social conditions in the Soviet Union for his own reasons, and not in response to Western demands. Had this not happened, and the West continued to insist on the prior satisfaction of its conditions, no real progress on peace with justice might ever have been possible.

Following Gorbachev's initiatives it has become possible to see his internal reforms as products of the Soviet culture, bearing international implications but not shaped or driven by them. It has become possible to approach the whole human-rights question in such a way that, to use law professor Harold Berman's formulation, "the interests of justice" do not have to clash with "the interests of peace." It has become possible to perceive that, in these matters, detachment can be more productive than demands.

The U.S. may hope that a reformed Soviet Union will be less disruptive than previously in its outward behavior. Secretary of State James Baker expressed this aim in 1989 when he said: "We want *perestroika* to succeed at home and abroad because we believe that it will bring about a less aggressive Soviet Union, restrained in the use of force and less hostile to democracy." Studies have shown a less violent history of relations between constitutional democracies than between other kinds of states; Americans may hope to benefit from that condition.

But the Soviet Union is not yet a constitutional democracy, nor is it headed ineluctably in that direction. If the Soviets do move that way, it will have to be in response to some set of inner dynamics that allows them to over-ride the inherited obstacles of economic backwardness, social antagonism, and political inertia. The motive power for this cannot be supplied from outside.

It may be that the inner turmoils of *perestroika* will one day build up a sufficient pressure to produce the needed impetus. Polls published in November 1989 showed, for example, that whereas 40 percent of Soviet citizens still favored extensive government controls over the market, another 40 percent—up strikingly from 25 percent the previous January—were ready to try a free market. This division of views was mirrored in published debates of the Politburo, which were similarly split between reformist and traditional stances. No outside encouragement can arbitrate that kind of division.

But there are routes toward a settlement that Western history and experience might suggest, and that Gorbachev could for his own reasons choose to adopt. One of these would employ what *Time* magazine called Gorbachev's talent for "calculated disorder," to postpone the resolution of inner conflicts until a sufficient demand can build up for more basic reform. This would match Gorbachev's early agenda; if successful now, it could parallel the reform path of French president Charles de Gaulle, whose calculated diffidence spurred his compatriots to self-assertion in the 1960's. By such means, an authentic dispersion of Soviet power within that society might perhaps be achieved, for the first time in history.

Another path toward fundamental reform, also potentially available to Gorbachev, would be that of scrupulously mediated constitutional change. Here the parallel might be with the American Constitutional Convention, which was conducted in a closed setting among political leaders of differing viewpoints, after an earlier experiment at confederation had failed. In America at the time the problem was too much decentralization, whereas in the Soviet Union today it is the reverse; but the procedural opportunity for a settlement is the same. Gorbachev has acknowledged that his power-allocation problems must be settled "at constitutional level." What could be helpful for this purpose would be a small assembly of representative leaders, each with his own political standing in some community of interest. From such a gathering, like that in Philadelphia in 1787 and unlike the mass Moscow Conference of 1988, it is conceivable that a durable scheme of institutionally limited powers might emerge—again, for the first time in history.

Such changes are unlikely to take place, however, unless and until all familiar avenues are tested and found wanting. A judgment on that issue is one that only the Soviets can reach. American example can beckon but not direct.

One contribution that Americans certainly can make to Soviet civic reform is to be themselves, to live up to their own historic calling of social and political freedom. Informally, through popular music and casual clothing and the adventurousness of its young, America has long exerted a magnetic influence on those in the Soviet population who are ready for greater freedom and self-expression. When that same confidence is not displayed by American governments, however, it gives recalcitrant Soviet authorities an excuse to remain unmoved. An America that is true to its own civil-liberties traditions, that breaks free from the reactive fears and suspicions of the 1950's—that repeals, for example, Cold War statutes barring discourse with people of uncongenial political beliefs—is an America that can continue to attract emulation from the vanguards of change in the Soviet Union and around the world.

There is a difference here again between example and intrusion. The Chinese government has frequently protested against American support for dissident leaders within China. That country, like Russia, is a proud nation, which historically has felt oppressed by the West. Chinese leaders tend to see human-rights claims as an impermissible continuation of Western interference in China's internal affairs. But when there is a spontaneous internal upsurge of democratic feeling, as there was in Tiananmen Square in the spring of 1989, the models and mottoes taken up by the Chinese protesters are typically Western and often specifically American: free press, free speech, Lady Liberty, Thomas Jefferson, Abraham Lincoln.

So also in the Soviet Union. Once Gorbachev had launched and legitimized his new initiatives of internal reform, Soviet officials at all levels became interested in examining Western standards of legal and political conduct. A new non-profit body, the International Foundation for the Survival and Development of Humanity, was established in Moscow in 1988 at Gorbachev's request to serve as a conveyor belt for advice and assistance from the West. An independent bar association, the first of its kind, was established in Moscow to interact with Western counterparts. Dialogues on criminal law and legislative procedure and similar matters were invited and pursued, in America and other Western countries, by Moscow institutes and associations.

Other ways can be found to provide non-intrusive assistance. One is to open up Soviet membership in international economic organizations, on established terms and conditions, when the Soviets are ready for it. The meshing of market and non-market economies, with all the potential for disruption this can imply, is a daunting prospect. Most Western experts agree, however, that "observer" status in international bodies can safely be accorded to the

Soviet Union, through transitional arrangements leading in time to membership based on economic behavior. President Bush endorsed that suggestion in his meeting at Malta with Chairman Gorbachev in December 1989. If the Soviets choose to accept the invitation, it could serve as an incubating opportunity.

The most important contribution the West can now make to the progress of internal Soviet reform is, however, to reduce East-West tensions in a prudent and orderly manner. American experts predominantly believe that the relaxation of international tensions will do more to loosen up internal controls in the Soviet Union than anything producible the other way around. Gorbachev made a start toward internal liberalization in the late 1980's; he also unrolled a string of initiatives aimed at international relaxation. They, and the Western reaction to them, form the subject of the third part of this book.

PART THREE

External Relations

10

Continuity and Change in Soviet External Policies

For Americans, accustomed as they are to two centuries and more of prosperous development in the shelter of two great oceans, the geopolitical precariousness of historic Russia is difficult to conceive. It is a huge country now, but it did not begin that way, and even today its low, flat boundaries offer little natural protection. In World War II—a statistic that can never fail to astound—the Soviet Union lost 20 million men, women, and children to 400,000 for the United States: a ratio of 50 to 1.

The birth of the Russian state was slow and painful, interrupted by rude external shocks. First Kiev and then Moscow emerged as dominant principalities around which the others could coalesce. Enemies and intruders rose up on all sides—Poles, Lithuanians, Swedes, and others from the West; Tatars and Mongols and Huns from the East. The Tatars swept across the land in the 13th century and controlled it for more than 200 years. Later the Poles made several incursions and occupied Moscow for a time in the 17th century. Two hundred years later Napoleon was to do the same; and, in World War II, Hitler laid devastating siege to both Stalingrad and Leningrad.

Each time the Russian state was crushed, it rose up stronger and reached out to extend its territorial hold. By the end of the 17th century it could boast a large and effective army, capable of intimidating and sometimes defeating adversaries. Much of Poland was taken under control in the 18th century, and in the 19th Russia seized parts of the crumbling Turkish empire. There were setbacks as well, in Crimea and later against Japan; but throughout all these struggles, it was Russian military power that defined and expressed relations with the rest of the world.

That left little room for cultural interchange of the kind customarily experienced among neighboring states. France and Germany in modern times have often gone to war against each other, but students in both countries read their Kant and Descartes. Both are inheritors of the modes of thinking opened up by the Renaissance and Reformation—neither of which (in another stunner to most Americans) ever reached the people or institutions of Russia. Even the deeply felt Christianity of millions of today's Russians came to them 1,000 years ago (from Byzantium) as an emblem of embattlement: Moscow became in its own eyes a "Third Rome," a font of medieval spiritualism by which to control, then convert, the faithless in alien lands.

There was more than a whiff of this assertive faith—Americans might call it "manifest destiny"—in the Leninist Communism that entered Russia in 1917. Some religious historians even suggest that the communist credo fashioned by Lenin can be understood as a heretical offshoot of orthodox Christianity. Whatever the case, the fervor of the Revolution was clearly universalist in its scope. If all mankind were to make common cause, there would be no more occupations or invasions or burdens of war. And so Lenin's vision of a single worldwide people's republic was inspirationally arrived at. It was only later, when the vision was not adopted by others, that it began to seem both menacing and menaced. That cast the new Soviet Union, along with its competitors, back to the ancient vocabulary of arms.

World War II greatly intensified this direction and connected the Communist Party, unmistakably, to the full long sweep of Russian culture and history. It also generated a new self-confidence, to stand alongside the traditional feelings of vulnerability. Anyone who wants to understand Soviet security policy must work his way through this watershed experience of the terrible triumph over Hitler.

The story began in ignominy, of course, with the Hitler-Stalin pact, leaving the Nazis free to invade Western Europe without fear of hostilities on their eastern flank. This was a sign, an acknowledgment, of Soviet military unpreparedness. At that time the USSR was not a major power; it had only one close ally, Outer Mongolia, and it was unable to work its will militarily even on little neighboring Finland. When, despite all this, the Soviets were able in due course to absorb the full brunt of a Wehrmacht invasion, to outlast it, and eventually to drive out the intruder, it was a major turning point in the nation's history. Russians and Ukrainians alike knew that Hitler had nearly succeeded, and that only their sacrifices had saved the Soviet state.

That state was not, after all, just a creature of Lenin and Stalin. It was, and the Soviet government let its people know that it was, an heir of the great Tsars and patriarchs and heroes paraded before them by their leaders during the darkest days of Leningrad and Stalingrad. This forged an emotional bond, perhaps for the first time, between the ordinary Soviet people and the Party. It also allowed the nation to feel proud of its ability to stand up to the worst that might come along and to emerge triumphant.

The postwar history of security dealings between Russia and the West can be seen as consisting, on the Soviet side, of differing ways to project that pride and to gain for it the respect it was deeply believed to have earned. There has been some overplaying of the Soviet hand, certainly, along with occasional underplaying, and there have been varying conceptual formulations; but there has also been a line or skein of consistency.

The Soviets have sought first of all, and continuously, what they consider "assured security" for the land within their borders. This search has been based, in light of experience, on the unilateral possession of military power. The only sure way to ward off the Tatars and the Mongols, they have judged—along with the Poles and the Swedes, the French and the Germans, and latterly the Americans—has been through ground and air and naval and missile forces directed from Moscow.

How much of this military capacity was actually needed, and how much might be counterproductive, were questions the Soviets have been slow to recognize. At times, especially under Stalin but not limited to that period, they opted for an almost paranoid concept of "equal security"—the maintenance of military forces equal in strength (and perhaps in specific symmetry) to those of all potential enemies taken together. This would mean of course that no single one of those powers, say the United States or even NATO, could stand up to the USSR; and so this posture generated stiff resistance and had, eventually, to be abandoned.

The impulse behind the concept may not die so quickly. It is the obsession with military force—again, understandable in the light of history—that tells the obsessor, if a little force makes you somewhat secure, more force will make you more so and absolute military strength will give you absolute political security. All this is false, however, and amply disproved by history. It fails to account for the perceptions of danger aroused in others, and the provocation it gives them to counter the threat with their own military buildups. Still, an immediate post-Hitler obsession with security is what best explains the Soviet refusal to demobilize their powerful land army, and their peremptory acquisition of control over the "buffer zone" of Eastern Europe. The alarm this produced in Western Europe and the United States, and the resulting decision to form and arm NATO, was the inevitable and in a sense stabilizing result; but it did not lead to unilaterally assured security for the Soviet Union or its people.

There is another, less unsettling security formulation that the Soviets have come to use, particularly in connection with the nuclear balance of forces, and that is "parity." Critical here is the perception of the Soviet Union as a superpower—a status hard-won by the devastating experiences of World War II and the deprivations since. There is persuasive evidence that what the Soviets have wanted most, after protection of their homeland, is to be seen as a global power and co-world leader alongside the United States. Nuclear weapons have been a price of admission to this club—and that entails, not just enough of the weapons to deter attack, but enough to measure up. "Sufficiency," from this perspective, is paradoxically not enough; "parity" is the ticket to the inner circle. That is one reason why the Soviets have stuck so faithfully to the strategic-arms (START/SALT) negotiating process, even when it was leading nowhere, and why they have pronounced themselves ready to move on to the more difficult discussion of intercontinental nuclear-force reductions: The very process of negotiation codifies the concept of nuclear parity and advertises the equality of the two major powers.

But parity has its limitations. To begin with, it is necessary to distinguish political-military parity with the West, which the Soviets have largely attained, from economic or social comparability, which is beyond their current grasp. Patriotic Soviets have been heard to remark, when they are being realistic, that the USSR today is little more than a heavily armed Third World country. Were it not for the arms, indeed, it seems doubtful that the U.S. or Western Europe would pay much attention to the Soviet Union—a very different situation from that of, say, lightly armed Japan.

Within the political-military sphere, the Soviet claim to parity relates to two distinct kinds of interests: (1) defensive security, which is strictly military; and (2) freedom of engagement in the Third World, which is a political exercise of superpower status. The Soviets have tended to take the United States as a model or justification for its conduct in both realms, but there is a need to be more clear about the dividing line between them.

History explains the Soviet Union's continuing desire to dominate or neutralize the countries on its border, wherever it can. (In the case of China, quite plainly it cannot.) The whole of its Eastern European policy stems from that concern. So does its brief postwar occupation of Iran, and its ten-year occupation of Afghanistan. But despite some strenuously voiced fears, at the time, that the Soviets would soon extend their 1979 Afghan invasion into other, non-neighboring, countries (thereby forming a "Red Crescent" in the Middle East), that neither happened nor was ever seriously threatened. The American commentators who joined in that chorus were simply off the mark.

The Soviets must accept some share of responsibility for this misconception, in that they have often couched their foreign excursions in a language of universalism, or ideology, that obscures the true geopolitical basis for their actions. Putting such verbalisms aside, there is broadly speaking a consistent distinction between Soviet conduct toward bordering and non-bordering states. The Soviets were determined to stay in Afghanistan, it appears, until the best possible security arrangement could be worked out—whereas, in non-contiguous places like Egypt, they have been content to leave when asked or when the cost of sticking it out exceeded the foreseeable gain. Cuba and Vietnam may have to be understood in this connection as special cases: non-bordering states where the costs of subvention are high but the unremitting antagonism of the United States has made it difficult to walk away.

There is, as well, a certain unreality to the Soviet insistence on superpower parity, even in its narrower sense of defensive security. The Soviet Union was once accurately described as the only country in the world entirely surrounded by hostile Communist states. The U.S. by contrast has had peaceful, if sporadically contentious, relations with Canada and Mexico, and it still enjoys the shelter of the vast Pacific and Atlantic oceans; there is no way of undoing those gifts. Also, the Soviet Union has been burdened for years by bureaucratic impediments to its technological productivity and innovation, which the U.S. (despite its own difficulties) has not experienced and is not likely to adopt. "Parity" in these important dimensions cannot be attained by shifts in security policy alone.

There remains, finally, the problem of perceptions: How does each side view the other's attempts to attain or keep parity, and what are the risks of misperception? The West has long seen the Soviet aim as being one of superiority, not just parity, and it has armed and positioned itself to deny the Soviets both. The resulting arms race, with its commitment to technological and military preparedness above all else, has diminished stability on both sides. The acts and the doctrines of the Soviet Union, as perceived in the West, have served to weaken parity.

This was perhaps inevitable. For much of Russian history, the best defense against invasion was thought to be an acquisitive offense. The nation expanded mightily over the centuries, without, however, gaining much in immunity from invasion. Even abstinence from hostilities brought no relief. The 1917 withdrawal from World War I was followed by the intervention of formerly allied military forces, the Hitler-Stalin pact by the invasion of the Wehrmacht. It cannot be judged surprising that after World War II Stalin should have seized control of Eastern Europe as a buffer against further attacks.

Western perceptions of Soviet foreign-policy aims have, in any case, long leaned to the expansionist view: The size and growth of the Soviet Union, the Asian despotism of its former rulers, the lure of pan-Slavism, all seemed to an often fractionated and internally warring West the signs of a territorial menace. When to that were added the ideological universalism of Lenin and the early Soviet Communist leaders, the basis was laid for the posture of Western hostility that Gorbachev found firmly seated when he took office.

For much of that the official Soviet ideology could take some blame. That ideology cast its world view in terms of an irreconcilable conflict between socialism and capitalism. Lenin could say, in the idealistic first flush of a Communist state, that "we aim at the firm union and full fusion of the workers and peasants of all nations of the world into a single worldwide Soviet republic." From Stalin through Chernenko, Soviet general secretaries persisted in describing world events as the emblems of an inescapable rivalry between the "two camps," only one of which could prevail. East-West competition was a zero-sum game, for which the East would take care always to be armed with adequate military strength. So went the dogma, and for years it was taken seriously by defense ministers of the West.

The official ideology of Marxism-Leninism has, however, never been an accurate or reliable guide to Soviet foreign policy. Much of the canon has recently been recast by Mikhail Gorbachev, but even before that happened it was not a controlling factor. The writings of Lenin have served always as a kind of "state religion," to be observed on ceremonial occasions and to be cited as a rationalization for pretty much any behavior Soviet leaders have wanted to pursue. In Harvard professor Adam Ulam's phrase, there are Marxist-Leninist sayings that still pop into usage when convenient, like "the involuntary sigh of a lapsed Catholic."

What has persisted beneath that level is an operational code of decision-making, which is ideological in a more basic sense. Ideology has been called, by the sociologist Daniel Bell, "a hardening of commitment, a freezing of opinion." At any given time such a mindset may exhibit elements of rigidity, or doctrinal commitment, that seek to shape and manage perceptions of reality. But it will also be open to the experience of learning, and therefore to change. This is the process that has led, in Gorbachev's time, to the reshaping and relaxation of Soviet ideology.

The United States and the Soviet Union are both exceptionally ideological in their foreign policies, in the sense that their views of the outside world have been shaped to an unusual degree by the internal values and principles of each country. A species of orthodoxy prevails in both places, and defines a range of "legitimate" perceptions about the world. The American orthodoxy has been broader and more flexible, readier to shift its emphasis in one direction or another. The Soviet progression has been all in one direction, away from the central core of faith that held sway in 1917.

Americans now are beginning to see and accept that evolution. It is a long way already from the American approach of 30 to 40 years ago, when John Foster Dulles could take the collected works of Marx and Lenin to Geneva in an effort to predict what the Soviets would do at a summit conference. Those writings are sufficiently prolix to yield anything a searcher wants to find, and they have had no real predictive value for anyone.

This is what the Soviets themselves have been discovering over the whole of their 70-year experience. The fundamental global ideas of the Russian Revolution—about capitalism, imperialism, and world revolution—have all had to be altered in the light of that experience. This has led to a shift in concepts, or operational codes, and at length to the kind of fresh initiatives and proposals that are embodied in Gorbachev's "new political thinking."

That thinking is the product of a historical learning experience that serves in its way to confirm the change. The Soviet view of the world has been progressively altered by what has happened since the days of Revolution—much of it unforeseen, and much flatly contrary to the expectations of that time. Lenin genuinely believed that the Communist revolutionary example would take a swift hold in Europe, which did not happen; so that in its earliest years the Soviet Union had to find a way of joining the international order and of playing the "game of nations." A similarly sudden adjustment was required in the post–World War II period, when the Soviets found themselves transformed from a participant in that order into one of its prime architects. The advent of nuclear weapons in the 1950's brought yet another major change, this one severing the connective link between war and foreign policy; for the first time, then, "peaceful coexistence" became an imperative and not just a stratagem.

Gorbachev, now, has added domestic structural reform to the forces impinging on Soviet foreign policy. This is not a private invention of his own, but a distillation of changes that had been gathering headway in Soviet society for some time. Back in 1945, and even as late as 1959, only one-third of the Soviet population lived in urban centers or received a secondary education. Today the figure is two-thirds. There is now the nucleus of a middle class in the Soviet Union, and it is looking for engagement and accountability. The resulting changes, which are both structural and attitudinal in nature, impose a fresh priority on the Soviet leadership that looks genuine and durable.

The new perspectives on foreign policy had been forming for more than a decade before they were embraced by the Soviet political leadership. Their essentials can be summarized as follows:

1. National security is interdependent and rests on a range of capacities, not just on military strength, which is often unusable and self-destructive.
2. International politics is not a zero-sum struggle against Western imperialism but a much more complex, interactive engagement.
3. Capitalism is not inherently or inevitably militaristic, but shares certain interests with state socialism, especially against nuclear devastation.
4. The Third World is not being swept by global revolution toward the Communist camp or cause, but consists of disparate countries and situations with which particularized foreign policies need to be formed.
5. Relations within the Socialist community, including China, are not just internal or even fraternal but increasingly international.

The adoption of these fresh attitudes, or perspectives, does not mean that the old global ambitions or self-images have all been eradicated. Most likely they remain—the old thinking alongside the new—and seek to be satisfied whenever conditions allow. But along with the new domestic priorities there is also a chastened sense of how costly and risky foreign adventurism can be. Among the lessons delivered to the Soviet hierarchy by the outside world in recent years are these:

1. The dynamic strengths of capitalism as an economic system, and the growing edge it has over state socialism in technology and services.
2. The breakdown of bipolar dominance over the world, and the emergence of unruly other forces.

3. The waywardness of economic and political development, leaving the Soviets often in a position opposed to Third World insurgencies.
4. The uncontrollability of the arms race, and the elusiveness of the strategic balance, by unilateral means.

These are all sharply challenging, and inescapable, factors for Soviet geopolitical calculation; they represent elements with which Mr. Gorbachev or any other leader would have to come to terms. Beyond all else, the Soviet leadership has learned it has no strategy for success that can ignore these factors.

There have been occasions when the Soviets have tried to act in the old way, and have come up conspicuously short. The Cuban missile crisis of 1962 was a case where Khrushchev sought to steal a march on a new U.S. administration, without sufficient thought for the consequences. The ignominy of the ensuing Soviet missile withdrawal, in full public view and after an American blockade, led in time to Khrushchev's dismissal in the 1960's, to Brezhnev's military build-up of the 1970's, and to President Reagan's answering build-up in the 1980's. That is the way an arms race can get started, to no one's ultimate advantage.

The Soviets had to learn the same lesson again, painfully, in the European missile environment of the 1980's. Brezhnev's advisers apparently told him he could safely position SS-20 surface missiles within range of targets in Western Europe without disturbing the perceived military equilibrium. There were experienced Western military leaders who were ready to agree. Admiral Noel Gayler, for example, a former National Security Agency director who once directed nuclear targeting at the Pentagon, thought the SS-20 emplacement was neither intelligent nor troublesome: It added nothing to the nuclear threat already presented by long-range Soviet missiles, whose trajectory could be readily depressed from intercontinental to intermediate range.

But, whatever the strictly military implications, the political reaction was sharp and adverse: Helmut Schmidt, then Chancellor of West Germany, persuaded his fellow Europeans that this was the occasion to plump for their own "equal security," in the form of American mid-range (INF) nuclear missiles fixed on European soil and targeted on the Soviet Union. When this view prevailed, the military leadership in the USSR saw that their security could be eroded; what they were facing now were serious instruments of regional deterrence. So, after a public-relations campaign to prevent the introduction of these U.S. weapons failed, the Soviets adjusted their negotiating stance to make possible a removal of all INF missiles from both sides. From their point of view, the whole exercise can scarcely have seemed worthwhile.

Part of the problem was the heavy-handed ineffectuality of Soviet diplomacy. Russian diplomacy, scholars tell us, has traditionally been a diplomacy of weakness. It originated in the Byzantine court, with all that implies about stratagems of manipulation. When power failed or fell short, this diplomacy sought through tactics of obfuscation and intimidation to achieve objectives that might not be obtainable directly. Nikita Khrushchev banging his shoe at the UN in 1960 to break up the regular order was flouting Western convention in the same way and for the same purpose as Peter the Great's negotiators in London in the early 18th century, who smashed up all the furniture in their rented house and were described at the time as little more than "baptized bears." People allowed them some room.

The question in recent times has been how much of the Soviet aspirations for world leadership could be carried out through intimidation of this sort. Certain kinds of Cold War negotiating behavior became repetitively familiar. There was a strong emphasis on security and secrecy in the conduct of discussions, coupled with tight central control: Foreign Secretary Andrei Gromyko could be made to sit on a cake of ice for as long as Nikita Khrushchev wanted him to. Power was respected more than sentiment, as in: "How many divisions has the Pope?"—a notorious Stalin expression. Little if any credit was extended for good will, and the toughness of the Soviet negotiator was legendary. President John F. Kennedy characterized the Soviet approach as: "What's mine is mine and what's yours is negotiable."

Throughout the 1960's and 70's, these tactics obliged American arms-control negotiators to be the first to put forth proposals, which the Soviets could then examine and revise. This was "safe" for them but very slow, and it meant among other things that arms technology began to outpace the arms negotiations. The multiple-warhead (MIRV) missile came along to confound the SALT I agreement, and by the time the SALT II treaty was ready for ratification the number of strategic warheads on both sides had tripled.

This low level of negotiating productivity contributed to an increasing militarization of diplomacy, first on the Soviet side and then—after Afghanistan—on the American side. For a while, in the early 1980's, there were effectively no political relations between the two powers at all; in September of 1983, Foreign Minister Gromyko was actually prevented from landing in New York to attend the annual ministerial session of the United Nations General Assembly.

General Secretary Gorbachev turned this situation around, with cooperation from President Reagan. Taking office as he did after the Brezhnev military build-up had been essentially completed, Gorbachev could feel objectively secure about the Soviet Union's invulnerability to attack. He also could conclude that his country's interests in the world were unlikely to be satisfied on an unchecked diet of escalating arms. This would lead him, and Reagan, to the extraordinary series of annual summit meetings that were held between them from 1985 to 1988, and the much greater number of ministerial and military as well as lower-level discussions that these spawned. The face of superpower diplomacy was changed in the process.

The change of substance that went with, and made possible, this procedural revision was the one announced by Gorbachev at the 27th Soviet Party Congress. Security, he there declared, was a political problem. One must think about the interests of both sides. "All must master . . . restraint and circumspection on the international scene." There could be vigorous competition, provided it was peaceful. But nuclear forces would have to be reckoned with: "The character of present-day weaponry leaves no country with any hope of safeguarding itself with military and technical means, for example, by building up a defense, even the most powerful. . . . [The] objective—I emphasize objective—conditions have taken shape in which confrontation between capitalism and socialism can proceed only and exclusively in forms of peaceful competition and peaceful contest."

Lenin of course had known nothing about nuclear weapons, any more than he could possibly have conceived of a billion hostile Communists in China. Factors like these are what led in time to the emergence of the "new political thinking," beginning as early as 1956. General Secretary Nikita Khrushchev announced that year, to the 20th Party Congress, that Lenin's theory of the inevitability of war was no longer a valid or acceptable doctrine. To this could be added, as it later was, Albert Einstein's celebrated observation, once the atom had been split, that "everything has now changed except man's way of thinking." To change that thinking, Gorbachev began saying, would require renunciation of advantage-seeking in favor of the common good.

This would be difficult for many to accept. The Soviet Union of the Berlin blockade and the Cuban missile emplacements and the SS-20s had been no stranger to advantage-seeking. The "new political thinking" might be simply a matter of public relations or of interim peace-seeking while the Soviets rebuilt their strength. There were reasons, therefore, to be cautious—but there were also new deeds to take into account.

Gorbachev followed up his 1986 declarations by agreeing in principle with President Reagan, at Reykjavik, on the reduction of strategic nuclear arms by up to 50 percent, and on the elimination of intermediate-range (INF) missiles by both sides. An INF agreement was then concluded, in 1987, and ratified in 1988.

Also in 1988, Gorbachev announced unilateral conventional force reductions totaling 500,000 men. In the Warsaw Pact countries of East Germany, Czechoslovakia, and Poland, 5,000 Soviet tanks and 50,000 Soviet troops in six tank divisions were marked for abolition, including their river-crossing and other assault elements. The remaining Soviet forces in Eastern Europe were to be restructured so as to make their missions "clearly defensive." On the European territory of the Soviet Union, Soviet tank forces were to be reduced by a further 5,000 tanks. Perhaps 30,000 Soviet troops ("a major portion") were to be withdrawn from Mongolia, leaving the bulk of the overall troop reductions—as much as 420,000 men—to be accomplished on Soviet territory.

NATO ministers meeting in Brussels the next day welcomed this initiative, while pointing out that even when fully accomplished the Warsaw Pact would still retain something on the order of a 2 to 1 advantage over NATO in tank forces. In troop strength, as well, 90 percent or more of Soviet military manpower would remain. More in the way of one-sided cuts would therefore be needed to dispel the image of a Soviet menace.

Still, Gorbachev's speech marked a step forward, particularly in qualitative terms. This was the first major troop reduction the Soviets had announced since Khrushchev demobilized 2 million men after the Korean War, an act that cost him the support of the Soviet defense establishment. On this occasion, too, Gorbachev's initiative provoked the resignation, "for health reasons," of his own chief of staff Marshal Sergei Akhromeyev, who took with him his ingrained World War II aversion to defensive force postures. His successor, General Mikhail Moiseyev, was described by the Soviet foreign ministry as a field commander too young to have participated in World War II.

More was to follow. In May 1989, the Warsaw Pact tabled what was essentially an acceptance of the NATO mutual force reduction proposals at the Conventional Forces in Europe (CFE) talks in Vienna. The Soviets and their allies agreed to parity in tanks, troops, artillery, and aircraft—even though the preponderance of the cuts would fall on the Soviet Union. President George Bush, attending his first NATO heads of government meeting that same month, embraced the Soviet position and proposed to extend it to troops and aircraft, despite the enforcement difficulties this would present. After these cuts both East and West would have—if all pertinent points could be brought into agreement—20,000 tanks in Europe, 28,000 armored vehicles, and 275,000 outside (U.S. and Soviet) troops; all the rest would be withdrawn and destroyed or demobilized.

Problems inevitably arose with respect to the definition of reducible forces and equipment. There were uncertainties too about the data base from which the changes would be measured. The Soviets were notorious about hiding their figures on defense spending and on troop and weapons dispositions. This was one of the factors sustaining a Western perception of menace. Now for the first time, a few weeks after the Gorbachev conventional force initiative, the Soviets published their version of the regional military balance and provided it to NATO negotiators. This summary took its own view, as expected, of the relevant numbers, but the subject was no longer excluded from discussion. As one Western attaché put it, the Soviet document represented "the first time that they have come forward with any kind of comprehensive data at all on Warsaw Pact capability."

The same was true also of the Soviet budget figures released in May 1989. The Soviets had never before produced an integrated report of their military spending, even for themselves. The occasion for doing so this time was the opening session of the new

Soviet Congress of People's Deputies, which would need some sort of expenditure benchmark if it was going to keep tabs on future defense spending. Here too, rough beginnings could lead to future refinements.

There was a pattern in all this, of emerging defense transparency. In 1986, the Soviets agreed at Stockholm to open up regional military maneuvers to outside observers. In 1987, the hierarchy overrode internal security objections to allow U.S. Congressmen and defense experts to visit and photograph the controversial radar installation at Krasnoyarsk. In 1988, the Soviets agreed to intrusive inspection of INF missile sites and accepted the principle of "challenge inspection" of suspected chemical-weapons sites. Also in 1988, while Marshal Akhromeyev was still in office he met with his U.S. counterpart Admiral William Crowe and initiated a series of high-level, reciprocal military visits by U.S. and Soviet commanders, actually inspecting equipment and force locations never before opened up to such examination. It was not that there remained no secrets, clearly there did; but the regime of pervasive secrecy was giving way.

This was not quite so unexpected as it may at first have seemed. On various earlier occasions, when the need arose and self-confidence permitted, the Soviets had shown themselves able to take a longer view of their own self-interest, to pursue common benefit rather than unilateral advantage. One example was supplied by the Mansfield Amendment of the early 1970's, which was a proposal by the then U.S. Senate majority leader to bring back American troops from Europe without any corresponding drawdown by the Soviets. This seemed like a ripe plum, a chance for the USSR to gain an edge over the United States at no cost; and yet the Soviets effectively blocked that possibility by entering into East-West negotiations on force reductions in Europe. Those talks proceeded thereafter for some 15 years, with no momentum and no troop withdrawals. The reason was, evidently, that the Soviets at that time preferred U.S. military leadership of European defense arrangements over the German leadership that might have followed an American pullout; put differently, they did not want West German military dominance to overflow the constraining channels afforded by NATO. This showed the capacity of the Soviets, on at least one occasion, to look beyond immediate self-interest to the more durable security implications of any proposed move.

There have been other occasions. The Polish "Solidarity" movement was not crushed in the early 1980's by Soviet garrison troops, as had been done earlier in Hungary and Czechoslovakia, because of the predictable outrage this would have provoked in the West, and the resulting loss of Soviet diplomatic opportunities with a new American administration. French and British nuclear weapons, likewise, were deleted from U.S.-Soviet INF negotiations, not because they were harmless to the Soviet Union but because they were clouding the superpower bargaining forum, which for the Soviets constituted an important instrument of their security.

Need and self-confidence are what converged again for Gorbachev in the late 1980's. The Brezhnev military build-up, for all that it may have worried and provoked Western leaders, did provide a measure of assurance for the Soviet Union, enough to let its leadership pursue negotiated force reductions. The Brezhnev blundering, for its part, in hostile places like Afghanistan and Cambodia, cost the Soviets enough in treasury and prestige to make some retrenchment imperative. Gorbachev was pursuing what he saw as the true national interest.

He was also following the advice of traditional diplomatists. François de Callières, the 18th-century codifier of Louis XIV's accomplished statecraft, could have had Soviet bullying in mind when he wrote:

> Menaces always do harm to negotiations, since they often push a party to extremes to which it would not have resorted but for provocation. . . . Success achieved by force or fraud rests on an insecure foundation; whereas conversely, success based on reciprocal advantage gives promise of even further successes to come.

The idea of Reciprocal Security, as applied to the closing years of the 20th century, is neither fanciful nor outdated. The march of modern technology (Space Wars), the evolution of current force doctrine (Electronic Battlefields), and the constraints of contemporary finance (Beleaguered Economies), all give a practical present-day impetus to the recognition of strategic interdependence.

These factors would compel some attention to Reciprocal Security even if there were no internal renewal at hand to give the idea vitality. The combination of the two elements, the practical and the political, are what propel the movement toward change.

In his speech to the United Nations on December 7, 1988, announcing the unilateral Soviet force reductions in Europe, Gorbachev declared his readiness to move beyond the traditional Marxist dogma of class struggle, and toward the acceptance of global diversity. "We are not abandoning our convictions," he said, "but neither do we have any intention of being hemmed in by our values." Inverting the metaphor, the dean of Soviet scholars George F. Kennan called the new policy a fencing-in of class struggle by "an objective limit": the inadmissibility of nuclear war.

There were those in the Soviet Union, to be sure, who would not agree to the curtailment of class struggle. Yegor Ligachev, the conservative leader on the Politburo, spoke earnestly about its continuing vitality. But he and others of like mind were outflanked both by history and by the diplomatic team assembled by Gorbachev to carry out the new security policies. This team, carefully put together, showed itself more accomplished and freer of friction than any in recent memory. In the Central Committee, the international department was headed at first by Anatoly Dobrynin, the long-time ambassador to the United States, who had served in that post with exceptional astuteness for 25 years. He was succeeded in 1988 by Alexander Yakovlev, the propaganda chief on Gorbachev's Central Committee who became a close supporter on the Politburo. Also in 1988, the veteran foreign minister and ceremonial president Andrei Gromyko—the embodiment of traditional Soviet security thinking—was retired from the Politburo; he died the following year. That cleared the path for Eduard Shevardnadze, the new foreign minister who rose from a leadership position in Georgian Party circles to become another strong supporter of the Gorbachev policies in the Politburo.

The new Soviet diplomacy showed itself more pragmatic and congenial than the old. It downplayed ideological declamation and widened the use of traditional techniques, such as reason and persuasion. It pursued articulated long-range goals, like the reduction of regional tensions and of arms levels in Europe, that appealed to affected populations. And it earned a considerable success. David Newsom, a former U.S. Undersecretary of State and later dean of Georgetown University's Institute for the Study of Diplomacy, cautioned that the new Soviet diplomacy might challenge U.S. interests more strenuously than the earlier military moves. It was time, suggested Mr. Newsom, to begin looking more carefully at the new Soviet effectiveness in the art of diplomacy.

11

U.S. and Western Receptivity or Resistance

The Soviet "new thinking" was grounded on two plausible and appealing premises: *strategic interdependence,* or Reciprocal Security, including the reciprocal perception of security; and *reasonable defense sufficiency,* as a way of escaping from the clutches of a "parity"-driven arms race. Together these two norms represented a down-grading of the military leverage the Soviets had previously used as their lead instrument of policy.

The new approach was addressed, however, to what was by then a thoroughly militarized and unreceptive American foreign policy. Eugene Rostow, the first arms control director for President Reagan, told a senior U.S. arms expert in 1982 that there was no point in discussing serious force limitations because "the Soviets are out to conquer the world." Fritz Ermarth, the leading Kremlinologist on the White House staff, told a university audience as late as 1987 that the "new thinking" made no difference: "If the Soviets have their way, by force or duplicity, people will lose their freedom, war or the threat of war will continue and vital U.S. security concerns will be jeopardized." These were a fair reflection of the official policy of the time.

The firm and unvarying predicate of the Reagan administration's attitude toward the Soviet Union, up to perhaps 1986 when the Iran-Contra scandal began forcing a search for more positive

international achievements, was that the Soviet leaders and policies of the 1980's were still, from a security standpoint, the same
as in the immediate post–World War II period. They were seen as
aggressive, expansionist, opportunistic, and above all obsessed
with the military balance of forces in the world. The only way to
check militarism was by militarism, it was thought; so U.S. foreign
policy became militarized. This was not without justification, of
course, in history and experience. But it failed to take into account
what the Soviets had been learning since the death of Stalin and
especially since their reverses of the 1970's—that short-term advantage can turn against the advantage-seeker and that, put simply, "no longer is your loss our gain." The early Reagan policies
were hammering in a seated nail.

Leading specialists like Robert Legvold and Seweryn Bialer at
Columbia University were saying in the mid-1980's that it was a
flaw in U.S. thinking to ignore the possibility that the Soviets had
been learning from experience. It was as if, some thought, there
was a quirk in the American political psyche that demanded an
enemy and would hold on to one no matter what the evidence
suggested. Yet the factors making for change were not shrouded
from view in either country; they were visible to, and affected,
both. Both countries had had impressed on them, in particular, the
impossibility in a nuclear era of playing out their differences to
the logical conclusion of war. This was not a Soviet invention, but
the teaching of reality. Einstein, put simply, was right, and a new
modulation of relations had to follow.

There was something in this logic, and in the way the Soviets
moved to adopt it, that could begin to engage the more perceptive
of the Western cold warriors. Writing about his own sense of
change a year before Gorbachev took office, the veteran analyst
and negotiator Paul Nitze put matters this way:

> During World War I, Lenin developed the Marxist-Leninist con-
> cept of peace, relating it to the socialist revolution of the prole-
> tariat. . . . At times it can only be realized by waging "wars of
> national and social liberation." . . . I have the impression, how-
> ever, that the doctrinal, almost religious belief of 30 years ago
> among Soviet officials in Marxism-Leninism has changed into a
> selective belief in the pragmatic utility of important aspects
> thereof. This may open an opportunity for us to borrow a phrase

the Soviets use—"peaceful coexistence"—and give it the meaning we believe it should have: . . . peace in the sense of live and let live.

This statement, coming from that source, was significant. Some 30 years earlier, Paul Nitze had presided over the drafting of the State Department document that first committed the United States to a different view: "The Soviet Union," said NSC-68 in 1950, "unlike previous aspirants to hegemony, is animated by a new fanatical faith, antithetical to ours, and seeks to impose its absolute authority over the rest of the world." That assessment would find little support among scholars or policy makers today, but there has been no movement since then to draw up a successor statement. This leaves a substantial gap.

The postwar evolution of foreign-policy attitudes in the United States has not been linear, as in the Soviet Union, but cyclical. Interdependence was a John F. Kennedy concept to begin with, articulated in an American University speech the year President Kennedy was killed. It was then woven into the Nixon-Kissinger policy called "détente," which flourished for a time but never caught on with important parts of political America. When it was succeeded in 1980 by a return to Cold War simplicities, the country was broadly supportive. By the end of the Reagan years that approach too had been played out, and the American body politic seemed ready to return to a view of the world as interdependent. The connection of this view with its counterpart in the Soviet Union may have to be firmly fixed if it is to last.

There have been objective reasons for American wariness, some perhaps sounder than others. The Soviets have in the past, for example, engaged in periodic and aptly named "peace offensives," designed to gain by diplomacy ends that had proved unattainable by threats or force. A successful peace offensive in the 1990's could relieve pressure on Soviet borders and budgets, allowing fuller concentration on the domestic goal of Soviet economic reconstruction. The seductive sound of Soviet reasonableness could also lull the West into foregoing repairs and improvements to its standing forces, allowing the Soviets over time to consolidate such military advantages as they might hold. These are properly matters to be watched, behind the surface of events.

There are also some elements in the "new thinking" itself that

look open to question. Certain of Gorbachev's security formulations, like strategic interdependence, are both original and realistic. Others, however, may owe more to their doctrinal derivations
than they do to reality. Gorbachev's 70th-anniversary speech, in
1987, contained passages that could strike an outsider as impracti-
cal and even romantic premises for policy, such as "disarmament
for development," with no discernible funding flows; denucleari-
zation and even demilitarization of forces; substitution of the
United Nations for a great-power balance of forces; and reliance
on global "class interests" to bring about peace. Mainly these were
secondary propositions, but they did have a tendency to detract
from the perceived seriousness of the overall message.

That tendency carried over into the Gorbachev treatment of
nuclear weapons, which in at least one respect sounded similarly
heedless of reality. The impression arose out of the millennial
nature of some of Gorbachev's more far-reaching arms-reduction
proposals, seeking to eliminate all nuclear weapons or all nuclear
tests when it had not proved possible to reach agreement on more
limited goals. On these matters Gorbachev seemed to be appealing
above the heads of Western negotiators to their populations, which
produced still another difficulty: It undermined NATO cohesion on
nuclear weapons, causing differences to emerge as among England, France, the United States, and the Federal Republic of Germany. This might operate to the short-term advantage of the
USSR, but not to the advancement of its long-term interest in
Reciprocal Security.

There was a further issue of longer range to be considered.
The Soviet strategic modifications, overall, may turn out to be
interim in character. The moderation of long-held Soviet aims and
policies could emerge as a step toward a future and more sustainable Soviet resurgence as a world power—using the pause, perhaps,
to build up a modernized industry capable of producing advanced
high-technology weapons systems by the end of the century. More
or less deliberately, the "new political thinking" could entail taking
a few losses now to strengthen the Soviets' superpower standing
in the long term. This too will be something to watch for.

As President Bush put it in a 1989 foreign policy speech at
Texas A & M University, "the national security of America and our
allies [cannot be] predicated on hope. It must be based on deeds."
The fact is, however, in those terms, that there have been a number

of validating deeds: the elimination of numerically superior Soviet INF missiles; the acceptance of on-site inspections; the unilateral reduction of conventional Soviet forces; and the acceptance of force parity as a standard for further reductions. It is not Soviet deeds so much as ultimate Soviet intentions that have remained uncertain to the West.

This uncertainty is to some extent homegrown. Skepticism has long been politically "safer" for Western leaders in their own countries than taking the Soviets seriously. The usual question asked among U.S. politicians has been, what if there is nothing to a particular Soviet initiative? The opposite question has now begun to demand at least equal attention: What if there is a great deal?

An overly militarized Western policy—one that concentrates on projecting force alone, and that declines to be drawn into serious talks—is a policy that can miss out on important bets. Secretary of State George Shultz recognized this point in a New York speech shortly after the re-election of President Reagan in 1984. "Americans have sometimes tended to think," he said, "that power and diplomacy are two distinct alternatives. This reflects a fundamental misunderstanding. The truth is, power and diplomacy must always go together, or we will accomplish very little in the world." Indeed, as that suggests, it does little good to try to counter skillful diplomacy with power alone. The conservative Cato Institute put it this way: "Clumsy military interventions, and such imitative subversion measures as the Reagan Doctrine, are not even well suited to countering the heavy-handed foreign policy pursued by Mr. Gorbachev's predecessors. Against a more sophisticated Soviet approach, they will fail utterly."

Conservative Western leaders like Presidents Reagan and Bush have been drawn to respond affirmatively to Mr. Gorbachev's diplomacy, in part because it has been well-considered and has attracted favorable attention among Western populations—but also because, as is often said in politics, you can't beat something with nothing. Having no broad-gauged new policy of their own to put foward, the West has had to make do as well as it could with the Soviet initiatives. Sometimes the results have been of questionable merit: INF missiles have been removed, for example, and short-range missiles kept in Germany, when from a strict security standpoint the reverse would have probably been much better.

This shows the need for the West to calculate its own interests and to develop its own initiatives, deciding for itself in the process what elements in the Soviet posture can prudently be taken as authentic and reliable. Neither skepticism alone, nor credulity, will substitute for the patient and thoughtful assessment this must entail.

12

Authentication of Change

The policy dialogue on view in Gorbachev's Soviet Union can be understood, in part, as a continuation in modern dress of the long-standing internal debate between unilateralism and comity, or Russification and Westernization. The latter set of forces was brought, by Gorbachev and his entourage, into ascendancy. Peter the Great had done much the same thing, however, without lasting effect. What was to keep Gorbachev's successors in turn from sliding back into the old way?

The answer has mainly to do with the costs and risks of a militarized diplomacy in the present age. The Soviets give signs of understanding that conduct on their part anywhere in the world that is offensive to Western sensibilities can stand in the way of lessening the arms burden. They have begun to downplay the role of force in their relations not just with NATO but with Japan and China, where Soviet military displays in the past had had the effect of hardening relations. They have also begun softening and diversifying their relations with the Third World.

Entanglement in Third World affairs since the 1960's had proven more burdensome than beneficial overall for the Soviet Union; in certain parts of the globe, like the Middle East, the entanglement carried with it the ongoing risk of superpower collision and hostilities. For economic as well as security reasons, the

Soviets were on the lookout for ways of tempering their regional involvements.

The forcing condition for Soviet policy change was almost certainly the risk of nuclear devastation. The accident to the nuclear power plant at Chernobyl, and the consequent damage to the countryside in the Ukraine, brought home with sudden clarity the fragility of high-tech nuclear delivery systems. What was true of power plants could also be true of high-speed long-range missiles. Particularly was this so after the introduction of so-called "smart" weapons, able to seek out and destroy ground targets with what was said to be pinpoint accuracy. The prospective shift to such weapons of discrimination, as they were called, helped to focus Soviet thinking on the value of defensive force dispositions, with deconcentrated units and command posts.

Another key factor was the age and experience of Mikhail Gorbachev and the people he assembled around him. All or almost all of them had gained their political education in the post-Stalin, post-World War II period. The new people and the new times, together, generated the "new political thinking."

That thinking was affected by external conditions but also by changes in internal Soviet constituencies, and in their expectations. The Polish Solidarity theorist and spokesman Adam Michnik put the proportions this way in an interview with *The New Yorker:*

> When I ask myself about the origins of the recent changes in the Soviet Union, I end up breaking it down like this: forty percent technological defeat; fifteen percent the changes going on in China; fifteen percent Reagan's foreign policy; and the rest— Solidarity. The entire team around Gorbachev realized that they had a choice, of setting up reforms or else some Russian version of Solidarity would move to create reforms *against* them. In this sense, Gorbachev is not a reformer but a counter-reformer.

Counter-reform is by definition something that must be kept going as long as the reform spirit is alive, and is not otherwise being satisfied.

There was some resistance to the new policy line within the Soviet Union, along with domestic as well as foreign policy tensions that had not been fully thought through or resolved. These included tensions, internally, between market and plan, between order and diversity, between initiative and obedience. If foreign-policy ambitions were being obliged to turn inward before such unsettled domestic imperatives, there were bound to be elements in the Party and leadership that would resist. That made it all the more important for Gorbachev and his colleagues to be able to show some successes with their new foreign-policy line.

The change in thinking, to the extent that it prevailed, was likely to unfold progressively over time. There were forces of inertial resistance to contend with, inside the Soviet political system and beyond. So, although there was movement toward retrenchment from excessive Soviet political-military entanglement in the Third World, some within the Soviet hierarchy persisted in seeing such engagement as a form of "just cause" from which no detachment was legitimate. So also, while the objective of reducing nuclear risks could be served by military disengagement from Eastern Europe, any precipitate or one-sided move in this direction could undo the security buffer assembled at great pains to guard against perceived conventional threats from the West. No sharp or sweeping reversals of form seemed likely in these circumstances.

What was going forward, however, in the way of "new thinking," showed itself in the main to be internally coherent and externally responsive to real needs and priorities. Nowhere was this truer or more significant than in the Soviet position on nuclear arms reduction. Despite ragged edges and questionable polemics, the core of the Soviet position was both realistic and understandable.

There was solid internal agreement, to begin with, among Soviet political and military leaders, on the need for an effective defense, on the nature of the NATO military challenge, and on the need for revitalization of the industrial base. What Soviet leaders began putting together for these purposes was: (1) a responsive battlefield strategy, (2) resource allocations to support that strategy, and (3) an arms-control posture that correlated with both.

Gorbachev and his generals went on record as saying not only that nuclear war was unwinnable but that nuclear weapons had no military use—which was not the same as saying that they had no political or dissuasive use. They further agreed that a non-nuclear war in Europe might be winnable, in strictly battlefield terms, provided means could be found to spare the Soviet homeland from nuclear destruction. And they joined in support of the Gorbachev economic reform program, which was supposed to get them a sophisticated electronic capability in time for its insertion, by the end of the century, into modernized Soviet forces.

These resource-allocating and strategic judgments taken together had a discernible effect on Soviet nuclear arms-control positions. They helped, for one thing, to explain the Soviet proposal for elimination of all nuclear weapons, which may never have been expected to gain Western acceptance. Other aims and achievements were more realizable. The intermediate-range (INF) missile treaty, by getting rid of the U.S. Pershing-2s with their very short flight time to Soviet targets, sealed an important USSR security objective. The intercontinental-range START agreement, in principle, to cut back strategic nuclear-arms delivery systems by up to 50 percent, would delete targets on both sides along with weapons, and so maintain an acceptable force balance. The Soviets began for like reasons to move away from reliance on highly targetable, fixed, multi-warhead systems like the SS-18 to deployment of more mobile and less vulnerable intercontinental missiles like the SS-25.

On the "Star Wars" (SDI) front, the Soviet military supported the Gorbachev effort to slow down or block further development of space-defense systems. This was not because they thought SDI would work as advertised, or could overcome simple countermeasures; that prospect was discounted by Soviet space scientists. In the near term, the Soviets believed they could handle the relatiely "low-tech" phase of SDI development. Their real concern was that U.S. electronic experiments might generate spin-off capabilities for terrestrial battle management. The "high ground" of SDI in their estimation would be here on earth.

Soviet interests, therefore, and the interest of global stability, called as they saw it for at least a stretch-out of SDI development, to allow for measured competitive planning. Those interests called also for offensive nuclear de-escalation, to the point where each side could be sure of its retaliatory capability but not of its ability to prevail in an exchange. The Soviet positions on nuclear arms reduction were consistent with these interests, and were therefore likely to be maintained regardless of the political fluctuations that might lie ahead.

Soviet diplomatic behavior in general also changed in the Gorbachev era, to reflect the newly perceived realities. There was an economic component now to Soviet international policy, illustrated by the mutual recognition in 1988 of the East European Common Market (CMEA) and the West European Economic Community. The Soviets expressed an interest in joining GATT and the IMF—the General Agreement on Tariffs and Trade, and the International Monetary Fund—and they restructured their internal bureaucracy to put economic diplomacy under the coordinating hand of a new State Commission on Foreign Economic Relations, chaired by a Deputy Prime Minister.

Discussing these changes in 1987, Foreign Minister Shevardnadze advised the Soviet foreign service that they reflected a new set of needs and priorities:

> In its day-to-day operations, comrades, the whole diplomatic apparatus cannot for a minute lose sight of the national economic interests of the country and should constantly remember that the most important function of our foreign policy is to create the optimal conditions for the economic and social development of our country.
>
> The leaders of the subdivisions in the central apparatus and the foreign missions along with all diplomatic colleagues should be aware of the fact that the party and the state, in allocating considerable funds for the conduct of foreign policy, expect that the political solution of important international problems will have great economic impact, have a favored effect on the development of the national economy and free up the material, labor and financial resources that are so essential to the solution of domestic economic and social problems; and they are expecting a real economic return from the work of the ministry.

Part of this new expectation was reflected in a Soviet emphasis on relations with the more economically advanced Third World countries. Gorbachev told the 27th Party Congress in 1986 that "real grounds exist for cooperation with young states which are traveling the capitalist road"—in regions, that is, like South America and the Persian Gulf with market economies and traditional ties to the West. The same report, and Soviet conduct thereafter, de-emphasized involvement with new socialist states and with movements of national liberation. The emphasis was placed instead on cutting losses and achieving gains in relation to the practical interests of the USSR.

There was also a new tolerance for Western-mindedness within the Warsaw Pact nations, beginning with Poland and Hungary, which were experimenting with multi-party democracy and with marketplace economics. In 1968 Soviet tanks had rolled into Prague to quell such indiscipline. In 1988, the Soviets were experiencing a "Prague Spring" of their own. "What is the difference between Prague 1968 and Moscow 1988?" went the joke. "Twenty years," was the answer. Now the only constraint imposed on Warsaw Pact members was that none should immediately renounce the Pact. Acting on that freedom, each of the remaining Warsaw countries cast off in 1989 its yoke of internal Communist oppression. The Soviets refrained from interference, calculating as it seemed that efforts to maintain control would simply divert resources away from *perestroika*, and prejudice advantageous relations with the West, to no beneficial effect.

The Soviets became willing to recognize as well a need to deal with the perceptions produced by its size and behavior. From a Western standpoint, even after its various reductions and retrenchments, the Soviet Union still had the strength and capacity to threaten or cause harm: (1) with nuclear or conventional forces; (2) by military and political intimidation; or (3) through the progressive domination of Third World resources. The Soviet readiness to relax political controls and eliminate force disparities in Europe, its withdrawal from overextended positions in Afghanistan and the Third World, and—not least—its manifestations of concern for Reciprocal Security, all bespoke a desire to reduce the perception as well as the reality of a Soviet threat to Western interests.

The doctrinal underpinnings for Reciprocal Security were not yet fully worked out by Soviet theorists but they were open to becoming so. The main elements proposed by Gorbachev were "strategic interdependence" and "defensive sufficiency." The first was of fundamental importance and made practical good sense, in the nuclear age, when either superpower's insecurity inevitably engages the other's. The second concept—"sufficiency"—was less clear. Within the Soviet military, it seemed to mean much the same as "parity" had done; General Yazov, the defense minister, said that U.S. deployments would establish what was sufficient for

Soviet forces. The politicians, Premier Ryzhkov among them, talked more boldly about moving to a Soviet self-definition of "reasonable sufficiency," aiming for no more than a counter-offensive capability.

The idea of sufficiency was thus, at the outset, a political initiative whose solidity and implementation remained to be established. The Soviet professional literature did suggest certain elements around which a fully fledged concept might be formed. These included: (1) a minimum secure second-strike nuclear weapons-delivery capability; (2) an ability to offset but not to replicate high-technology, high-cost U.S. initiatives like "Star Wars" (SDI); (3) a conventional force structure capable of deterring any attack but not of sustaining an attack of it own; and (4) the provision of Third World military assistance only to places (unlike Afghanistan) where the local regime was capable of sustaining itself in power. Taken together, these elements operated as a kind of invitation to the other superpower to join in a debate about "sufficiency," and to develop for it a shared political content to which both military establishments might then be expected to subscribe and add content.

Such a process could well serve, over time, as a basis for shared confidence in the stability of change. It allowed for reality, as jointly perceived, to serve as the basis for policy. Taking security as a political problem, in Gorbachev's phrase; mastering restraint and circumspection on the international scene; and respecting the interests of both friend and foe—all tended to promote the acceptance of long-run national interests as something transcending short-term advantage. All tended thereby to promote the carrying out in practice of what had been begun in concept: the progressive de-ideologization of Soviet and American foreign policies, and their increasing foundation in realistic self-interest.

13

Test Cases

The most vital interests of the Soviet Union are to avoid nuclear extinction, or conventional hostilities that could lead to such extinction, while also avoiding financial bankruptcy. Those are the chief interests also of the United States and of the West. Neither side's interests can be satisfied without the cooperation of the other. This furnishes an instance of what Alexander George has called, usefully, "high interest symmetry"—and it is what underlies the movement toward replacement of advantage-seeking by Reciprocal Security.

The Soviets in the main have recognized this imperative, in their pronouncements and also in their conduct since Gorbachev's accession. The record is not wholly uniform on this matter; there are deviations and disparities. But overall it displays a mutuality of dealing on matters of strong mutual interest.

There are matters of less vital interest, of course, where an accommodation might be valuable but is not essential. So long as both sides agree on what these matters are, there is no particular danger in leaving them open for competition. The problem is that sometimes the two sides do not agree, or their politicians seize on lesser interests to inflate them into larger ones—with resulting potential harm to the security relationship. It should be instructive to examine the record for what the Soviets have made of the various opportunities, and to see what hierarchy of mutual interests may emerge.

Human rights in the Gorbachev era is not the deeply divisive issue it once was in East-West relations, although substantial differences persist and will no doubt continue to engage leadership attention on both sides. In May 1988, President Reagan was able to visit Moscow and "get off his chest" what he had long wanted to tell the Soviets about their failings with respect to civil liberties. Mikhail Gorbachev bristled at the hectoring tone, but did not intervene when Reagan met with dissidents or lectured students. He let it go.

Gorbachev could feel comfortable, overall, with the inroads into world opinion he had made since 1985 through his domestic human-rights performance. The noted dissenters Sakharov and Shcharansky had been released, along with scores of prisoners of conscience. Public demonstrations and news conferences had been held with some regularity by proponents of social change. Nationality protests had been allowed in places like the Trans-Caucasus and Crimea, mostly in the name of the central authorities. Other nationality groups, like ethnic Germans and Soviet Jews, had been allowed to emigrate in substantially greater numbers. Religious repression had been eased, and the Orthodox church at least partly embraced. There had been a flowering of independent public-policy groups. The daily press and television had been opened up for exploration of civic and governmental shortcomings. Bukharin had been rehabilitated, *Repentance* shown, and *Doctor Zhivago* cleared for publication. It was a remarkable series of steps.

If these reforms were taken more for instrumental than for doctrinal reasons—more for public relations and for *perestroika* than to satisfy the claims of law or morality—that did not make them any the less effective, or authentic. It meant that the Soviets wanted to institute reforms for their own reasons, including but not limited to the satisfaction of outside opinion. Gorbachev found that he needed to stimulate sagging internal morale, and for this purpose to give his population a sense of engagement or participation in social renewal. At the same time as this top-down transformation was taking place, there were demands for social involvement arising from the bottom up, which the Soviet leadership would in any event have had at some point to recognize and deal with. The combination of the two revolutions, leadership and popular, meant that reforms initiated for instrumental reasons could in Seweryn Bialer's phrase take on an eventually normative significance.

But this was not brought about by international law or negotiation; they by themselves had produced very little. That is because "human rights," a plastic phrase, means one thing in Western traditions and another in Eastern. Agreements to protect them are agreements in the air. Also, as we have seen, there is no way short of conquest and occupation to impose outside views of human rights on a society. Pressures are resented, and coercion hardens resistance. The whole history of Western efforts to enforce outside views of social civility on the Soviet Union has been a history, very largely, of futility.

Human-rights performance, as the West would define it, has improved in the Soviet Union since 1985 not because the Soviet leaders were obliged to improve it but because they chose for internal reasons to do so. No doubt this has bettered the climate for superpower dealings on issues of national survival; but the two sets of issues are not the same, and Soviet domestic objectives could conceivably change without altering their external security imperatives.

Another point of diminishing division, and now a goal of Soviet diplomacy, is economic interaction with the West. The Soviets want to husband their investments, and to maximize their returns, both at home and abroad. This has led them to open up somewhat to expanded trade and investment flows with the economically advanced industrial democracies.

But that of itself does not afford political leverage to the United States. The Soviet economy is too big, too self-reliant for that; and past attempts to exercise leverage—the Carter grain embargo, the Reagan pipeline boycott—have proved deeply divisive within the U.S. and the West. They are not a winning game.

United Nations statistics, compiled for the U.S. Congress' Joint Economic Committee in 1987, showed that in the early 1980's exports from the United States accounted for less than 5 percent of Soviet hard-currency trade—and this included steeply declining U.S. grain sales. As Gorbachev told American businessmen in Moscow in 1985, the Soviet Union would like their trade but does not need it. The leading independent authority on the subject, the economist Ed Hewett, says that the Soviets need neither American credits nor technology to meet their development goals. If all U.S. economic inputs were somehow excluded from the Soviet Union, the impact on Soviet welfare and security would not be significant.

A high-level monthly forum on U.S.-Soviet trade relations, conducted in Washington, D.C. in 1986, heard American business leaders offer their perspectives on this subject. These experienced traders made the case that the curtailment of East-West economic relations—apart from goods or services of direct military application—cannot alter the course of Soviet policy, domestically or internationally. The United States has no monopoly on restricted items today, as it may have had 30 years before. Business refused goes to non-American competitors, some of whom may thereby achieve the scale economies needed to become low-cost producers for the world, including the U.S. market.

The Soviets for their own reasons value trade and commerce with the West, and this can be mutually beneficial. As many moderate and even conservative economists agree, a progressive integration of the Soviet Union into the world's economy is likely to produce a generally tempering or "civilizing" effect on that country's institutions and policies. If fear of the world has lain behind much of the excessive security preoccupation of the USSR, confidence in the world could begin to change that. In this sense President Bush's 1989 declaration of openness to Soviet integration was both timely and appropriate—although it will be up to the Soviets to accept and act on the invitation.

To sum up, the U.S. and the West share with the Soviet Union an interest in developing humane and civilized social and economic interactions. When they can avoid offending each other on these matters, they will presumably do so. When they can do better than that, it will benefit the general climate. But neither trade nor human rights is a first-order, external concern like nuclear security. They are valued but lesser interests, and asymmetrical in that they respond primarily to shifting internal priorities. This order of things is unlikely to change, so that the potential for friction will remain—until the day when (if ever) the Soviet Union so transforms itself that it is no longer meaningful to talk about differing Eastern and Western perspectives on commerce or human rights.

* * *

The Soviets have moved extensively since 1985 to harmonize their policies toward the Third World with those of the West. This has happened not because East-West interests in the developing countries are of a high order but because they are largely symmetrical. Neither side wants to get overextended, or to blunder into an unintended shooting war with the other; and the fact that "high politics" are not usually involved may have made it somewhat easier for the two sides to be accommodative.

The Soviets have accumulated a number of expensive Third World clients, some of which will continue to cost them considerably for a time. From a few of these, notably Afghanistan and Angola and Kampuchea, the Soviets have withdrawn or begun withdrawing combat support while continuing to offer military and economic supplies. Cuba and Vietnam, as inner members of the socialist "family," constitute a continuing substantial drain on Soviet resources. For the other, second-echelon clients like India and Syria and Ethiopia, which are not embattled with the West, the ruble levels of support are showing signs of decline. The Soviets at the same time have stepped up their engagement with the growth economies of the "young states which are traveling the capitalist road," as Gorbachev has described them.

This pattern of reduced commitments and enhanced opportunity is one that is being played out particularly in two areas of global importance and traditional Western interest: the Asian/Pacific theater, and the Persian Gulf.

Gorbachev's policy toward Asia has been shaped by a felt need to improve Soviet standing in a region of growing economic and political significance. Before his accession, Soviet prospects for influence in the region looked bleak. Despite (and also because of) a steady and continuing Soviet military buildup along the eastern front and in key client states, the Soviets were generally perceived as an extraneous menace—part of the problem, not of the solution. Their political and economic position in Asia as a whole was weaker in 1985 than it had been 30 years before. Brezhnev's Asian policy was accounted very largely a disaster.

Gorbachev moved swiftly after his installation to show that he intended to change this situation, to reduce tensions and to broaden non-military engagement. He began with his much-publicized Vladivostok speech of July 28, 1986, laying out a comprehensive Asia policy. The first significance of this address was that it descended from the level of customary Soviet generalities to deal with concrete specifics, such as troop withdrawals, that responded to outstanding Asian grievances. Beyond that, the speech exhibited a sense of overall strategy and of priorities, starting with China, which was plainly central to the new Soviet approach.

The Gorbachev aim toward China was for an improvement in relations leading over time to normalcy, not warmth. China was too concerned about Soviet involvement in areas essential to its security—Afghanistan, Manchuria, and especially Vietnam and North Korea—to offer more; but Chinese leaders did show themselves open to a lower-risk foreign policy. By the late Spring of 1989, when Gorbachev arrived in Beijing for a long-sought summit meeting, he was able to display enough in the way of regional military de-escalation to secure his desired normalization of relations.

In the near term, however, China seems likely to continue to find the United States more pertinent than the USSR to its desire for strengthened security and economic growth. The same holds true for Japan, the Number Two Soviet priority in the region. The Japanese are unlikely to want to broaden or deepen their relations with the Soviet Union unless it is in tandem with the U.S. Bilaterally, there are unsolved Japanese-Soviet issues left over from World War II, the most prominent of which concern retention or return of the Northern Islands. That question tests the political-military balance within the USSR, with the Soviet military wanting to hold on to the islands for security reasons. There are also emotional stresses in the relationship, particularly on the Japanese side. Against all that there is the possibility in the coming years of some demonstrations of good will—though by themselves, such motions may affect little more than the surface of events.

Finally, of course, among the top Soviet priorities in Asia is the checking of U.S. influence, which since the end of the Vietnam War has enjoyed a widening field. Whether and how far the Soviets can achieve this goal is a complex function of the interrelationship between their foreign-policy goals and their domestic reforms. The extent of Soviet engagement with China and with other Asian states depends on how far the Soviet economy and social structure can be brought into congruence with theirs. The region's avowed economic reforms carry well beyond anything Mikhail Gorbachev has called for or that his program ostensibly contemplates. If that disparity persists, Soviet enterprises may have only a limited entrée into Asian transactions. And, on the social side, until and unless Soviet populations come to grips with their racial attitudes, ethnic antagonism and suspicion of the "yellow peril" can be expected also to limit the scope of Soviet regional penetration.

Some of this calculus applies on the American side as well. The economic strength of the United States, drained in the 1980's by very large trade and budget deficits, is essential to the maintenance of the U.S. position in the Far East. Deficit policy, in a very real sense, is becoming strategic policy—and it is so perceived by America's Asian partners no less than by its Soviet rival.

For that rival, as for America, the regional prize is of great importance. The volume of U.S. trade with countries of the Pacific Rim some time ago surpassed that with Europe. On the Soviet side, Gorbachev was reportedly much impressed with an IMEMO study, conducted by Ivan Ivanov, projecting a shift of world economic primacy to the Pacific region by the year 2000. The Soviets must certainly have perceived that they could not afford to be left out. Hence the assertive thrust of the Vladivostok speech, which was drafted by Gorbachev's most influential foreign-policy adviser, Politburo member Alexander Yakovlev.

Translating the new conceptual emphasis into working reality will not be easy. The Soviet literature speaks of a "natural fit" between Eastern Siberian resources and Far Eastern markets, but the process of achieving that fit is not obvious. The Baikal-Amur railroad development was supposed at one point to mark the connection, but without hugely capital-intensive development projects along the right of way nothing substantial can be expected to come of it; and the Soviets have been obliged for budgetary reasons to put such development projects on "hold." Gorbachev's overall priorities are for intensification of existing investments, which are located in European Russia. To shift the focus to Asia would require heavy joint-venture participation by Japanese and/or American firms, which is not in prospect and will not become so until and unless there is some major political realignment.

The Soviets could offer for such purposes very substantial energy and other extractive resources in the Eastern USSR, but with virtually no infrastructural support—towns, roads, factories—in place to permit their exploitation. The Japanese (in comparison to many American businessmen) tend to take a long view of investment opportunities, and could conceivably be attracted to joint-venture participation in eventual infrastructure and resource development. This would be seen as a political undertaking, however, and would not be entered into under current thinking against U.S. opposition or (probably) without the participation of American co-venturers. Economics by themselves will continue to direct Japanese attention more to the markets of Western Russia, where sales of established Japanese products are possible.

Anticipating that the current trade frictions between Japan and the United States may continue or even intensify, there could be some rise in Japanese nationalism and anti-American sentiment, particularly among business and government elites. The Soviets could expect to gain little near-term advantage from such a development, however, given the narrowness of their market for Japanese consumer goods of the kind that would get backed out of the U.S. market in a trade war (autos, TV sets, and the like). In the longer run, a Soviet move toward "market socialism" might eventually open up wider opportunities for Japanese trade and investment.

The Gorbachev reforms have conspicuously not been moving toward adoption of market socialism on the Hungarian model, or of the broader structural reforms attempted in China. That may limit Soviet economic prospects not only with China and Japan but also with the newly industrializing countries of East Asia, the so-called NIC's (Singapore, Hong Kong, Taiwan, and South Korea). Some substantial liberation of market forces within the Soviet Union seems essential to engaging the market economies of these nations. There has of course been liberalization in the Soviet Union, as there has been in the NIC's and China; the signs of change are equally striking when measured against any of these countries' past performance. When the countries are measured against each other, however, the pace and degree of change in the Soviet Union look markedly inferior to those in the NIC's or China—despite severe social disturbances in the PRC.

To summarize, then, it can be said that the Soviets' need to find proper answers to their Asian predicament commands an increasing but not yet top-priority claim on leadership attentions, and that the specific Soviet interests to be served by policy change have not yet been fully sorted out. Europe and North America are still predominant in Soviet political, economic, and military thinking. The USSR does need expanded markets elsewhere and lower-cost security everywhere, as part of a lower-risk foreign policy and a pause to promote internal restructuring. Further, geopolitics make their expected claim: The Soviets want to be, and to be considered as, a global power that is excluded nowhere. They also worry on security grounds about the long-term containment of China; a *modus vivendi* with that power is defensively important. Finally, the Soviets continue to draw some guidance from the actions of the United States, and to take as a model the scope of expression in Asia as elsewhere of American strategic interests.

When it comes to the Persian Gulf, there is a long historical pattern of Russian involvement in that region, which is natural in view of the geography. The Soviets have at times used military power in support of their interests, notably in Iran from 1941–46 and in Afghanistan from 1979–89. They left Iran fairly promptly in 1946, however (as they had in 1921), when a continued tenure became unmanageable; and they decided in 1987 to begin a full departure from Afghanistan. Throughout the period, despite these episodes, the Soviets have looked mainly to non-military means of exercising leverage. It has been a matter, for them, of assessing the costs and benefits of comparative approaches.

Soviet assets in the region are considerable. They are believed to include some 30 army divisions stationed near the Soviet-Iranian border. The Soviet Union has been the chief political sponsor of Syria, and was the chief supplier of Iraq in its 1980's war with Iran. The Soviets are the potential beneficiary of such leftist discontent as exists within Iran, and they have re-established or strengthened diplomatic ties with the government of that country and of other oil-rich states along the Gulf. The USSR further supports the OPEC cartel in its maintenance of high oil prices in Western markets.

These resources are offset, however, by the substantial burdens and shortcomings of the Soviet position: (1) The tide of Arab nationalism, which brought the Soviets into regional prominence as a supporting power in the 1950's and 1960's, has all but entirely receded. (2) The relative decline of the PLO has deprived the Soviets of another entrée into influence. (3) The waning of Soviet-style socialism as a perceived model for regional development had dried up still another avenue for the USSR. (4) The emergence of alternative arms suppliers in Europe has, for most of the states in the region, diluted the strictly U.S.-Soviet character of their outside dependence. (5) The Soviets were long mired in Afghanistan, thereby earning for themselves a mixture of Islamic enmity and Arab disdain. (6) The rise of Islamic fundamentalism throughout the region has brought with it a virulent animus against all "foreign devils," including specifically the irreligious Soviet Communist Party. And finally, (7) the Soviets' own priority of engagement in the Middle East (apart from *defensive* contingencies) has declined—in levels of trade, political involvement, and arms supplies—since Gorbachev's accession and indeed for several years before that.

The Soviet Union has a continuing, strong, *defensive* interest, as has the United States, in damping down explosive potentialities in the region and in maintaining the capacity to counteract power moves by others that might threaten the balance of local and outside forces. No one can predict with certainty what would happen if Iran should at some point disintegrate into factional struggles, but rival invitations to Soviet and American intervention are one clear possibility—with all the attendant dangers to world peace this might imply. (Neither side now conceives that it can afford to let the other assume control of that country.) Former Secretary of State Cyrus Vance has termed the Middle East one of the prime potential locales for a superpower collision; and the Soviet leaders around Gorbachev have indicated agreement by placing priority emphasis on the Gulf region in their crisis-avoidance consultations with the United States.

All of this relates to the presumably shared U.S.-Soviet *defensive* goal, of preventing regional disruptions and curtailing their spread. The main focus of Western speculation has, however, been on the opposite possibility: that the Soviets might take unilateral, *assertive* action to increase their standing or influence in the region at the expense of the United States and the West. Concern about this possibility has twice in recent years (1979 and 1986) given rise to a spate of nervous, ultimately self-defeating, American reactions. It should be useful to undertake a realistic assessment of the prospects for assertiveness as seen from a Soviet perspective.

There is an extensive history of regional diplomatic engagement by the USSR, stretching back to the 1920's, and the Soviets have in recent times renewed their emphasis on political relations with the moderate Gulf states. U.S. influence and prestige in those states undoubtedly declined in the wake of the Reagan arms deal with Iran, at the same time as Gorbachev's diplomacy was showing itself to be uncommonly astute. It is possible to estimate both that Soviet regional standing is higher as a result than its objective circumstances would warrant, and that the way lies open to some further gains for the Soviet Union in the future.

Conceding that possibility, the scale of Soviet involvement in the region is likely to remain very different, for the foreseeable future, from that of the 1950's or 1960's. Full diplomatic relations with Oman or with the UAE, for example, might put 50 Russians on the ground as compared with the 20,000 that once were to be found in Egypt. Soviet diplomacy may be adroit, but the resources it can draw on today are stretched thin by other preoccupations and priorities—Central Europe, China, arms reduction, and the domestic USSR economy. The indigenous obstacles to contend with in the Gulf region are, moreover, daunting: Islamic fundamentalism, oil-backed conservatism, and the deteriorated standing in the Middle East of leftist secular parties, all serve as barriers to extensive Soviet penetration.

In 1987–89 Gorbachev moved to improve his regional position by withdrawing Soviet forces from Afghanistan. The Soviets under Brezhnev had invaded that country in 1979 to head off the feared "defection" of a pro-Soviet buffer state and its transformation into an anti-Soviet prong for Western and Chinese designs. The Kremlin plainly miscalculated the costs and resistance this would provoke, along with the impetus the invasion would give to the spread of anti-Soviet feelings throughout Afghanistan. In due course, Brezhnev's error became Gorbachev's open wound. The new General Secretary judged it advisable to withdraw without political preconditions—leaving it to the local Communist party to secure whatever position it could in the future Afghan government. This was an act of realism, recognizing in effect that the 1978 Afghan revolution had been premature, and that no central government has ever been able to extend effective power to the highlands. It was also a politically courageous act of risk-taking, somewhat on the scale of Charles de Gaulle's withdrawal of French forces from Algeria in the late 1950's; and it earned the Soviet leader a comparable international esteem.

Arms control for the two superpowers is a matter of "high-interest symmetry," carrying opportunities for harmony along with temptations to advantage-seeking. Gorbachev has responded at varying times to each.

At the Reykjavik Summit in 1986, and on other occasions, Gorbachev has taken the unrealistic position that the aim of nuclear-arms negotiations should be to eliminate all nuclear weapons. This sounds attractive to untutored minds, but it is unwise and unattainable. Nuclear weapons have helped to keep a peace that conventional arms by themselves—judging from the overall record of the 20th century—might never have been able to keep. And even if it were thought desirable to remove this deterrent, there is no effective means of doing so.

Nuclear weapons cannot be willed out of existence by any means known to the human imagination. They are held, more or less as of right, by the five permanent members of the United Nations Security Council (China, France, USSR, U.K., U.S.). India acknowledges having them, while Pakistan and Israel and a considerable list of other suspected nuclear-weapons states do not. A few years ago *Progressive* magazine published a "how-to" set of instructions on building your own hydrogen bomb. There is no way to stuff the nuclear genie back into the bottle. It must be lived with and somehow tamed. That is what serious arms control has always been about.

As Supreme Court Justice Oliver Wendell Holmes, Jr., liked to say, public policy must deal with matters that are "not a theory, but a condition." That is an apt description of nuclear deterrence. It is an existential, or unavoidable, reality. To propose its elimination is to court unreality and all the disturbance that entails. It is also to risk being discounted as a serious partner in the sober evolution, by the international community, of a stable security environment. Gorbachev's repeated public insistence—even as arms reduction talks have become productive—that nuclear deterrence cannot stand, serves, perhaps more than anything else, to undercut in sensible minds the leadership position he has otherwise laid claim to in international security politics.

That seems ironic when one considers that an equally unrealistic aversion to nuclear deterrence lies at the heart of his bugaboo, SDI. That too was conceived as a way of "ending" mutual assured destruction, or deterrence, although virtually all independent scientists agree that it can do no such thing. For Gorbachev to insist on replacing nuclear deterrence is to feed the fantasy that lies behind SDI. It is a curious, self-defeating thing for him to do.

Of course an international audience is not the only one a national leader needs to, or does, address. Some years ago French President Charles de Gaulle took to tweaking the United States in public about its difficulties in Vietnam, not because this would have any real effect on U.S. policy (beyond the sound of grinding molars in parts of the Pentagon), but because it would hearten a French morale depressed by Dienbienphu. Later, U.S. President Jimmy Carter took to calling publicly for American-style human rights in the Soviet Union, not because there was then any serious prospect of obtaining them but because American morale needed lifting after Watergate and Vietnam. So here, General Secretary Mikhail Gorbachev may have felt the need to shake up and elevate a Soviet morale downcast by years of stagnation under Brezhnev; and, for this purpose, he may have sought fresh moral ground that, strictly speaking, had little prospect of engaging his international partners or of producing real-world results.

A leader who thus takes charge of his own society and government may be, as British Prime Minister Margaret Thatcher once said, "a man we can deal with"—even if certain of his pronouncements along the way have to be disregarded.

It remains important, however, to distinguish serious from showboat proposals, and not to have to make the distinction too often. There was some question about the solidity of Mr. Gorbachev's unilateral force-reduction announcement, made at the UN in December 1988, when his chief of staff Marshal Akhromeyev immediately resigned. If political pronouncements are thought to lack military reality or backing, they are less likely to be taken seriously. In this case it turned out that Marshal Akhromeyev was not out of favor, but would remain as a close adviser to the General Secretary. That, and the subsequent negotiating behavior of the

Soviet Union at Vienna, affirmed the solidity of the Gorbachev initiative.

Another token of seriousness, for which both Soviet and American leaders must share the responsibility, is the sequence or priority of arms-control negotiations. In the second Reagan term, the two sides put nuclear reductions ahead of conventional limitations, and INF (mid-range missile) elimination ahead of everything else. This made doubtful sense in security terms, indeed it was probably backwards: Conventional reductions should really have come first, along with removal of battlefield nuclear weapons, followed by strategic reductions and a cut—not an elimination—of the INF weapons that had by then become the nuclear peacekeepers in Europe. The "walk in the woods" type of formula for partial INF reduction, proposed by Paul Nitze and his Soviet counterpart Yuli Kvitzinsky in 1983, would have worked very nicely for this purpose, as national security adviser General Brent Scowcroft and NATO commander General Bernard Rogers later argued. But President Reagan in 1983 would accept no arms-control agreement regardless of its merit; whereas by 1987 (after the Iran-Contra revelations), he seemed to want almost any agreement he could get regardless of its demerit. INF elimination was available quickly, whereas conventional and strategic reductions would be less conclusive and would take longer. So Reagan settled for what, with Gorbachev's assistance, he could get, and arms-control coherence was the loser.

The two leaders went down this path together between 1986 and 1988, talking from time to time about a nuclear-free world, articulating their vision in sweeping gestures that tended to catch the popular fancy. Perhaps this was needed to shake loose what had been an essentially intractable arms-control stalemate: no agreements of any sort, no limitations, until 1987 no diplomacy at senior level. As late as 1989, after Gorbachev had started accepting U.S. positions and had offered a number of his own initiatives, there was still more illusion than reality to parts of the U.S.-Soviet agenda. The strategic nuclear arms (START) negotiations, for example, had by then identified a 50 percent overall reduction in warheads, and certain weapons sublimits, as goals of the strategic discussions. But the U.S. had no agreement internally, or with its allies, as to what Western systems should survive the cut—which, by established counting rules, ran closer to 30 percent than to 50.

There was no agreement either on the treatment of mobile missiles, which American negotiators were seeking to eliminate or immobilize (for verification reasons) while strategic analysts like Brent Scowcroft were insisting they should be promoted (for invulnerability reasons). When Scowcroft resumed the position of National Security Adviser in 1989, his views on this matter prevailed; but President Bush was still unable to decide between the MX and Midgetman for his mobile missile, so he threw that decision to Congress—further clouding U.S. preparations for a serious negotiation.

Gorbachev may thus have been acting in this period less as a spoiler than as a catalyst for needed American and Western rethinking. His talk of zero nuclear weapons has become muted as the process has gone forward, and the legitimacy of "minimum nuclear deterrence" as at least a Western position has been conceded. The Soviet stance on conventional arms reduction has also become more substantive than showy, and in key respects has approached or even led the NATO position. There have been important disclosures of previously shielded information—some of it, inevitably, rudimentary—on Soviet force deployments and defense expenditures. The Soviet stand since Reykjavik has become appreciably more constructive than flamboyant.

That progression has been helped by the inauguration of senior-level military-to-military talks, beginning in the closing months of the Reagan administration. These have by common understanding not been negotiations, but shared assessments of the practical and doctrinal factors that can support or complicate negotiations. The Soviets claim for example to be moving to a "defensive" military posture, which is something susceptible to observation. Admiral William Crowe and his successors as chairman of the U.S. Joint Chiefs of Staff have put themselves in a position where they can conduct and evaluate such observations. That is a form of confidence-building, from the ground up, by a Soviet administration with enough self-confidence to open itself to this degree of examination.

There remains, however, one important field of "high-interest symmetry" in which advantage-seeking remains a strong temptation for both sides: the integrity of Eastern and Western alliances. For years it was the manifest objective of the Soviet Union to enfeeble its adversaries by breaking up NATO. As Moscow governments rarely had any success in this direction, their goal was little more than a debating point in East-West polemics. Since the advent of Mikhail Gorbachev, however, with his more supple and engaging diplomacy, the fragmentation of NATO has become of considerably more practical concern—especially in relation to a united Germany.

The prospect is not one that ought to appeal to enlightened statesmen on either side. A Germany released from alliance restraints, without more, would become a rogue factor in the security calculations of countries on both sides of the Oder-Neisse line. So also, any Warsaw Pact dismemberment that threatened the Soviet sense of security would destabilize the balance of restraints throughout the continent. Both sides will need to proceed carefully and by degrees toward the ultimate dissolution of pacts, when security assurances may be providable by other means—the work, in all likelihood, of years.

The test case here is provided by short-range nuclear missiles (SNF), positioned on West German soil and capable of reaching only East European targets. These missiles have never been prime instruments of dissuasion: They cannot reach targets in the Soviet Union, and they could be swiftly over-run and dismantled in a conventional attack. In an orderly sequence of arms diplomacy, they would have probably been slated for reduction or removal alongside conventional forces, leaving a contingent of INF missiles to keep the peace. This is what the French and British would have preferred, and the West Germans would have accepted, as indeed they did when the INF missiles were installed on European territory in 1982–83. The overriding objective of the nations that survived the great European wars of the 20th century has been to prevent their territories ever again becoming "safe" for the dreadful scourge of conventional war. The INF missiles were well-suited to that purpose, which is, in part, why Chancellor Helmut Schmidt invited them into Europe in 1979; but a decade later all of them had been removed, leaving nothing but the conspicuously inferior SNF weapons in their place. The French and British were reduced to asking that these weapons take up the slack, at which the West Germans understandably balked—and the Soviets had the openings of the split they had long been looking for in the alliance.

Such a result, if it ripened into a full division, would be incompatible with vital American interests. The historic antagonisms within Western and Central Europe that have drawn America into two world wars in this century—and that could still unleash the last of general wars, if not restrained—are reconciled within NATO today under American political chairmanship, in a way that would not otherwise occur. This is a reflection not of U.S. superiority but of the need for a disinterested chairmanship that all NATO countries can accept. Federal Germany cannot fill that role as yet, nor England, nor France: The political cohesion of Western Europe has not carried that far. If the idea of an integrating alliance now fades, and major members start going their own way, the whole structure of Western self-containment on which postwar stability has been built could begin to break apart.

Faced with such consequences, future American administrations are almost certain to want to repair past errors of diplomacy, as far as they can, and to pursue common interests once again with their NATO allies. President George Bush began doing so at his first NATO summit in May 1989, where he adroitly maneuvered a short-term resolution of conflicting French and British and German positions on the SNF question. But the Gorbachev diplomacy has not stood still. In July of 1989, to the Council of Europe, he proposed a conference among nuclear-weapons states and those European countries "on whose territories nuclear weapons are stationed"—i.e., Federal Germany—to discuss the appropriate limits of nuclear deterrence within the region. That conference idea could be dismissed, as it was, but the political vulnerability to which it was addressed would remain.

The U.S. will have to find ways to repair that vulnerability in the coming years. Where NATO doctrine has fallen out of step with present or future reality, it will have to be reviewed and revised collegially—not by unilateral or superpower dictate. The United States must also recognize, despite some Congressional posturing to the contrary, that its contributions to a "forward defense" are acts not of charity but of enlightened self-interest—in deterring a war that would surely engage it, at much greater cost and risk, if there were no deterrence. The West Europeans for their part can find concrete ways, appropriate to their circumstances, of displaying their own continuing belief in the importance of a concerted Western military-political posture.

The Soviet Union itself must at some level appreciate the value to it of an armed but non-nuclear Federal Republic of Germany, integrated as it has been into Western political, economic, and security structures. Despite the habit of decades, it would be more in line with Gorbachev's "new political thinking" for the USSR to give up its alliance-division efforts and to focus instead on the long-term process of evolving stable, successor, security structures for all of Europe. A Europe at loose ends, at this stage of its security development, would be hazardous to Soviet and world peace. It would be contrary to Russian interests.

14

Adjustment of Competing Superpower Interests

For Washington as for Moscow, the challenge of the coming era is to join strength with skill, power with diplomacy, to arrive at what is in the long-term national and global interest. The rivalry of the two superpowers is not going to disappear, but it can be modulated. For this to happen and to persist, astuteness must be met with astuteness and not with mere coercion, which so often has proved counter-productive. When on the other hand it appears that either side has yielded to the short-term temptations of advantage-seeking—whether by efforts at alliance-splitting or otherwise—the other must respond with firmness to restore the balance. Mettle meeting mettle can forge in this way a durable alignment of competing interests.

The evolution of the Soviet interest in a non-provocative (or "defensive") defense provides a good opening example. It grew out of the conspicuous Soviet failures with provocative defense—with the Berlin blockade, the Cuban missile emplacements, and more recently the SS-20 deployments in Europe. These united NATO and summoned into being American weapons placing Soviet territory at greater risk, from Western Europe, than ever before. The Soviets decided in due course that they could not afford such experiences.

Soviet military strategy since World War II, when the country was ravaged with invasion, has however centered on offensive capability—the ability to wage battles outside Soviet borders and to avoid a repetition of that deeply destructive war. The problem was that the resulting force orientations, many divisions deep and in advanced positions, came across to Western defenders as menacing. They counteracted the politics of tension reduction that Gorbachev was trying to conduct in Western Europe. The political incentive thus became one of finding ways to move Soviet tanks and troops back behind Soviet borders and of equipping them to fight defensive engagements.

The new strategy proposed was to absorb a presumed Western blow, giving ground and destroying the attackers as they advanced, in somewhat the same way that Hitler's and Napoleon's advances had been defeated; the difference being, this time, that high-technology instruments might allow the defenders to prevail much sooner. It was attractive in theory, but at the outset it failed to attract very much in the way of professional Army support. When Marshal Akhromeyev resigned in the wake of Gorbachev's 1988 unilateral force reductions, it suggested among other things that "defensive defense" might have a hard time getting established in actual military practice.

It may be that that is now changing. Alexei Arbatov, the young civilian conventional-force theorist at the Academy of Sciences in Moscow, told visiting friends in 1989 that Soviet military strategists were no longer ignoring him. General Makhmut Gareyev, deputy chief of the Soviet general staff, wrote in the *Bulletin of Atomic Scientists*—with high-level and, one assumes, peer approval—that there are distinct and observable stages on the way to a non-provocative defense. The first entails a reduction of forces, already underway. The second involves the withdrawal of strike forces a sufficient distance away from a contact point to rule out sudden or surprise attacks. Then, so as to be able to tolerate the appearance of an opposing threat without having to launch a preemptive attack, the forces and their weapons are deployed in non-vulnerable positions; combat readiness is bolstered with highly mobile reserves; and high-technology scanning and response equipment are supplied. Finally—although this may be the first to show up in the field—the defensive disposition of the forces is expressed in operational plans, exercise manuals, and training maneuvers.

These changes, Gareyev wrote, cannot be accomplished by either Warsaw Pact or NATO echelons acting alone: "The problem of sufficiency of defense cannot be solved unilaterally." But the Soviets can seek to display their own interest in the matter sufficiently to draw NATO into constructive discussions.

One way to do this, and to strengthen the military involvement in defensive defense, is to explore its ramifications in senior professional consultations. NATO gave its blessing to such an enterprise, on December 8, 1988, when its foreign ministers approved "an organized exchange of views on military doctrine tied to actual force structures, capacities, and dispositions in Europe." Admiral William Crowe, the chairman of the U.S. Joint Chiefs of Staff, said after his first round of meetings with Marshal Akhromeyev in 1988 that he would be watching for signs of an unambiguous doctrinal shift; and his Soviet hosts in the USSR the following year went out of their way to show him as much of that as they could.

Translating even an agreed doctrinal shift into assured force restructurings is an enterprise of considerable complexity—far more so than the negotiations to limit nuclear weapons. The Conventional Forces in Europe (CFE) talks in Vienna are, to begin with, a set not of bilateral but of multilateral negotiations among 23 countries with very differently organized forces, and with hundreds of different types of armaments whose total number reaches into the hundreds of thousands. Most of these weapons are smaller than missiles and very much easier to conceal. Verification of reductions will be correspondingly very difficult. So, although President Bush in 1989 set an optimistic target date of 1990 for completion of the CFE negotiations and of 1992 for their implementation, actual achievement of mutually non-provocative defense is almost certain to take longer—and to repay, if it can be accomplished, all the pains it may summon.

While the two superpowers and their allies are forming their minds for these negotiations, the shape of the battlefield they are confronting has been changing before them. Technology is the moving force in this change, particularly computers and other electronic instruments of surveillance and control. They have opened up a potential new generation of lasers, battle management systems, and self-contained "smart" (high-precision) weapons, capable of seeking out and destroying specific military targets no matter where located. What this portends in military planning terms is a high-technology replay of World War II, with even greater though less random destruction.

The prospective shift to weapons of discrimination, as they are called, has implications for the deployment of both conventional and nuclear forces. It supports and makes more palatable a defensive reorientation of both. In the face of "smart" weapons the mass tank or infantry attack could become as obsolete as the mounted cavalry charge had earlier become against the machine gun. Ground forces and mechanized units and aircraft and command posts may all have to be dispersed or deconcentrated to lessen their target potential. Nuclear bombers and missiles, too, may find themselves driven more and more away from the front lines, acquiring in the process a much more clearly secondary character as instruments of deterrence.

All of this could produce, in time, a considerably more stable and less anxious security stand-off in the European theater—if the two major powers see it that way and act in tandem to bring it about. But there is a significant catch, if they do not. For if either side reasonably believes, in the coming years, that the other is stealing a march on it in weapons of discrimination, it may be provoked by that concern to move its nuclear weapons back up from reserve to early or even first-use disposition. Such a development could destabilize rather than calm the battlefield.

For these reasons, as General Gareyev has suggested, the achievement and maintenance of a non-provocative defense regime will have to be made a matter of comprehensive, high-priority, and continuing attention.

Priority of interests is in general a matter of rank-ordering, which for stability's sake must find some correspondence as between the two sides. Fortunately that seems to exist. The Soviets give highest priority in their security thinking to East-West relations, including arms control, as does the United States. They give second priority to Eastern Europe, for them a "high-interest asymmetry" region whose peaceful evolution they now accept must entail some Western involvement. And they give third place, currently, to the developing world, with whose ideological zealots they used to make common cause to the prejudice of good relations with the West.

The most vital interests of the Soviet Union, as now perceived, are to avoid nuclear extinction and financial bankruptcy. In Central Europe, where the forces of East and West have been arrayed against each other as nowhere else, both sides hold clear security interests and both have defended them persistently for more than four decades. A stalemate of sorts has settled onto the field, enough so that it has become possible for the rival forces to begin looking for lower-cost ways of maintaining the peace.

There are some on both sides who continue looking for ways to destabilize whatever peace there is, in search of some unilateral advantage; but that has proven elusive over the years, and its seekers are not currently in the ascendant on either side. Both the Soviet Union and the United States are over-stretched economically, and both need to find prudent ways to retrench. At the beginning of the 1990's there is accordingly a better prospect than previously of coming to terms on negotiated reductions to lower, less costly, and more stable force levels.

Past Soviet negotiating patterns may be instructive as to what will happen next. Arms control for the Soviets has traditionally been more of a psychological than a war-gaming exercise. "It is not the refined structuring of deterrence that matters most to them," writes Robert Legvold, "but rather the management of the political environment." The Soviet view of deterrence differs in this respect from that in the West. Spurred by the memory of Hitler's invasion, and Napoleon's, and all that went before, they consider that war may be senseless but that it can happen all the same. Fyodor Burlatsky, an influential adviser to both Khrushchev and Gorbachev, has written that the roots of hostilities are political and not technical: One must get at the basic conflict and not just the balance of armaments. Pending that kind of resolution, the Soviets have tended to treat arms control as an aspect of arms deployment, on the not illogical premise that war is an unpredictable affair demanding sure and redundant forces.

Insofar as this perspective derives from a historical sense of inferiority, or vulnerability, it began to be altered by the Brezhnev military buildup of the 1970's. The contribution of that buildup, psychologically, was to allow Soviet leaders and elites to believe in the security of their country against plausible threats of attack, whether nuclear or conventional. The problem then became one of convincing Soviet leaders to give up some part of their hard-won security.

The Soviets traditionally have tried to use arms control to limit or remove perceived destabilizing Western weapons systems: the anti-ballistic or ABM missile (later SDI), Trident I and II, the MX, and INF. With the exception of the INF and ABM Treaties, however, they have been loath to give up any destabilizing systems of their own. That is why the SALT I and II strategic-weapon agreements, for example, capped weapons growth but did not eliminate any systems already in place. They introduced predictability into arms planning—an undoubted achievement—but not reduction.

Gorbachev shifted to talking about reductions, in a big way. He first proposed a sweeping 50 percent cut in all strategic warheads, then accepted sub-limits that would eliminate substantial numbers of Soviet ICBMs already in place, and suggested far-reaching reductions also in European conventional forces on both sides. The latter may be especially significant: If the two sides could succeed in bringing about the restructuring of the conventional balance, this would transform the problem that has been at the heart of the whole postwar East-West confrontation.

What this might produce in turn is a new political environment, one that would allow the parties to begin accepting some generalized arms and hostility reductions. Given historic Soviet attitudes, however, there may be need both for hard bargaining and for persistent policies en route to the new plateau of stable relations. That will test the seriousness of both Western and Soviet priorities.

In Eastern Europe, the dominant purpose of the massive postwar Soviet troop concentrations was never so much to attack or intimidate NATO as to keep control over East Germany, Poland, Hungary, and Czechoslovakia. This is shown by the course of conduct of the Red Army over the years, which never moved against Western Europe but twice intervened and once threatened intervention against East European states (Hungary 1956, Czechoslovakia 1968, and Poland 1981) that took a path at variance with Soviet-imposed uniformity. The appearance of a threat to Western Europe remained, of course, and interfered with the Soviet interests we have just examined; to remove that interfering appearance would require some reassessment of Soviet interests in the East.

Those interests were traditionally to preserve stability, to maintain a buffer against perceived Western menaces, and to promote economic integration. By the end of the 1980's these objectives were no longer all attainable. The East European states, drawing in part on the Gorbachev reform model, were reaching for internal growth and self-expression. The Soviets themselves needed to reduce their subsidies and other expenses of control. These newer aims were largely incompatible with the old: The Soviets could not keep control over the region, cut expenses, and secure a peaceful interval for their own *perestroika* all at the same time. They had to allow some freedom of movement and experimentation; when the change came, it was all in a rush.

The cascade began cautiously, in Poland, where months of negotiation produced an April 1989 agreement with the Warsaw government legalizing the Solidarity trade union and opening up designated seats in the Polish parliament to contested election. In June, the local Communist Party suffered a sweeping defeat when Solidarity candidates won 260 of the 261 seats they were allowed to seek; by August, Solidarity was confirmed as the new governing majority and elected its own prime minister—the first postwar transfer of power away from a communist government. The Soviets watched, were consulted, and did not interfere.

The signal this gave was immediately picked up in the region. In May, Hungary's by-now multiparty state began dismantling the Cold War barbed-wire fence separating its territory from Austria. In September, floods of East Germans began pouring through that fence, and through Czechoslovakia and Poland, to West Germany. East German officials looked to Moscow to help them block this hemorrhage, and were told, in effect, to acquiesce. In November, the East Berlin government and Party leadership resigned en masse and were replaced by relative moderates. On November 9, the country's borders and the Berlin Wall—that long-standing emblem of East-West separation—were opened up.

The spark of sovereign self-expression then shifted to Czechoslovakia. In late November, huge demonstrations took place in Prague and other cities, demanding open elections. Hard-line Communists were forced to resign, leading by December to the parliamentary formation of a non-communist government and the overwhelming election as president of the playwright-dissident

Vaclav Havel. Also at this time, in Bulgaria, the Communist Party leadership was replaced after 35 years, leading to large popular rallies in Sofia for open elections and an end to police repression.

All of this, to that point, occurred peacefully. The case was otherwise in the last of the Warsaw Pact countries, Rumania, whose surviving Communist dictator Nicolae Ceausescu confronted the popular reform movement with deadly force. Government massacres of unarmed civilians were reported in Timisoara and Bucharest. Soviet authorities looked on, took counsel, and refrained from intervention. On December 22, regular forces of the Rumanian army threw in their lot with the insurgents, engaging and overcoming the Ceausescu security guard. On Christmas Day, the dictator himself was captured and executed. A new provisional government was installed.

The transformation was sweeping, swift, and unpredicted— but not inexplicable: when a stopped drain is cleared, the dirty water goes out quickly. Here the obstruction had for years been the threat of Soviet armed intervention. Once that was gone, the rest could follow.

But only the first step could follow right away. The structure of Stalinism was everywhere torn down, but successor regimes were not quickly defined. In each of the countries of the region, a coalition or provisional government was put in place, with a promise of early free elections. The levers of advantage in these elections, of experience and party machinery, were still predominantly held by the out-of-favor Communists, many now changing their party names to improve their electoral prospects. Reform forces might be able to evict them, but not necessarily to install a full-fledged Western-style democracy. There was a tradition of democratic self-government in Czechoslovakia, less so in Poland, and almost none in Rumania. Variations and vacillations were to be expected, with associated East-West maneuverings for internal influence. The full results might not be known for several years.

Some things could be decided more quickly. The new governments of Czechoslovakia and Hungary began asking at once for removal of Soviet troops. They asked that this be done swiftly, within a year or two, while Gorbachev was still in power. The Soviets seemed likely to acquiesce. The same Eastern governments could be expected to draw down or eliminate their own armed forces, on the theory that the threat of regional conflict was receding and that funds were needed for higher domestic priorities.

Such alterations of force, assuming they take place as suggested, will not appreciably modify the East-West security balance in Europe or displace Soviet security predominance in the region. Apart from East German forces, the Soviets have always been unsure of the combat reliability of its Warsaw Pact allies. War plans have had to be based on the assumption that the Red Army, which makes up 80 percent of the Warsaw total, would do most of the fighting. This will not change, if that Army now withdraws to more defensive positions within the USSR and the smaller Pact forces are dismantled.

The Warsaw alliance itself, with continued Soviet political and military leadership, can have an important role still to play. It can ease concerns about the power of a combined or confederated Germany, particularly as that affects the Oder-Neisse border with Poland. It can serve, along with NATO, as an instrument of political transition to an eventual European-wide structure for security. And it can provide needed interim stability within Eastern Europe, constraining the ethnic and territorial antagonisms that divide, for example, Hungary and Rumania.

The Soviets must be left to judge very largely for themselves the timing and dimension of their disentanglement from the region. Eastern Europe is still an arena, to borrow Alexander George's classification, of "interest asymmetry favoring the Soviet Union." It is a locale in which Soviet geopolitical interests are substantially more immediate and important than those of the United States—the mirror image, one might say, of what the Caribbean region represents for American interests. An outside power cannot demand a reappraisal of such localized interests, although it may make one marginally easier by its circumspection.

There will be temptations, all the same, for the West to intercede and to disrupt the process of realignment. Former President Nixon suggested in his book, *1999: Victory Without War,* that outside support for internal and East European nationalism could help to baffle Soviet power. Against that suggestion lies the whole history of regional instability that twice in this century has drawn America and the West into war, and whose upheavals have invariably been accompanied not by liberalization but by increased internal repression and authoritarianism. It is not in the interest of either East or West to seek the abrupt undoing of security structures in Europe—as Lech Walesa of Poland's Solidarity, for one, has consistently recognized. The healing vision, like his, must be long-term.

Nor would it be in the Western interest to try to conclude some sort of "second Yalta agreement" with the Soviet Union, as Nixon's erstwhile secretary of state Henry Kissinger reportedly proposed, giving that country guarantees of Western non-intervention in return for its assurance of East European autonomy. If the Soviet leaders saw their interest as lying in that direction, there would be no need for an agreement; if they did not, the agreement would have little value. There are risks enough of frustration and disappointment in the region without adding to them.

There is, as a result of the developments of 1989 in Eastern Europe, a likely near-term *increase* in the precariousness of the European political balance. This will demand from both sides, not gimmicks or stratagems, but a clear mutual understanding, some steadiness of purpose, and an active attention to Reciprocal Security.

The periodic use of direct military force by the Soviet Union within Europe, to discipline its Eastern neighbors, has paradoxically produced fewer tensions between East and West than have Soviet indirect military intrusions into the Third World. Here are the territories that Alexander George identifies with "low-interest symmetry," in that—objectively speaking—both superpowers hold only modest geopolitical interests in their alignment. Despite this concordance there has been a great deal of subjective friction over Third World activities by both sides.

The Soviet Union has assisted militarily since World War II in the establishment of communist regimes in the following Third World countries: Afghanistan, Angola, Kampuchea, Cuba, Ethiopia, Mozambique, Nicaragua, South Yemen, and Vietnam—not a large haul, certainly, but each or nearly each an affront to presidents of the United States, who have felt their global standing diminished whenever there was a successful communist intervention. The Soviets have perceived themselves as acting the part of the superpower, with a proper regard for the objectively authentic interests of its rival, albeit not much sensitivity to its internal politics. The whole postwar evolution of Soviet policy toward the developing world can be understood as a matter of global muscle-flexing with its satisfactions on the one side versus mounting costs and setbacks (including setbacks to the "central" relationship with America and the West) on the other side. When the debits at length outran the credits, the Soviets took action to curtail their losses.

To begin with, however, there was the exhilaration of un-thwarted action. The Soviets initially hoped and believed that the newly independent countries of the world would be drawn to communism. When Fidel Castro moved Cuba in that direction, only 90 miles from America's shores, it was as great a vindication politically for the Soviet leaders as it was an injury to the American. A shining prize had been gained, at little cost, or so it must have seemed before the Bay of Pigs and the Cuban Missile Crisis.

Angola, Ethiopia, South Yemen, and Vietnam all offered their own opportunities for low-cost, seemingly low-risk Soviet leverage in the Third World in the 1970's. The invasion of Afghanistan in 1979 was a different case—an exercise not of opportunism, as then perceived, but of reaction to a feared hostile encirclement. The concern for defensive security entailed in that case put Afghanistan in a class with the countries of Eastern Europe, and established no real precedent for Soviet behavior toward other, non-bordering parts of the Persian Gulf region.

Elsewhere, Soviet opportunism and Soviet influence in the 1970's were attracted to local conditions and circumstances. They reflected also, to a growing degree, the perceived geopolitical power balance between the U.S. and the USSR. This changing balance shaped what would look like opportunities to the Soviets, and also what could be projected as Soviet influence—even with-out active Soviet intervention—in the Third World. The loss of automatic and pervasive U.S. dominance in the world, after the 1960's, became a pertinent factor. Very likely this shift in the power balance was inescapable and, in the "North," was stabilizing; in the "South," however, its immediate tendency was to re-lease the Soviets from previously observed constraints and to open up a wider competition.

That competition, even in the adventurous 1970's, was never uncontrolled. The Soviets sought to extract a lesson from Vietnam, for example, by drawing a distinction between proclaimed U.S.

interests and those that the U.S. political culture as a whole—including Congress and the American public—would regard as such. On matters understood as being broadly vital, the Soviets stayed clear.

This formulation of course left room for miscalculation and for differences of perception, which took place. The Soviets believed for example that, after the Moscow Summit in 1972, the U.S. would not be troubled by Soviet intervention in secondary locales like Angola. They were unprepared for the sharply disruptive effect on American political opinion that Angola produced.

The Soviets had thought they were taking "instruction" from the American example of how a superpower behaves in the world. The Americans might fail (as the French had before them) in Vietnam, but once the U.S. had gone down that road it should not be heard to complain of Soviet interventions on behalf of their own Third World clients. The Soviet decision to build a blue-water navy, as an instrument of power projection in the developing world, may likewise have stemmed from this perceived "instruction." And the idea that Third World conflicts should not unduly roil the surface of superpower relations could certainly have been derived from President Nixon's presence at the 1972 Moscow Summit, at the very time he was openly mining Haiphong Harbor and bombing Hanoi.

But the message changed, or perhaps it was misperceived. Henry Kissinger, the secretary of state most visibly identified with the concept of détente, told *Time* magazine after leaving office that "détente means a restrained international conduct." Never mind that this was contrary both to the dictionary meaning of the word (a "loosening") and to its settled diplomatic usage; it was what the internal political necessities of the United States seemed to demand and did not get. The Soviets had not received that message. The result was confrontation and a military buildup that cost the U.S. taxpayers heavily and that eventually cost the Soviet Union its jaunty freedom of action.

U.S.-Soviet perceptions and misperceptions were not the only factors in this shift. The Third World itself was proving more costly and refractory to deal with than the Soviets had expected. Rivalries for power within developing countries, which seemed to invite East-West intervention, were often rooted in tribal animosities or other distinctly local conditions having nothing to do with superpower competition and impervious to outside resolution. A country that adopted the word "Socialist" as its prefix did not by that action become socialist in the Soviet sense. Alliances (as with Syria) proved shaky and short-term ways of exercising influence, while direct political control (as in Mozambique) did not produce reliable disciples. The costs of persistence, and of military and economic subsidies mounted, while the returns on investment waned. In the late 1970's and 1980's, Soviet-supported regimes in Africa and elsewhere began encountering substantial local armed resistance, some of it aided by China or the West. The champion of "national liberation" was now itself in some cases on the receiving end of insurrection.

By the end of the 1970's, also, the Soviets had their own internal slowdown to contend with. They began moving toward a posture of what could be called "assertive retrenchment." As early as 1983, then General Secretary Yuri Andropov told the Central Committee that the Soviet Union should not invariably support self-styled "Marxist-Leninist" governments in the developing world. The Soviets should instead pick the revolutionary regimes it wished to underwrite, looking for those with some promise of political stability and economic self-reliance. More than that, in effect, would be an imprudent claim on Soviet resources.

In 1986 Andropov's political heir Mikhail Gorbachev took this position one step further. The declarations of the 27th Party Congress, his first as General Secretary, changed what until then had been the customary treatment of Third World issues. The role of "national liberation," for one thing, was greatly downplayed. Outside encouragement of such movements, and "doubly so by military means," was described as "futile and inadmissible." Gorbachev acknowledged the persistence of capitalist influence in the developing world, as a fact of life. The program adopted by the Party Congress explicitly encouraged Third World countries to resolve disputes among themselves, and with the capitalist powers where necessary, "by means of talks." In all these ways, by tone and content, the 1986 Party Congress moderated Soviet policy toward the independent world, giving an apparent victory to those within the Soviet Union who had been arguing that regional conflicts undermine the central Soviet interest in stable superpower relations.

It is possible to suggest a rough resulting hierarchy of Soviet engagements in the developing world. There are two countries, Cuba and Vietnam, that have been in effect abstracted from the Third World and placed in the Second, alongside the East European allies; they are members of Comecon, and their portfolios are managed by the Socialist Countries Department, not the International Department, of the Central Committee. This may reflect a felt need to declare a "high-interest asymmetry" as regards the communist regimes in these two countries, vis-a-vis the United States, which has in the past expended large political and military capital on their attempted overthrow. If so, it would stand at the opposite pole from the reticence the Soviets display about military intrusion in Central America. Soviet bases there, the experts advise, are seen as a quick loss in the event of an armed conflict and so command no priority among the Soviet general staff.

That leaves in the balance the "low-interest symmetry" countries, where the Soviets may feel they have a continuing right to intervene but where doing so could injure their interests either as self-determined or in relation to the United States. By the summer of 1988, the Soviets were proposing a managed phase-down of the indirect conflicts then being waged in Angola and Kampuchea. This did not mean, necessarily, that the Soviets would be striking all their tents in the Third World. Nor did it mean that they were yielding to U.S. discipline. The Soviets would be looking to the establishment of their own balance, including the taking of any fruitful (low-cost, low-risk) opportunities that might be open to them. Overall, however, the posture for the coming years would be one of Soviet retrenchment from Third World activism as measured by 1970's standards.

The reasons for this retrenchment, again, were a compound of high economic costs, poor political results, and adverse impact on U.S.-Soviet relations. The 1970's piled up huge multibillion-dollar annual Soviet assistance obligations—to Vietnam, Afghanistan, Ethiopia, and Angola—on top of the estimated $5 billion annual subsidy to Cuba. These chosen clients and their enterprises fared generally badly in their first decades of socialist economic development efforts: Ethiopians starved on a highly publicized mass scale, and socialism in large parts of the world came to be identified with poverty. As for relations with the United States, the invasion of Afghanistan became the immediate cause of shelving the SALT II arms control treaty and also helped to elect a proclaimed anti-Soviet candidate to the presidency in Ronald Reagan.

A question left unanswered as the 1980's were drawing to a close was how far it would be necessary, or appropriate, for the two superpowers to keep raising the costs of each other's Third World interventions. That was the evident purpose of the so-called "Reagan Doctrine," which aimed to find (some would say, to create) and assist non-communist armed resistances to communist regimes. In theory, anything that could serve to reinforce superpower reticence toward Third World activism, as this might do, should be helpful. In practice, however, such guerrilla measures tend over time to raise costs and intransigence on both sides. The Soviets dig in, as they did in their 1980's policies toward Nicaragua, to avoid being pictured as a loser in the superpower stakes; whereas for the United States, the costs and internal divisiveness of sustaining a high-cost, protracted policy in places like Nicaragua grow to exceed any achievable gain. Superpower relations can easily go sour in this setting. Some discrimination accordingly seems called for on both sides; and as the developing countries have shown, they may be entirely capable on their own of "raising the costs" unacceptably against anyone presuming to intrude with outside force.

In any case there are other, non-military, ways in which the Soviets can exercise a global calling. There are non-communist developing countries in the world, some of whom may have interests or aspirations in common with the USSR and others of whom may represent removable obstacles in the way of Soviet ambitions. The program of the 27th Party Congress spoke to this set of opportunities in 1986. It asserted the existence of a realistic basis for cooperation with those states that follow the "capitalist road" of development. "Whatever road they follow," the program declared, "their peoples are united by a desire to develop independently, on their own, and to run their affairs without foreign interference."

This was in essence a declaration of open competition in areas of traditional Western activity and interest, provided the means were non-military. It gave rise to a need for new modes of effective interest-adjustment.

To avoid or reduce potentially hazardous friction with the West in the Third World, the Soviets have pursued or proposed a wide array of risk-limiting techniques. These have included: conferences, condominiums, consultations (both political and military), codes of conduct, good offices, force withdrawal (pure and simple), withdrawal with co-guarantees, cooperative or competitive nation-building, and submission to UN mediation. Each has its own attractions and limitations.

Conferences

In Asia and in the Middle East—two areas where the interests of the two superpowers are in competition—the Soviets have proposed a conference mechanism as a way of harmonizing these interests and, not incidentally, of asserting their political parity with the United States. The Asia proposal, set forth in Gorbachev's Vladivostok speech on July 28, 1986, was to convene a meeting of all interested states on the model of the Helsinki Conference for Europe. This aroused little interest among Asian states, each of whom had an agenda of more specific and practical measures it was looking to the Soviets to meet. The Asian conference idea became, for the time being at least, a dead issue.

Not so in the Middle East, where the Soviets have long pushed the idea of an international conference chaired by the two superpowers to oversee an Arab-Israeli settlement. After periods of resistance, followed by frustration at the lack of success of its own peace initiatives, the United States in the late Reagan period came around to favoring some form of an international conference. In 1988, Secretary of State George Shultz put substantial time and effort into promoting this idea among America's regional clients—Israel, Egypt, and Jordan—without visible success. The question remained on the table for the Bush administration.

Whether it would be in the interest of regional stability, or of the United States, to allow the USSR a hand in Arab-Israeli settlement efforts, is a matter of some debate—turning in the main on whether the Soviets are seen as already occupying a blocking position, and on what negotiating role is assigned to the two superpowers. Assuming a passive conference role, and that the Soviets would encourage constructive negotiation by their Arab clients, such a development could be useful. On differing assumptions, one could conclude that drawing the Soviets in would hand them a stick with which to belabor U.S. relations in the region.

The Shultz idea, to which the Soviets gave no clear answer, was to convene an international conference that would have a ceremonial role but no authority over the actual negotiations, which would be conducted among the states of the region. This would recognize the underlying reality, which is that the Arab-Israeli conflict arises out of ancient antagonisms having nothing to do with the rivalry between present-day superpowers: Neither the Soviet Union nor the United States, nor the two together, can devise or impose a lasting solution.

These two states do, however, have their own clear *defensive* interest in the stability of the region. If Iran or Israel or Syria were to explode in fragmented pieces, the temptation and threat of superpower intervention would mount precipitously. So there is a need to find some way of harmonizing U.S. and Soviet policies. A conference may be too passive and too slow an instrument to serve that purpose. Systematic information-sharing and crisis-avoidance between the superpowers would be alternative, perhaps surer ways of affording the Soviets a constructive hand in the Middle East peace process.

Condominium

At the Moscow Summit in 1972, President Nixon and General Secretary Brezhnev signed a short document with the grandiloquent title, "Basic Principles of Mutual Relations Between the USA and the USSR." It purported to legislate a state of peaceful coexistence between the two states—without, on the U.S. side, submitting the results to Congress or to the American people for discussion. Two years later, when Mr. Nixon resigned his office, the "Basic Principles" went with him—but not before having worked a fair amount of mischief in the relationship.

Article II of the 1972 declaration called for the "recognition of the security interests of the parties based on the principle of equality and the renunciation of the use or threat of force." The immediate reference was doubtless to the Helsinki Final Act, then in negotiation, which would seal the prevailing European borders. But the principle could be read as pertaining also to the persistent Soviet desire for a global condominium with the United States.

That would entail the imposition of a joint directorate over regional disputants which, as Alexander George has suggested, would be neither feasible nor desirable.

The world is not the United States' to manage or hand over. Care must be taken to avoid misunderstanding and frustration on this point. Traditionally, the Soviets with their "diplomacy of weakness" have taken a more managerial or *dirigiste* approach to regional issues than has the United States. There obviously are American and Soviet spheres of interest, in the sense of relative importance—Afghanistan for them, Nicaragua for us—but the U.S. has customarily been unwilling to acknowledge any departure from the Wilsonian ideal of self-determination everywhere. The Soviet penchant for superpower co-management in the Third World is therefore not an idea that the U.S. is able to accept, or one that should remain undisabused.

Consultations

Since 1985 the two superpowers have been meeting periodically at expert level to conduct case-by-case consultations about regional trouble spots. This course was first proposed by President Reagan in an address to the United Nations on September 24, 1984, then ratified at his Geneva Summit meeting with General Secretary Gorbachev on November 21, 1985. Meetings have followed on the Middle East, the Persian Gulf, South Africa, Afghanistan, and the Far East. No untoward experiences have been reported.

There is some doubt about how positive a contribution these sessions have made. Alexander George portrayed them, at the beginning, as a "sterile exchange of mostly familiar positions and views." Senior officers at the Department of State, in a 1986 briefing for analysts, said that the consultations had yielded some fairly effective, though haphazard, information exchange on superpower motives and movements in conflicted regions.

The practice of pre-crisis consultation deserves to be continued and expanded—not with the aim of devising solutions, but with the narrower goal of avoiding misunderstandings. Case-by-case consultation can lead to mutual forbearance, which is in the interest of Reciprocal Security. The meetings deserve in fact to be widened to encompass the "high-interest asymmetry" regions of

Latin America and Eastern Europe, where temptations to intervene or to anticipate intervention may be strong in the coming
decade.

Such an expansion can be tolerated on both sides if it is made
clear both that no security measures will be proposed in these
meetings, and that the discussions will not be limited to the reitera-
tion of fixed position papers. (The continued absence of detailed
publicity should help in both regards.) How far to carry things
beyond that is a matter for joint deliberation. The consultations
should not extend, in practice, to interest definition, which as
experience has shown can be a chancy business: Neither side can
know for certain what its or the other's interests are before they
are tested in a crisis. The two parties should content themselves
with exchanging informed current perceptions of regional developments, and of each other's actions in or affecting the region.
From that small seed some useful plants can grow.

Military Restraint

One measure that could help substantially in this respect is the
"Dangerous Military Activities Agreement" signed in Moscow on
June 12, 1989, between the chiefs of the two military staffs. The
first concrete product of senior staff talks begun a year earlier, this
agreement commits both nations to take designated steps to avoid,
among other things, inadvertent military tensions in "special cau-
tion" areas like the Persian Gulf. If potentially dangerous incidents
nonetheless occur, the two nations are supposed to take measures
to resolve them "without resort to the threat or use of force." The
agreement sets up a Joint Military Commission to oversee and
evaluate the new system.

The DMA agreement grew out of a series of prior incidents—
the shooting of a U.S. Army officer in East Berlin, the hazardous
use of lasers against aircraft—in which Soviet forces had harmed
American military forces or jeopardized their equipment. It also
grew out of Soviet security concerns, for example about the pene-
trability of Soviet airspace. But the agreement drew for its specific
provisions on a highly successful 1972 Incidents at Sea Agreement,
which for nearly 20 years had prevented naval conflicts by the use

of practical collision-avoidance techniques. This was the kind of restraint that seemed likely to work.

Codes of Conduct

There have been periodic efforts over the years to go beyond flash-point avoidance and to formulate more or less definite codes of behavior—to regulate Soviet and American conduct in Third World environments. In the heyday of the détente period, 1972–73, the Soviets successfully pushed two such "codes" to adoption as part of the summit process of those years. Language for this purpose was included in the first three articles of the Basic Principles Agreement signed at Moscow in May 1972, and again in the Agreement on Prevention of Nuclear War signed at San Clemente, California in June 1973.

The first of these two agreements said in pertinent part that:

> The USA and USSR . . . will do their utmost to avoid military confrontations and to prevent the outbreak of nuclear war. . . . Both sides recognize that efforts to obtain unilateral advantage at the expense of the other, directly or indirectly, are inconsistent with these objectives.

Article II of the second agreement, a year later, carried these principles a step further and applied them explicitly to conflicts involving third parties:

> Each Party will refrain from the threat or use of force against the other Party, against allies of the other Party and against other countries in circumstances which endanger international peace and security.

Although President Nixon described these provisions to Congress as having established a "code of conduct," there was neither a substantive nor a procedural consensus about what restraints would apply. The parties came away with different understandings both about what was intended and about how seriously that should be taken. The result in due course was a setback to peaceful adjustment rather than an advance.

The Soviets read the two agreements narrowly but took them seriously. Brezhnev pronounced them the principal achievements of the 1972 and 1973 summits, outshining even SALT I and the ABM Treaty. For the Soviets, the documents promised important political protection against the outbreak of nuclear war, by establishing a regime of consultations and constraints in the case of threatened confrontation with the United States. This freed the USSR, as Brezhnev and the Politburo saw it, to pursue its own agenda in parts of the Third World where the United States had not staked out countervailing interests. That understanding led in turn to the Angolan intervention of 1975, which the Soviets believed would not trouble American policy concerns, but which in fact contributed substantially to the unraveling of détente.

The U.S. understanding, or hope, was that the two agreements would somehow induce a general restraint on the part of the Soviet Union, regardless of whether any immediate superpower confrontation was threatened. The goal was to curtail Soviet influence of all kinds in the developing world. No language to this effect can be found in either of the agreements, however, nor was the U.S. aim effectively communicated to the Soviets; on top of which, the American leaders did not take the agreements as a serious limitation on their own freedom of action. Less than 24 hours after signing the Basic Principles Agreement in 1972, President Nixon visited the Shah of Iran and agreed to provide covert assistance to the Kurdish rebels inside Iraq—a state that had just concluded a friendship treaty with the Soviet Union. This was Nixon's interpretation of the ban on "efforts to obtain unilateral advantage" he had just signed.

The two agreements were not as a legal matter binding or enforceable against either party. They set forth no procedures, prescribed no penalties, established no criteria, contained no methods of verification. They expressed simply a "spirit," which is what the Soviets seem to have wanted and to have taken seriously, while withholding any of the substance that might have made that spirit effective. Part of the confusion may have been attributable to the differing legal traditions of the two sides, which customarily lead the Soviets to favor rhetorical principles while the Americans look for practical provisions. In this case the Soviets appear genuinely to have believed that they had an agreement, while the Americans may have signed on knowing that they did not—a shortsighted, and inevitably self-damaging, posture.

If the Soviets had been better advised, they would have suspected from the outset that such "codes of conduct" have no standing in American law or politics. Restraints on the exercise of armed force are by tradition a matter for U.S. treaty determination, not for executive agreements. Congress was not invited to participate in the formulation or approval of either of these documents. Nor for that matter were the Secretaries of State or Defense or the Joint Chiefs of Staff. The NATO allies were advised only minimally and at the last moment. Even the President was left largely in the dark as to what he was signing—all in all, an ominous harbinger of the Iran-Contra affair some fourteen years later.

There were serious concerns among U.S. allies, then as later, that the U.S. was moving to establish a consultation exclusivity, or condominium, between the two superpowers, that would monitor the application of force by other parties all over the world. Soviet claims on behalf of the two agreements tended at times to support this extravagant reading, which the absence of any limiting language or process made difficult to refute. All of this was a lot of fuss to stir up over what was, in reality, no more than a personal declaration of the moment by a President under siege and on his way out of office. The Soviets, by now, must have come to understand, if they did not earlier, that these two "codes of conduct" lost all force the moment Mr. Nixon resigned in August 1974.

Another and more deliberate effort to spell out self-limiting measures, and to make them legally effective, emerged in 1988 from a joint three-year study by U.S. and Soviet unofficial teams headed by Georgi Arbatov and Arthur Macy Cox; its members included such figures as William Colby, a former director of the CIA, and Fyodor Burlatsky, a seasoned adviser to both Khrushchev and Gorbachev. The stated aim of this panel was to demilitarize all U.S.-Soviet competition in the Third World.

For that purpose it recommended a comprehensive agreement that would commit the two superpowers, in areas of regional conflict:

1. not to intervene directly or indirectly with military force;
2. not to transfer, and to engage other suppliers not to transfer, sophisticated weapons;

3. not to introduce proxy military forces or volunteer forces or covert paramilitary forces;
4. not to organize, fund, equip or advise insurgencies or counterinsurgencies;
5. to limit military assistance programs to equipment and training necessary only for legitimate defense;
6. to offer military protection to friends and allies only against a crossborder invasion; and
7. to establish machinery to insure adequate verification of these agreements.

One thing that emerges immediately from inspection of this list is a distinction between those proposals—1, 3, and 6—that would limit the introduction of outside military forces, and the rest. The distinction is that outside invasions, whether direct or indirect, challenge the other superpower to a potentially mortal riposte; whereas the same is not true, judging from past experience, as regards weapons supply or insurgent assistance. Restraints on the latter may also be desirable, but they are not so necessary or attainable or enforceable as restraints on the former. In this respect, the narrower scope of the 1972–1973 agreements, as they were read by the Soviets, seems preferable.

Proposal 2, cutting off sophisticated arms shipments to the Third World, is certainly desirable but it bumps up against the interest held by all developed countries—not least the Soviet Union—in maximizing arms-export earnings. No practical way has yet been found of imposing reliable limitations on this traffic.

Proposal 4, banning outside support to insurgencies, looks difficult to police and again seems less necessary than its companion proposals.

Proposal 5, limiting equipment and training assistance to what is "necessary only for legitimate defense," sets up an indeterminate standard for judging what is permitted and what is not. It invites conflict and confusion.

A group of senior officials from the national security agencies of the U.S. government, invited to consider these proposals in the fall of 1986, expressed doubt that any of these provisions, even if initially accepted, would comport in the long run with superpower appetites or interests. They pointed out that a regime of military constraints sufficiently specific and verifiable to keep the Soviets out of future Afghanistans and Nicaraguas would also operate to keep the United States out of those places, as well as others, whose engagement by one military means or another the U.S. might not be prepared in all circumstances to foreswear. Unless sharply focused, in their view, a regime of this sort would be likely to become unstable over time. As Alexander George has suggested, such a regime would imply that the United States and the Soviet Union are "willing to accept any outcome of a regional conflict, however harmful to their individual interests the outcome might turn out to be." Agreements of that sweep tend not to hold.

As for verification, the Arbatov-Cox report suggested the use of "existing U.S. and Soviet intelligence assets," backed up by consultation machinery. The evidence of outside military support is, however, typically prolix and ambiguous as well as elusive. It is difficult to pin down, and not at all on a par with the surveillance of large-scale nuclear-weapons sites with which both superpowers have monitoring experience.

A code of conduct that reaches for more than it can verify or assure, is a code that may cause more harm than good. The end result of adopting such measures could be to aggravate rather than allay superpower hostility and recrimination, as in fact occurred after the summit agreements of 1972–73.

Even to deal with direct invasions—proposals 1, 3, and 6—it may be preferable to look not to the machinery of legal agreements but to less formal understandings and practices. The two superpowers have been gaining in appreciation, as we have seen, for a diet of military self-denial growing out of informed, mutual self-interest. At the same time, Third World countries have been showing themselves increasingly adept at reinforcing such restraint.

When it really matters, the U.S. and the Soviet Union know how to follow a tacit code of conduct. They have done so successfully, under the trying circumstances of cross-loyalties to regional combatants, in the Arab-Israeli wars of 1967 and 1973. Both of those wars featured one or the other superpower keeping its regional ally short of the decisive victory that would have threatened to draw in the other superpower. The formula is not perfectly stable—it would obviously be preferable to temper the regional antagonisms—but it has worked better, in all probability, than an ambiguous or overstated formal restraint.

Some continuing modest effort to codify restraints is doubtless desirable. The Arbatov-Cox study quoted former Soviet Ambassador to the United States Anatoly Dobrynin as endorsing the idea of "norms of behavior to limit military action and to regulate regional conflicts that could escalate into world war." That is the langauge of balance and discrimination—"norms . . . to limit . . . conflicts that could escalate"—and it leaves open the form in which such self-denying strictures should be expressed. It can serve, appropriately, as a starting point for the further reflection that seems warranted.

Good Offices

The Soviets have found that they can act on their own to damp down instabilities, in areas of security interest to themselves, when the U.S. is not prepared to join in. This became clear during the latter part of the Reagan administration, when Soviet diplomacy in the Persian Gulf and the Middle East began outpacing their supporting resources, whereas for the U.S. at that time the exact reverse was the case. The Soviet Union offered its "good offices" for resolving regional antagonisms—in conjunction with the United States if possible, but separately if not.

The motivation behind this Soviet maneuvering was only partly competitive, to discomfit the United States. The Soviets hold an obvious, defensive security interest of their own in this region of political volatility adjoining its borders. The Soviet leadership seems also to have realized—taking a leaf from the earlier American book at Camp David—that the development of businesslike relations with the parties to a regional dispute can equip an outside power to behave as a mediator, or broker, with ensuing political credit and leverage.

The U.S. for a time forgot that lesson, and created a vacuum for the Soviets to step into. The Iran arms sales, coming to light in 1986, were a major regional embarrassment to the Reagan administration. To recover lost face, the administration overcorrected in the other direction, taking a position overtly against Iran by aligning the United States with Iraq's informal ally, Kuwait. The Soviets thereby became the only major power in the region that enjoyed a working relationship with both sides in the Iran-Iraq war. At the same time, the U.S. moved summarily to close ranks with Israel—its active partner in the covert Iran arms sales—in a way that reinforced Arab concerns about a lack of U.S. evenhandedness toward their interests. The U.S. seemed almost for a while to be reading itself out of diplomatic usefulness in the region, which tended to highlight the emergence of the Soviet Union as the party that was reading itself in.

That may have been only a momentary development. Without substantial economic and military sustenance to back it up, the Soviets' long-term political contribution to Persian Gulf stability may be limited to reawakening the United States. By the summer of 1988 the Soviets had carried their diplomatic position about as far as it could go, given the higher priority claims on their resources for Europe, China, *perestroika,* and the like. For the U.S., the enduring lesson seemed to be that leaner resources and a more supple diplomacy can often produce a more positive return.

Withdrawal

The Soviets have shown that they are capable of cutting their own losses. In 1987–88, General Secretary Gorbachev initiated action to withdraw Soviet troops or troop support from the long-draining conflicts in Afghanistan, Angola, and Kampuchea. In each case, following the American precedent in Vietnam, the Soviets made no effort to exact an internal settlement as a precondition for the troop withdrawal. Quite probably this would not have worked in any case; but as with President Nixon's policy of "Vietnamization" in the 1970's, necessity was clothed as a virtue. In June of 1988, speaking of the projected Angola withdrawal, Soviet Deputy Foreign Minister Anatoly Adaimshin simply predicted that an internal settlement would be achieved "very easily" once foreign troops were retired.

That seemed unlikely. Regional conflicts arise in the main from local antagonisms having nothing to do with East-West rivalry. The center's dispute with the highlands in Afghanistan, the tribal frictions in Angola, the secular battles in Indochina, all antedated the entry of the superpowers and all will survive their retirement. (The same could be said with at least equal justice about the Arab-Israel, Iran-Iraq, and Libya-Chad hostilities.) The wars in these places may be reduced in intensity, and one day sputter out; but the main effect of superpower force withdrawal will be to remove these locales as flash-points for a global war. That is a sufficient advantage, and a benefit, for the superpowers and the world, so long as it holds.

Co-guarantees

To make a withdrawal secure, the Soviets have taken to suggesting that it be accompanied by a joint superpower guarantee against the reintroduction of outside forces. Such a pledge was included in the Afghanistan settlement, negotiated under UN auspices, and was proposed for Angola and Kampuchea as well. The U.S. would commit itself, side by side with the Soviet Union—and perhaps with the other permanent members of the UN Security Council—not to send military forces directly or indirectly into a named country and to refrain from helping others to do so.

The problem, as with codes of conduct, lay in definition and enforcement, and also in perceptions of national interest. Where should one draw the restrictive line? In the Afghanistan settlement, internal political resistance in the United States led to an insistence that arms cutoffs be executed simultaneously on both sides, which meant in practice that the reduction of fighting intensity was delayed. In Angola as well, where the U.S. made available its own good offices for withdrawal pledges by South Africa and Cuba, the U.S. insisted that it should remain free to send weapons and ammunition to Angolan rebels.

This was not just a peculiarity of American policy. The Soviets too have been major suppliers of military equipment to the Angolan and Afghan theaters. For them, a cutoff of arms supplies could affect not only future political leverage but also and more immediately the security of withdrawing troops. The scope and effect of co-guarantee clauses seem for such reasons to be likely to come under increasingly close review, in coming years, by the superpowers and by other parties involved in a withdrawal.

Nation-building

Gorbachev's book *Perestroika,* published in 1987, called among other things for a joint U.S.-Soviet effort to defuse Third World conflicts by diverting resources from the arms race to economic development. Little detailed attention was given to what this might mean, or to what the Soviets could be expected as a practical matter to contribute.

A less confrontational superpower competition in the developing world could assist development by rerouting local resources and by making the countries in question more attractive to private and outside investors. U.S. patterns of assistance might conceivably become more straightforwardly developmental—although, in the absence of a communist "menace," past history suggests they could dry up altogether.

The U.S. has paid small attention in recent years to the long, hard, step-by-step business of building an independent and self-sustaining core of countries in the uncommitted Third World. Here lie the future markets for Western goods and services, and the bases of future global stability, but they have received no sustained nation-building support from either Americans or Soviets. As former president Richard Nixon once observed, when the Communists see a development problem they at least have tried to get credit for dealing with it, whereas the American tendency has been to "see only the Communists."

The overwhelming share of America's aid program in the 1980's went not into nation-building but into military and security assistance. General economic aid fell steeply. The poor countries of Africa and the struggling democracies of Latin America—objects of rhetorical solicitude in the 1980's—have gotten very little practical support. They have been crowded out by earmarked and military aid to a few selected "cockpit" countries like Israel and Egypt and Pakistan.

One thing that might serve to alter these trends, and perhaps to turn them around, would be evidence of authentic Soviet development assistance, of the sort that Gorbachev was describing. Here again, a healthy competition could be beneficial. Past patterns and present intimations both, however, give grounds for considerable skepticism.

The Soviets have for decades focused their aid on embattled

client states. These have included Cuba and Vietnam—now considered Second World, socialist states—but also non-communist supporters and economic partners like India and the states of North Africa. The USSR fished in troubled waters in the 1960's, drew a poor catch, and withdrew. It has until now stayed out of the major international aid-giving institutions like the World Bank, the IMF, and the regional banks. Neither independently nor multilaterally, since World War II, have the Soviets been a force for disinterested development of the kind they are currently proposing.

Gorbachev made a pertinent gesture at the UN in December 1988, when he offered to excuse the external debts of the poorest Third World countries. The fact was however, that the Soviets held very little in the way of such debt, so that for those who look beyond the headlines the gesture seemed largely empty.

There are, to be fair, some practical obstacles in the way of a substantial Soviet contribution. Many of the kinds of technology and know-how most suited to transformational development are not available in the Soviet Union at present or are more easily obtainable from others. Under current budgetary strictures, moreover, the Soviets are not in a good position to offer preferential rates of interest or repayment terms.

Gorbachev may have had it in mind to dedicate savings from the demilitarization of Third World engagements, into a development "pool" containing like monies from the United States and perhaps from other developed countries. There would be a need for some kind of cooperation, tacit or otherwise, to achieve demilitarization, and that cooperation could in theory carry over into funding. But the effort would still tend to leave the technology-backward Soviets in a passive or lesser role, following the more active lead of the Western countries—which would be difficult for the Soviets to accept, politically, while the expected non-military rivalry between East and West for regional influence continues. The aim of Gorbachev's development policy, in summary, seems more ideal than real, at least in the coming period.

UN Mediation

On September 17, 1987, Mikhail Gorbachev published an unusual signed article in *Pravda* and *Izvestia.* Reversing the Soviet practice of decades, Gorbachev declared his government and party to be in favor of strengthening the United Nations: building up the mediative capacities of the UN Security Council and Secretary General, making wider use of regional peacekeeping forces under UN command, broadening the compulsory jurisdiction of the International Court of Justice, and establishing overall what Gorbachev called a "comprehensive system of international security."

The initiative aroused immediate skepticism. The Soviet Union, a superpower solicitous of its status, had long opposed any dilution of its independence. Nikita Khrushchev on these grounds had opposed UN peacekeeping in the Congo and refused to contribute to its operations. More recently, the Soviets had withheld payment for UN forces at the Golan Heights and in Southern Lebanon, among other places. Yet here was Gorbachev volunteering to pay all past dues, and actually making a substantial downpayment; accepting the mandatory submission of identified cases to the International Court, if other permanent members of the Security Council would do the same; and allowing Soviet nationals to become long-term UN civil servants, rather than short-term agents of the USSR, as in the past. It was not an offer that could be easily disregarded.

There were parts of the proposal, inevitably, that sounded less well-considered than others. Gorbachev suggested use of the United Nations to verify arms-control and ceasefire agreements, apparently forgetting how a UN observer post was obliged by Egyptian authorities to fold up its Sinai operations just before the start of the 1973 Arab-Israeli War; no verification scheme that is dependent on the withdrawable consent of an interested party is going to make much of a contribution to stability. Likewise, a Gorbachev proposal for an enforceable, harmonized UN code of human rights appeared to ignore the failed history of such efforts and the underlying cultural divisions that rule out any easy harmonization.

Other ideas put forward in the General Secretary's speech were less objectionable but still offputting to experienced international diplomats. The notion of placing Eastern and Western escort navies in the Persian Gulf under UN command seemed to put the clothing ahead of the body. A UN tribunal to investigate international acts of terrorism might be expected to slow down rather than expedite police action, and to summon the glare of publicity that is often at the heart of terrorist objectives. Giving the Security Council a role in settling international economic conflicts, such as Third World debt, could similarly risk ensnaring such settlements in the sloganeering politics of development nationalism that habitually attend such issues.

Gorbachev and his advisers may have chosen to include such proposals in the Soviet initiative as a way of attracting quick Third World support in the General Assembly. If so, they were only partly successful. On December 7, 1987, by a vote of 76 to 12, the Assembly adopted Soviet-sponsored Resolution 42/93, favoring a "Comprehensive System of International Peace and Security," with the abstention however of a remarkable total of 63 developed and developing states. On a companion resolution not incorporating Gorbachev's phraseology, but stressing the need to enhance the authority and effectiveness of the Security Council, the vote was a more robust 131 in favor, 1 opposed (the United States), and only 23—all industrial democracies—abstaining.

As this latter vote suggests, part of Gorbachev's motivation may have been to isolate the United States. The U.S. in the 1980's had been slashing its own UN dues payments and publicly belittling the value of the institution. At the time of Gorbachev's proposals, the U.S. owed more than $400 million in past dues and was continuing to withhold payment until a series of administrative reforms—including a U.S. veto over UN budgets—was adopted. The United States had also withdrawn during the decade from the compulsory jurisdiction of the International Court, and ignored that Court's finding that the U.S. had violated international law by mining the approaches to Nicaraguan waters. America was ripe for a challenge to such practices, so far as international opinion was concerned, and Gorbachev must certainly have been alive to that opportunity.

But there was more to it than this. The Soviet Union needed the help of a strengthened international system to advance its own national agenda. At a tactical level, becoming a paid-up supporter of that system would be likely to aid the Soviets' IMF and GATT applications, which they had reason to hope would help them modernize their economy. In strategic terms, engaging the cooperation of the other permanent Security Council members could help to neutralize regional power plays, and open up a face-saving way of disentangling Soviet prestige from foreign misadventures.

There were other potential advantages. The Arbatov-Cox report endorsed UN responsibility as a way of overcoming suspicion that U.S.-Soviet cooperation might produce a superpower condominium. Beyond that, the over-riding goal of global stability could be furthered by giving up a measure of independent national control over its attainment. That had long been the hope, however idealistic, of the architects of the UN system, and the Soviet move in September 1987 made it possible to begin thinking once more of its possible achievement.

There were also some limits to what the Soviets were proposing, but these served in their way to strengthen its realism and hence its credibility. The Soviets did not ask for an augmentation of General Assembly powers, despite (or probably because of) the "democratic" character of that one-nation, one-vote body. It was the General Assembly that had condemned the Soviet invasion of Afghanistan, and the Soviets would not have wished to submerge their sovereignty in that mass. Much better, they would have thought, to rely on the Security Council, where the USSR has a veto and can bargain as an equal with the other major powers.

No role was proposed, moreover, for the Security Council, or for that matter the Secretary General, in settling non-border conflicts—such as Cambodia and Nicaragua—that engaged the other major powers. Dragging the UN into such cases might offend regional sensitivities, and could not be done without the consent of the rival powers, principally China and the United States, whose interests would be affected. As if to prove the point, when China in 1988 manifested its consent by becoming a participant in Cambodian settlement discussions, the UN began readying itself for Indochinese peacekeeping duties. The Soviets in such ways appeared to be treating their UN peacekeeping proposals as a part of the politics of the possible.

This seemed to confirm that the Soviets overall were pursuing a real-world, reciprocatable, diplomacy of national interest.

15

The Trustworthiness of Soviet Commitments

A constant refrain in American politics since World War II has been that you can't trust the Russians; there is, as we know, some support for this position in the record. Experienced negotiators like Averell Harriman and George F. Kennan have long maintained, however, that the Soviets *can* be trusted—to pursue their own interests. The record shows that they will abide by well-prepared mutual agreements, like the Limited Test Ban Treaty of 1963, which Harriman brought home after two weeks of negotiation and which has never been violated.

There have been other kinds of agreements, like the Litvinov and Yalta and Helsinki accords, that have not been fully complied with because they were not well considered or well prepared. John Lewis Gaddis describes the divergence, persuasively, as follows:

> The point is that agreements between great nations are no better than the interests that lie behind them; no government is going to allow vital interests to be circumscribed by ink. Where those interests conflict, no number of carefully worded and lofty-sounding agreements is going to resolve the issue. But where interests are congruent—and despite the intensity and persistence of the Soviet-American rivalry, there are such areas of

214

congruent interest—diplomacy can be useful, provided means
exist to verify compliance.

Gaddis lists several agreements that have met these criteria, including the Austrian State Treaty of 1955, the Limited Test Ban
Treaty, and the ABM Treaty (whose durability was roundly tested
and found worthy during the Reagan years).

Their success has been a matter not of form but of substance.
When conditions are right, a tacit agreement or reciprocal action
can do just as well as, or even better than, a formal treaty. Eisenhower and Khrushchev arrived at a nuclear test moratorium by
informal means, just as Kennedy and Khrushchev agreed on a
mutual hands-off posture in Cuba (no Soviet offensive weapons, no
American invasion) without adopting any formal paper. There has
long been a tacit agreement to tolerate each other's "spy" satellites,
in the common interest of enforcing arms agreements and of
avoiding surprises. These are all matters of considerable importance, whose informal treatment has succeeded—where more formal agreements might have failed—because it responded to mutual security interests and was verifiable.

The successful agreements have also been free of the trappings
of so-called "linkage"—an instrument of contractual coercion that
has repeatedly been found wanting. The delusion has been that if
there is no direct way to secure Soviet compliance with a preferred
behavioral norm (on something like human rights), it could be
pried out of Moscow by making the award of some unrelated
benefit contingent on the desired Soviet performance. The benefit
might be diplomatic recognition (1933), postwar cooperation
(1945), normalized trade (1974), secure borders (1975), nuclear
arms limitation (periodically)—or anything else that came to
hand. All of these instruments of leverage, without exception, have
failed to produce the intended result, for the reason identified by
the French diplomatist de Callières, namely, that coercion repels
while only a perceived mutuality of interest can procure a lasting
success.

There are actually two kinds of linkage: one that uses inducements to get another party to join an agreement, which may be
called positive linkage; and another that sets unrelated preconditions on one's own entry into an agreement, which is negative
linkage. The 1972 Moscow accords, putting together a package on

Berlin and Eastern Europe, arms control and trade, was an example of positive linkage. There was a commonly perceived practical
relation among the various parts, each of whose achievement
could help to fortify the others. There is nothing at all wrong with
that; it was this kind of balancing, of benefits and burdens, that
kept the peace among the Concert of Europe parties for a hundred
years. Positive linkage, practiced quietly between states, is a well-
established diplomatic instrument.

It is a quite different matter, however, to assert that one will
not join an agreement, even when it is in one's own perceived
interest, unless the other party does something unrelated that is
not in its perceived interest. That is a practice of negative linkage,
for which there is no warrant in diplomatic history. The U.S. did
a lot of that with the Soviet Union—much of it noisily—in the years
after 1972. It imposed or threatened sanctions for behavior Americans did not like, and included in its threats the abrogation or
non-performance of existing arrangements as well as the shelving
of new agreements. American interests, and the sanctity of contracts, were not advanced in the process.

National Security Assistant Henry Kissinger coined the word
"linkage" in 1969, to tie the opening of SALT negotiations to Soviet
willingness to bail the U.S. out in Vietnam and the Middle East.
The Soviets of course never did any such thing, but the connection
slowed the SALT I process down considerably. Secretary of State
Cyrus Vance, coming next, renounced linkage; but Security Assistant Zbigniew Brzezinski persuaded President Jimmy Carter to reverse policy again, after Angola and Afghanistan. This time SALT
II was the victim. Here were two prominent examples of negative
linkage to arms control, neither of them beneficial to nuclear restraint.

On any fair consideration such linkage makes no sense. Nuclear arms control cannot be linked to anything else, because
avoiding nuclear war is an objective without equal. There is no
parity with any other issue, and without parity there can be no
linkage. Put differently, realistic and effective nuclear arms limitation is in the paramount security interest of the United States. To
attach any preconditions, penalties, or sanctions to this objective
is therefore to diminish the national security.

Besides which, linkage just does not work. Americans have
learned since 1972 that to attach side issues to any negotiations

with the Soviet Union is to make it somewhat less likely that we can influence its behavior on those unrelated issues. This is a very human matter. Ask someone in private whether he will do something that can make it easier for you to sign a mutually beneficial agreement, and he will probably try to accommodate you. Tell him in public that he must meet your unrelated demands, and he will walk away. It has happened time after time: SALT I and SALT II are leading examples, but so is the Jackson-Vanik amendment, which for many years shut the door on Jewish emigration rather than opening it. There is not a single authentic "success" story to be chalked up in the whole postwar history of negative linkage. That is arresting, or ought to be.

If, then, the only damage has been to America's own interests—grain farming, manufacturing, nuclear security—is there any proper place for negative linkage? Some believe it should be used as an instrument of limitation on Third World activism by the Soviet Union, and others see it as potential leverage against Soviet human-rights abuses. As to the first, it seems sometimes to be forgotten that when President Nixon went to see Brezhnev in 1972 the U.S. was at that very moment mining Haiphong Harbor and bombing Hanoi. Brezhnev signed onto SALT I and the ABM Treaty despite this behavior and perhaps even because of it. No doubt he hoped to get the U.S. out of Vietnam, just as the U.S. later worked to get Russian troops out of Afghanistan—but by instruments other than negative linkage.

Human rights affords another, perhaps more sensitive, illustration of the same point. Avoiding nuclear war is quite probably the over-riding issue of human rights for all mankind. Westerners may bemoan the fact that the civil traditions in Russia, having never absorbed the Renaissance or the Reformation or the Enlightenment, have carried forward a different view of human life and liberty than the one we espouse. But the West cannot successfully impose a change on the Soviet culture from outside. And U.S. leaders cannot ignore the distorting effect on American public opinion of continuing to hold onto that unreachable goal. It can only ideologize, and constrict, the popular willingness to find real-world solutions of matters where a mutuality of interest exists.

It is useful to observe that, in the Nixon and Carter administrations, the persons keenest on negative linkage—Security Assistants Kissinger and Brzezinski—were those least attuned by experience to its domestic political consequences. Diplomats and politicians with a habit of taking the wider view—people like Cyrus Vance— renounced linkage. And so, ultimately, did President Nixon. In his book *Real Peace,* published in 1983, Nixon took the view that profound and irreconcilable differences between the societies of the Soviet Union and the United States must be accepted and dealt with. He urged a continuing process for managing and containing those conflicts.

The failure to follow that counsel has had unfortunate domestic as well as international effects. When it was first introduced, the idea of Cold War diplomacy or "détente" had no broad supportive public constituency. The American people had been nurtured for 25 years on an unremitting diet of hostility. President Nixon at the time was unwilling or unable to educate the public about the broad value of what he was doing. So, when "linkage" was proclaimed as part of the negotiating approach, it stirred up a sea of opportunism along with pre-existing doubts that the Soviets could be trusted.

Those doubts had been fostered by a human-rights diplomacy long intertwined with domestic political posturing. There is probably no instance in which Western ideals or values have profited. The Litvinov letters in 1933, formalizing the establishment of U.S.-Soviet diplomatic relations, purported to guarantee the free exercise of religious conscience and worship in the USSR—without effect. The Yalta conference in 1945 declared the right of all peoples in liberated Europe to choose the form of government under which they would live—without effect. The Helsinki Final Act in 1975 pledged sovereign regard for "human rights and fundamental freedoms, including the freedom of thought, conscience, religion or belief"—once more without effect. The only thing affected, and that adversely, has been international respect for the sanctity of negotiated agreements.

This long and dismaying experience should prompt a sober awareness of the limited role of such agreements. That role is not to parade expressions of hope or to proclaim an unrealizable morality, but to pin down a realizable common interest. There is always room for idealistic instruments such as the 1948 UN Declaration of Human Rights—provided they are recognized as prayers for peace, no part of which is designed to be enforceable. The problem with tucking such provisions into more businesslike documents (Litvinov, Yalta, Helsinki) is that they give the impression of being enforceable agreements and so serve to discredit the process of negotiation when that impression proves unfounded.

John Lewis Gaddis reminds us that the success of U.S.-Soviet diplomacy, and more especially of negotiated superpower agreements, depends upon two things: (1) obtaining an accurate reflection of the real-world interests of the two sides, and (2) securing the ability to induce compliance. None of the human-rights agreements we have looked at qualifies on either of those counts. Organized religion was seen as an enemy of the Soviet state in 1933, an independent Poland was contrary to the security needs of the Soviet Union as perceived in 1945, and the Soviets still felt threatened by internal dissidence in 1975. Similar things can be said about unilateral impositions, like the Jackson-Vanik amendment, which demanded of the Soviets a relaxed view about Jewish emigration that in 1974 they did not have. Add to all this that there was no way of securing compliance with any of these provisions, without hurting important American interests—in stable economic and political and military relations—and you have an array of clauses that should never have been included in any serious agreement.

That they were so included is an illustration of the tendency of American domestic politics to short-change its own constituency interests. Americans understandably have been skeptical of Soviet intentions in the world, and resistant to taking approbative steps like diplomatic recognition or postwar cooperation or the settlement of borders. So their leaders on occasion—rather than seeking to explain the value of a step being proposed—have thrown the public a "human-rights" bone. The problem is that the bone has had no meat on it, and the skepticism has simply been reinforced.

To its credit the Reagan administration in its closing years moved American policy away from this unproductive course. Recognizing perhaps that past errors had been equally divided between Democratic (1933, 1945) and Republican (1974, 1975) administrations, President Reagan abandoned linkage in his second term and moved to the more promising technique of parallel advance.

Nothing symbolized this change more completely than President Reagan's state toast to General Secretary Gorbachev at the White House dinner on December 8, 1987, when the INF treaty was signed:

By now, Mr. General Secretary, you may have concluded that, while we have fundamental disagreements about how human communities should govern themselves, it is possible all the same for us to work together.

A century and a half ago, the brilliant French observer de Tocqueville foresaw that our two countries would be the major two countries of the world. History, geography, the blessings of resources and the hard work of our people have made it so.

And between us there has always been a profound competition of political and economic philosophy, making us the protagonists in a drama with the greatest importance for the future of all mankind.

Man's most fundamental beliefs about the relationship of the citizen to the state and of man to his creator lie at the core of the competition between our two countries. History has indeed endowed our relationship with a profound meaning. Certainly we will not settle those issues this week, but the tasks before us require a full awareness of those issues and of a responsibility that is binding on us both.

I speak of a responsibility we dare not compromise or shirk.
I speak of the responsibility to settle our differences in peace.

That challenge was met by the Washington Summit. It produced an agreement on matters of clear mutual interest—nuclear arms control—between two parties much of whose values remained in disagreement. The Joint Statement issued at the close of the Summit made this plain. It cited "the continuing differences between the sides and their understanding that these differences are not insurmountable obstacles to progress in areas of mutual interest."

The agreement on this point was not simply rhetorical. It showed up concretely in the leaders' treatment of human rights, so often in the past an obstacle to agreement, which this time was summarized in one simple sentence: "The leaders held a thorough and candid discussion of human rights and humanitarian questions and their place in the U.S.-Soviet dialogue." That was all that was said, on the record.

This was not an oversight. It was deliberate, the culmination of the de-linkage policy that Secretary of State George Shultz had begun putting into place shortly after he took office. That policy holds that if an arms-control or other security initiative is in the American national interest, it should be pursued without political preconditions. It also holds that human rights deserve to be addressed on their own footing, as an appeal to conscience and community and not as an externally imposed legal obligation. Judging from their favorable reaction to the Washington Summit it seems probable that the American people would agree, if asked, that nuclear sanity and social civility are indeed complementary rather than competitive goals, neither of which should be allowed to obstruct a realization of the other.

Another figure who would agree, and who has acted on his agreement, is Mikhail Gorbachev. He bristled in his NBC television interview before the Washington Summit, and again six months later during Mr. Reagan's Moscow forays with the Soviet dissident community, that his government could not accept outside interference into Soviet internal affairs, and that he would not remain long in office if it did. But Gorbachev also knew that his own, self-motivated, human-rights performance would make it easier, politically, for Western leaders to do business with him on other fronts. This was no longer, for him, a matter of yielding to negative linkage; it was an offer of positive linkage, in the form not of promises or contingencies but of completed and ongoing actions.

At the United Nations General Assembly in December 1988, the General Secretary proclaimed that all prisoners of conscience had by then been released, and that strict time limits had been placed on the "state-secret" reason for barring emigration. With an eye to the diplomatic arena, Mr. Gorbachev told his audience: "This removes from the agenda the problem of the so-called 'refuseniks.'" Never mind that actual criminals—including some whose crime was speech offensive to the state—would remain in prison, or that there were other bases in Soviet law for holding on to some "refuseniks"; at least the more arbitrary imprisonments were ended, and this was enough of a change to invite recognition.

That recognition took the form, concretely, of Western approval for the international human-rights conference the Soviets were proposing to hold in Moscow in 1991. The January 1989 final document of the Vienna CSCE Conference, conferring that approval, was instructive. It was, like its predecessors, not a binding legal document but a joint statement of political hopes and expectations. The likelihood of its full performance was in some respects questionable: Tolerance for religious education and for "state-secret" emigration was already in evidence in the Soviet Union, but removal of anti-religious discrimination and of barriers to free internal movement was not. The Soviets nevertheless took the drafting exercise seriously, telling their Western counterparts that they hoped to find ways of affirming what their authorities would actually allow. They were acting out their own internal dynamics, trying to find positive inducements but not in response to outside impositions.

Another factor that bears on Soviet trustworthiness is their relationship to international terrorism, which some in the United States have believed to be one of sponsorship. If the Soviets were seeking to assassinate the Pope, or to aid the hostage-takers in Iran, the argument would run, how could they be taken as constructive partners in fashioning a stable world order?

Most often this question has arisen out of hostage-takings in the Middle East, which in the decade 1979–1988 proved intermittently capable of preoccupying the United States and of tying up its resources. While Soviet interests may have benefited marginally from this preoccupation, there is little credible evidence to demonstrate Soviet sponsorship of regional terrorism. The Soviets do have client relationships, including military and intelligence ties, with nations and groups on the State Department's list of terrorism sponsors—Syria, Libya, and the PLO among them. But the degree of effective control that these relationships afford is probably no greater in practice than that enjoyed by the United States with its supposed clients in the Middle East.

Whatever may have once been the case, the Soviets today have come to recognize that they too can be targets for terrorism. The 1985 seizure of four Soviet diplomats in Lebanon, one of whom was immediately murdered, was for them a watershed experience. In recent years the USSR has climbed to fifth place (behind the U.S., Israel, France, and Britain) as a victim of terrorist attacks. And Soviet leaders confess a quiet anxiety about the potential of sudden, unexplained terrorist incidents to provoke a military confrontation between the two superpowers.

A constructive Soviet approach to counterterrorism cooperation has recently emerged. The deputy director of the KGB, Lieutenant General Vitaly Ponomarev, declared in January 1989 that:

"We realize we have to coordinate efforts to prevent terrorist acts, including hijacking of planes. We are willing, if there's a need, to cooperate even with the CIA, the British intelligence service, the Israeli Mossad, and other services in the West." That same winter, a group of Soviet and American counterterrorism experts met in Moscow under unofficial auspices and reached agreement on the following recommendations:

1. Creation of a standing bilateral group and of a channel of communications for the exchange of information about terrorists, before and during crises;
2. Provision of mutual assistance in the investigation of terrorist incidents;
3. Mutual constraints on the movement of terrorist-prone weapons, such as the American Stinger and Soviet SAM-7 portable missiles; and
4. Joint action to strengthen anti-terrorism law and institutions.

Official interest in these matters was exhibited, at about the same time, by an unprecedented meeting between U.S. ambassador Jack Matlock and KGB director Vladimir Kryuchkov. Both sides expressed a desire to pursue avenues of practical cooperation. Then in June of 1989, a first consultation was held between national authorities from the two sides, seeking to identify (in the words of the State Department press guidance) "areas of practical cooperation that go beyond rhetoric." The proceedings were otherwise unpublicized, which suggested their seriousness of purpose.

All of this was consistent with a general shift in the thrust of the Soviet presence, not only in the Middle East but elsewhere, from one of radical, anti-Western, ideologically driven activism in the 1950's to one of great-power, geopolitical, stability-seeking today.

Serious agreements entered into by serious parties still need to be enforceable, which means in the first instance that compliance with them must be verifiable. "Trust but verify," as President Reagan liked to say; verifiability seals the trustworthiness of a commitment.

On the nuclear-weapons front, verification presents new problems as the sides move away from fixed and toward mobile weapons systems. These offer greater stability at the cost of greater elusiveness. New ways must be found to deal with the verification challenges they present; and Mr. Gorbachev, with his openness to on-site inspections for chemical and INF weapons, has shown some willingness to make constructive contributions to this search.

One measure that could make a contribution would be resurrection of the Special Consultative Commission, an expert body established in 1972 to investigate and resolve arms-control compliance questions, which was unaccountably shelved by the first Reagan administration. The SCC had shown that it could transform political arguments into practical solutions, thus strengthening the regime of agreements.

Another useful step could be the one proposed by the Bush administration in the summer of 1989, and swiftly accepted by the Soviet government. It was to hold up the unfinished START (strategic nuclear arms reduction) agreement until adequate verification measures could be selected and tested. This would assure the seriousness of an eventual START treaty, if suitable arrangements can be found.

The "intrusive" inspection regime associated in public pronouncements with the INF Treaty will not, however, be of very much help with this problem. There are extensive on-site provisions in the INF Treaty, and they do break new conceptual ground. As a practical matter, however, their value is modest. As Senator Sam Nunn, chairman of the Senate Armed Services Committee, said after his review of that treaty, if the Soviets were intent on cheating they would put forbidden INF missiles back somewhere else than at the specific sites that are open to inspection. Verification experts agree that perhaps 95 percent of INF monitoring will take place through satellite and other national technical means of inspection, and that these are adequate for enforcement.

On-site inspection will add little to this—indeed, it could detract somewhat. Whenever the complicated multi-page code of INF challenge procedures fails to produce a letter-perfect, timely response—as is bound on occasion to happen—those in America or in the USSR who distrust the other side will be handed an argument of a concreteness and specificity they have not had

before. It will be a political argument, of no great military significance, but potentially harmful all the same to the conduct of arms
control.

INF itself is likely to survive such questioning, because the
Soviet self-interest in preserving that treaty is clear enough to
over-ride technical suspicions of non-compliance. As Senator
Nunn also observed, there is little incentive in that regime for the
Soviets to cheat. The same is not necessarily true, however, of
follow-on strategic or conventional arms treaties, where the incentives and opportunities on both sides will be different. Indeed, it
is generally accepted that the INF model as such will not fit future
agreements, like these, that call for the removal of some but not
all of a given class of weapons.

Conventional arms limitations, of the kind being discussed for
Europe, may have to include far-reaching and intrusive verification measures. Jonathan Dean, the former U.S. ambassador to the
Mutual and Balanced Force Reduction Talks, has estimated that at
least 500 on-site inspections—many of them of the short-notice,
"challenge" variety—will have to be conducted each year for each
alliance. And that may not be enough. The absence of small forces
or moveable munitions from a designated region is immensely
difficult to verify, without a virtual occupation regime that would
be unacceptable to host governments. In the United States, there
are Constitutional restraints on warrantless inspection of private
premises that, under U.S. law, can over-ride any inconsistent
treaty provisions. Within the Western alliance, there may be problems of political discrimination. The U.S. has proposed a regime
for policing conventional force reductions that would place treaty
inspectors in French and British armament plants, but not in Soviet or American plants. Measures of this sort can be highly divisive.

Troop and aircraft reductions, originally rejected by NATO on
grounds of unverifiability, will need special verification attention.
The ability of the two superpowers to redeploy withdrawn aircraft
rapidly to Europe argues, in the minds of some experts, not just for
the destruction of the planes, as proposed, but also for a worldwide
U.S.-Soviet commitment not to replace them. The complexities
and intrusiveness of the verification measures needed to enforce
such a scheme had not, by the end of 1989 at least, been taken into
account.

As for troop reductions, these have long been recognized as being difficult to monitor. Gross violations can be detected, but exact and continuing surveillance of all troop movements may never be feasible. President Bush took a stab at the problem with his revival of former President Dwight Eisenhower's 1955 "open skies" proposal, suggesting in a May 1989 speech that "surveillance flights, complementing satellites, would provide regular scrutiny for both sides." The technical sufficiency of such scrutiny was open to question, however, and politically it gained only tepid endorsement.

Unilateral measures, for all the flexibility they enjoy, do not escape the necessity of verification. General Secretary Gorbachev attracted widely favorable attention, in December 1988, by his announcement of a 500,000-man Soviet troop cut. But he was unable by this gesture alone to instill in his Western counterparts the sense of security that could lead to a course of stabilizing force reductions. That will require the negotiation of reliable verification measures, against the day when East-West suspicions may eventually be set aside.

That, ultimately, is the problem: the legacy of postwar distrust. If, in 1945, fresh from their common victory over the Nazis, the Soviets and their Western allies had moved promptly in tandem to demobilize their forces, little thought would have probably been given to verification techniques. Each side would have simply watched the other, expecting a peacetime reversion and contributing to it.

When that did not happen—when, instead, rearmament and an arms race gave rise to a Cold War—there was a broaching of the 40 years of mutual mistrust whose legacy only now is in prospect of dissipation. To let that dissipation take place, in the face of all the practical difficulties, may have to entail some adjustment, over time, in the relative proportions of "trust" and "verify." At the outset, as previously, trust may have to depend very largely on verification; later, with experience, more of the verification may come to be rested on trust.

That will not happen all at once, or quickly. It took a long time to build up the mutual mistrust and it will take time, and patience, to overcome it.

16

Implications and Options for the U.S. and the West

The way to improved trust and confidence lies through reciprocal pursuit of geopolitical self-interest. The West should watch Soviet conduct with some uncertainty but not with skepticism. The Soviet measure of success for its external reforms is sure to include some sign of openness toward change on the part of the United States. What is important politically is less what the West can "do" for Mr. Gorbachev than how much it shows it is paying attention.

The testing or probing of Soviet intentions is, for this purpose, unnecessary and inappropriate. It assumes a tutorial leverage the West does not possess, distorts the behavior that is being examined, and hands the initiative in security relations over to the Soviet Union.

What Mr. Gorbachev may choose to do with his initiative—how much of his objectives are short-term or long, unilateral or mutual—is difficult and again unnecessary to sort out. Traces of all these objectives can probably be found in any of his actions; in the ideal case, he may hope to realize advantages for each. The part of Western diplomacy should be to ascertain what gains are in its security interest, and not very much to mind what associated advantages may accrue to the USSR.

Some signs of Soviet behavioral change to watch for in the coming years include the following:

227

1. Soviet transformation of the character of their European forces from offensive to defensive.
2. Institutional adjustments in Soviet pricing and market mechanisms to qualify for GATT membership.
3. Forbearance from intrusion into stable non-communist regimes in Eastern Europe.
4. Abstention from intervention in an Angola- or Mozambique-type of Third World situation.
5. Satisfaction of international expectations for the emigration of subject peoples.

Each of these steps, quite inconceivable a few years ago, is now within the realm of attainability. Yet a Soviet Union that meets all these benchmarks will still have a political and economic system very different from ours, will still be heavily armed, and will still be capable of intervening in unstable, low-risk situations around the world. The bear may be more equable, but it will not have been transformed into a deer.

The West and particularly the United States must now re-learn the art of great-power relations. They must school themselves to act on the basis of realistic self-interest, including a realistic awareness of how each side's conduct is perceived by the other. That can afford a tacit, mutual leverage more effective than the overt or unilateral coercion each has attempted in the past.

Eastern Europe and Central America offer two illustrations of how this may work. Each is a region of "high-interest asymmetry"—the first for the Soviet Union, the second for the United States. But the Soviets need Western participation in the economic and political evolution of Eastern Europe, if only to stabilize that region while the USSR winds down its commanding presence. The one thing to which the Soviets are bound to be sensitive, and which could slow down or stop their retrenchment, would be a resurgence of the German hegemony that preceded World War II. Chancellor Helmut Kohl of the Federal Republic of Germany showed some awareness of this concern at the Western Economic Summit in July 1989, when he proposed—and President Bush among others agreed—that Western engagement in Eastern Europe should be modulated by the multi-member European Community, thus muffling the involvement of any one nation.

The Soviets have displayed a comparable recent awareness of

U.S. "asymmetrical" sensitivities in the Western Hemisphere, and particularly in Central America. Bases in the Western Hemisphere, or force deployments there, are viewed—according to the experts—as quick losses in any East-West conflict; they command a very low priority for the Soviet military. General Secretary Gorbachev, when he took part in the 1987 Washington Summit, told President Reagan he was prepared to assist in a military disengagement from Nicaragua by curtailing Soviet arms shipments there. No agreement was reportedly reached, but after that the conflict in Nicaragua began moving in a decidedly more political direction, and Soviet readiness to cooperate seems to have played a part.

These two "asymmetrical" regions, with their high potential for destabilization of superpower relations, should qualify for future inclusion among the subjects of regular, quiet, U.S.-Soviet trouble-spot consultation. They can in this way become part of an enlarged and effective peacekeeping diplomacy.

The first Reagan administration tended to disparage such diplomacy. Improvement in the U.S. geopolitical position, through the buildup and deployment of armed force, was thought at the time to be sufficient by itself to shift the burden of adjustment to the Soviet Union. This policy proved unsound and ineffective, for the reasons identified by the French diplomatist de Callières: It narrowed the bases for sustainable interaction. In December 1984, four months before the accession of Mikhail Gorbachev, U.S. Secretary of State George Shultz forecast the changing perspective of the second Reagan term when he declared:

> Americans have sometimes tended to think that power and diplomacy are two distinct alternatives. This reflects a fundamental misunderstanding. The truth is, power and diplomacy must always go together, or we will accomplish very little in this world.

This is so, not because of anything the Soviets have done, but because it is the only fruitful course of action open to the United States. A friendlier, sleeker Soviet bear will not be free of menace to the U.S. or the West. President Bush's policy advisers played him short when they had him say, in a 1989 speech on U.S.-Soviet relations: "We seek a friendship that knows no season of suspicion, no chill of distrust." That failed to describe the state of relations even within the NATO alliance, let alone with a major geopolitical rival. The proper goal is not friendship, but stability resting on reciprocal interest.

The same Bush speech said that the Soviet Union had sought cooperation before, "only to reverse course and return to militarism." There was truth in this; but it is also true that the West has the capacity, broadly speaking, to monitor and limit Soviet resurgence. The Soviet "new thinking" may be likened to the launch of an exploratory satellite, whose aim is to ease into low orbit where it will remain unless there is something to be gained by shooting into higher orbit. The U.S. and its allies have the means to limit the attractiveness of an unduly assertive second-stage resurgence on the part of the USSR.

Prior Soviet shifts of position have, moreover, emerged from very different strategic circumstances. The destructive reach of nuclear weapons, the financial strains of world empire, and the competitive rise of regional power centers all combine to transform the objective calculus by which the USSR, the U.S., and other countries and blocs are now bound. It would take an act of rare self-destructiveness to try to escape those restraints.

Planners of course must worry about extreme cases; up to a point, this is both prudent and necessary. But as the degree of improbability of a feared event mounts, it becomes difficult to the point of impossibility to bring democratic publics along. The worst security posture the West could probably adopt would be insistence on a level of defense readiness its internal constituencies were unwilling to support. Prudent and balanced military security, patrolled by an active diplomacy, is the key.

An active diplomacy is one that can meet skill with skill in the forum of power politics and can do so cost-effectively. It is the opposite in these respects of the inflated and only marginally effective military leverage deployed in the Persian Gulf by the Reagan administration during the Iran-Iraq war. Well before the USS *Vincennes* mistakenly shot an Iranian airliner out of the sky, with a loss of 290 civilian lives, the Soviet Union had positioned itself as the only peacemaker in the region that could claim a working relationship with both parties to the war. It profited first of all from the U.S. covert arms sales to Iran, which when disclosed painted the U.S. as a perfidious party, and then from the American counterreaction, which took a distinctly anti-Iranian line. American escort operations in the Gulf, which grew to the dimensions of an occupying navy, at a reported operating cost of $1 million a day, were used exclusively to combat Iranian, never Iraqi, attacks on neutral shipping. When the Iranian airline disaster paradoxically helped generate momentum to end the war, the Soviets found themselves in an advantageously neutral position from which to engage all parties, while the U.S. had to scramble indecorously for a renewal of contacts with Iran. In the end the United States incurred a large expenditure, and opprobrium, for essentially no gain; the Soviets were enabled at small expense to pick up the political pieces.

America and the West must accept that there is now a new, less ponderous, non-military rivalry with the Soviet Union in the Third World. This competition, rightly addressed, can be healthy and even beneficial. The Soviets have for example begun angling for position among the industrialized countries of the Far East, such as Singapore, where a heavy-footed American economic diplomacy has tended in recent years to alienate both official and public opinion. *Glasnost* and the withdrawal of forces from Afghanistan and Cambodia have attracted favorable attention to the USSR, at the very time that U.S. trade muscle was being exercised in a coercive and self-damaging fashion: Trade preferences were withdrawn from Singapore, and copyright "piracy" charged, at the behest of American private interests with little foreign-policy direction from Washington. In the short term at least, an opportunity was opened up for the Soviets in this significant and growing market.

The new economic rivalry may emerge in this setting as a useful corrective force. American high-handedness toward a vital maritime and financial and commercial center like Singapore is something that, on self-interest grounds, should never have been allowed to happen. If the internal U.S. protections against self-damage of this sort somehow break down, and it takes the presence of a Soviet alternative to alert American policy circles, then to that extent and for that purpose American interests can be served by the rivalry.

The American diplomacy of the future should include among its goals regularized trade and investment relations with the Soviet Union itself. This can serve both the economic and the political interests of the United States. Long-range, the Soviet Union remains one of the world's largest unopened markets, with vast untapped resources and large unserved consumer needs. Although it may take decades to achieve the transformations that can open up these markets to the international community, the effort to do so can begin in a much shorter period to temper and "civilize" Soviet attitudes toward the world.

Economic interaction can also contribute to foreign policy by developing an alternative, non-governmental channel of discourse with the Soviets. American business leaders tend to be respected figures in this country, and their reports on the Soviet performance of contracts and other similar matters will tend to carry weight. In as highly politicized a field as East-West relations, the more informed points of view one can hear, the more protection there is against perceptual distortion.

What has been seen in recent years is not, however, a long-range pursuit of American interests but a short-term effort to manage U.S.-Soviet trade for coercive purposes. The effort has signally failed, with detriments to both trade and foreign policy. It has produced losses to American employers and employees, and caused strains to U.S. relations with allied nations. The instruments of futility have ranged from grain and gas-pipeline embargoes to the Jackson-Vanik (tariff) and Stevenson (credit) prohibitions, and on to assorted foreign-policy controls and restrictions.

Speaking at a Washington trade forum in 1986, PepsiCo executive (and one-time Nixon mentor) Donald M. Kendall summed up the need and the opportunity for American international economic policy very simply as follows:

1. We should differentiate our trade policy from our foreign policy.
2. We should bring an end to sanctions against non-strategic trade.
3. We should make economic and trade advantage to the United States the sole basis for conferring tariff parity, or "most favored nation" status, on the Soviet Union.
4. We should likewise grant customary export credit to the Soviet Union strictly on the basis of economic risk.

The effect of such measures, if adopted, would be to begin to regularize East-West trade, and other economic transactions, on the basis of comparative advantage—leaving military goods and services out of the bargain. It would restore the precepts of Adam Smith, or more exactly begin introducing the Soviets to his concept of market-driven interchange. The effects over time should be beneficial both to the Soviets and to the West, and beyond that to the world at large.

In security relations, on the other hand, there needs to be a movement away from the more idealistic goals and pronouncements of recent years. President Reagan began moving in this direction, actually, before he left office. At the Moscow Summit in 1988 he was importuned by Mr. Gorbachev to sign another unexamined security declaration, but this time Reagan deferred to his advisers and ultimately declined to accept it. The Gorbachev draft said that: "The two leaders believe that no problem in dispute can be resolved, nor should it be resolved, by military means." Gorbachev expressed some dismay that this offspring of Locarno, and the Kellogg-Briand Pact, was not accepted, although he must surely have known that such declarations have a dismal record of effectiveness. On the Western side, in particular, the forswearing of "military means" could have been read to rule out the stationing of forces; this would have (a) engaged the NATO alliance, without consultation and (b) undercut established NATO military doctrine—the precise double sin of Reykjavik. The U.S. alternative draft, which was eventually accepted, not only was better but was actually quite good. It endorsed "a realistic approach to the problems of strengthening stability and reducing the risk of conflict . . . [despite] the real differences of history, tradition, and ideology that continue to characterize the U.S.-Soviet relationship." One of those differences, notably, is embodied in the NATO alliance.

That alliance needs to take time now to digest and reflect upon the changes in the security environment that have been taking place. President Bush opened his 1989 term with a four-month Washington pause for reflection on these matters, which was useful as far as it went; but NATO as a body has not done the same thing. It needs to do so, both to heal the strains of Reykjavik and to gird itself against the further alliance-dividing tactics that Mr. Gorbachev may be prompted to resort to in future.

Central to this process of review should be the determination of force missions and structures that can meet minimal U.S. and NATO security requirements for the coming period. Missions come first in this needed analysis, then force structures and levels, then dollar expenditures—not the other way around, as has too often been the case. The analysis will be complicated by the fact that Soviet force missions are in the apparent early stages of being changed, toward a posture of "reasonable sufficiency" and defensive defense. On the NATO side, defense doctrines have not been searchingly re-examined since "flexible response" was first adopted in the 1960's; technology and politics have both changed substantially since then, but the doctrine has not. Looking to the 1990's, and beyond, the West does not know where the Soviets may be going, or where it itself should go.

This uncertainty affects among other things NATO's nuclear doctrine, which as confirmed by Western heads of government in May of 1989 embraces "an appropriate mix of adequate and effective nuclear and conventional forces which will continue to be kept up to date where necessary." But what nuclear forces are truly "adequate and effective" for future European deterrence? It seems unlikely that short-range (SNF) missiles, which detonate on German territory and can be quickly overrun if not used promptly in a conflict, would have been chosen by a rational planner for this assignment. The mid-range INF missiles were much better suited, but these have all now been negotiated into extinction. That leaves only the French and British theater weapons, which are located in Europe but are politically unpalatable to the Soviets and the Germans; and U.S. strategic weapons, which are politically suitable but are not physically bound to Europe.

A conventional-only deterrence, if it came to that, would undo the NATO consensus and would raise in many minds the specter of a return to pre-1940 conditions. The Maginot Line was a species of conventional deterrence.

So, if "adequate and effective" alliance security is to be maintained for the protracted period of reciprocal force reduction that lies ahead, it will be necessary for NATO to think through its doctrinal adaptation to the nuclear-force mix it has left itself. This could form a centerpiece of the kind of internal, "wise man" review that has been proposed by a number of NATO's more experienced friends.

As that process unfolds, and older doctrines become reconciled with newer realities, one beneficial effect could be to lessen the felt necessity for arms-control negotiating feints and stunts. It could for example take the pressure away from serving up "bargaining chips" of dubious military value as a means of procuring concessions at the bargaining table. Both the MX missile and SDI, widely considered to be destabilizing and even invulnerating weapons systems, survived Congressional review in the 1980's by being painted as potential bargaining counters; in the end, neither was offered up and each acquired a procurement life of its own, despite being judged by most impartial authorities to have diminished the security of the United States.

The next candidates for this kind of treatment may be "smart" weapons, capable of destroying fixed military targets with precision-guided conventional munitions. By the 21st century, if they work as advertised (there is some doubt about that), these artifacts of the Electronic Battlefield may come to be substituted quite widely for the tanks and troops and nuclear weapons that are now relied upon to keep the peace. That could, in turn, destabilize the strategic balance, at the same time as it contributes to the short-run moderation of perceived tensions. The party that felt itself behind in "smart" weapons would sooner or later be drawn back toward increased reliance on nuclear deterrence and on preemptive strikes to remove the inequality. That would be hazardous for both sides.

It would therefore seem unwise to toss "smart" weapons on to the bargaining table as bare negotiating counters; they are all too likely to survive and to acquire their own standing as unconstrained systems in the fashion of past similar chips. And yet there is evidence that the Soviet interest in "defensive defense" has been inspired at least in part by the development of precision weapons, so that their introduction at the table could prove enticing for Western negotiators. At a consultation with senior Soviet arms-control advisers in Moscow in April 1988, Westerners were told that preemptive countermeasures were being readied against "smart" weapons but that the Soviets would not bargain away their tank superiority just to get rid of what were still, at that point, paper systems. This was similar to the position that the Soviets took on the INF question in 1982, before the deployment of American Pershing-2 and cruise missiles. The Pershing-2 was itself a destabilizing weapon, but its deployment was probably a key factor—along with new Moscow leadership—in changing the Soviet position and bringing about the eventual INF agreement.

That is perhaps the key. The Pershing-2 deployment was used, in the end, not as a general negotiating lever to put the Soviets at a disadvantage, but as a specific offset to the SS-20 and other counterpart Soviet weapons. INF missiles were traded against INF missiles, not against tanks or troops. So also here, an agreed ceiling on "smart" weapons—assuming one can be negotiated and enforced—would preserve East-West stability while maintaining an impetus in favor of defensive defense. This again is an argument in favor of a reflective NATO pause.

PART FOUR

The View Ahead

17

Reciprocal Security

There are no sure things about the future of Soviet internal reform, or of Soviet external reorientation. Both are pre-eminently political matters dependent for their outcome on the progress of events over which even so highly talented a politician as Mikhail Gorbachev has only limited control. The problems of inter-ethnic hostility, of economic weakness, of Party incompetence, can be overcome only by a combination of luck and patience and persistence for whose occurrence the long-suffering Soviet people may not in the end be willing to sit still. It seems plausible that Gorbachev, who has done much, and his followers, who have witnessed much, should be able to find the compelling chord that can keep their countrymen together for the times of uphill struggle that remain ahead. But this cannot be assured. The quick-answer people, the Boris Yeltsins of the left and the *Pamyat* people on the right, will have an easier resonance to propose. After four months in Moscow in 1989, during which the first elections to the new People's Congress were held, the senior and respected American scholar Marshall Shulman returned with the judgment that the future of *perestroika* was uncertain.

For American policy makers with an eye on their own country's long-term interests, however, the essential thing is that this does not finally matter. The Gorbachev reform era, if it were to end now, would already have shown enough in the way of changed political dynamics to warrant a new approach to great-power relations, or more exactly a return to earlier approaches. The internal fortunes of *perestroika*, while absorbing, are not decisive for the external relationship of the two powers.

The Soviet Union must work out its own national character and identity by itself. We in the West may not like the result, and, even if we do, we cannot suppose that the rivalry will have ended. Whatever happens, the Soviets and the Americans will continue to act out the competition foretold for them 150 years ago by Alexis de Tocqueville. The difference, in future—and this is the lasting change—is that both must accede to the outside realities that neither can wish away: the devastating power of high-speed, remorselessly accurate, nuclear-weapons systems; the economic impossibility of sustaining an all-out arms race; and the prickly resistance of regional conflicts to superpower resolution. Both of today's great powers must find a way to moderate their competition.

They cannot do that, of course, if they insist on seeing their rivalry in all-or-nothing, ideological terms. So, both must learn to practice what we have called a Constructive Detachment from each other's perceived faults and annoying conduct. Both must draw a line between such annoyances and authentic threats, reserving their security responses for the latter. And they must limit themselves to a military force no greater than that required for this responsive purpose, forming their own judgments in respect to their own security needs and not in reflexive imitation of each other. This is what we have called Reciprocal Security.

To recall the diagram at the close of Part One, in simplified form it reads as follows:

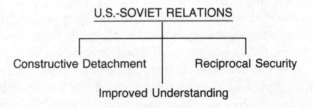

We begin our conclusions with Reciprocal Security.

*   *   *

There is a foundation point for the acceptance of Reciprocal Security in the Joint Statement adopted at the Washington Summit in December 1987. It said: "The sides shall discuss ways to ensure predictability in the development of the U.S.-Soviet strategic relationship under conditions of strategic stability. . . . They will not seek to achieve nuclear superiority." In a nuclear world, as this implies, no great power or power bloc can be more secure than its adversary. Each must exert itself to avoid, and where necessary to correct, destabilizing disparities of power.

But nuclear weapons, having no strictly military or battlefield usage, offer no advantage to either side once they exceed a certain number. The West does not need to match or counter every last weapons system the Soviets may possess. The doctrine of Mutual Assured Destruction, conventionally called "MAD," does not have to be mindless. An evolution toward something called "MIND"— Minimum Invulnerable Nuclear Deterrence—would work to improve security at reduced cost. It would guard against outward assault and inward insolvency.

President Eisenhower used to say that in military procurement "we need what we need" and not what the Russians happen to have. He also said that "the problem in defense is how far you can go without destroying from within that which you are trying to defend from without." This, by the way, was a classic expression of political conservatism as traditionally understood.

We may apply this logic to the Reagan administration's early preoccupation with a feared Soviet advantage in something called "hard-target kill capability"—the ability to destroy fixed, multi-warhead missile systems. This was the rationale offered for building both the MX missile and (in its later versions) SDI, or "Star Wars." But the huge Soviet land-based missiles that caused the concern can be disarmed both better and more cheaply, simply by taking down the U.S. fixed installations—the "hard targets." The U.S. would retain an overwhelming second-strike capability housed in far less vulnerable weapons systems on submarines, on aircraft, and in land-based mobile missiles. The big Soviet missiles, by this means, would have lost their mission. Score one, if you like, for the United States.

There is small but significant support in respected circles for a MIND approach to national defense. In his Palfrey Lecture at

Columbia University in 1984, former National Security Assistant McGeorge Bundy made the essential points:

> Once you have thermonuclear weapons and effective means of delivery, the situation achieved by both great nations in the 1950s, there remains only one requirement which makes continuing and serious demands upon the capabilities of your forces—the requirement of survivability.
>
> When any one element of our deterrent becomes even partially vulnerable to attack, it makes sense to redeploy that element in a more survivable mode.
>
> Survivability is important much more for deterrence than for war-fighting. What we need is a credible capacity for unpredictable and repeatable reply.

To similar effect is a report by Michael May, assistant director of the Lawrence Livermore Laboratory, prepared for the Reagan administration's Department of Energy and thereafter published in *International Security* (Spring 1985). Stable deterrence, May asserted, depends on survivability. The MX missile fares poorly by this criterion; so for that matter does the proposed, not-all-that-mobile, Midgetman. Survivability is a function of such factors as speed, hardness, and maneuvering room. The new and proposed U.S. deployments do not by May's estimates enhance deterrence, as more survivable systems would.

Space weapons like SDI are of course vulnerable in themselves, and they also threaten the survivability of vital military satellite systems, used by the United States for navigation, command and control, intelligence, and the verification of Soviet arms dispositions. Space weapons therefore degrade, rather than promote, deterrence.

U.S. and allied military strategists are coming to similar conclusions. Retired Lieutenant General Glenn Kent, then with the RAND Corporation, told the *Wall Street Journal* in October 1985 that the U.S. could get the benefits of SDI for much less money by adopting what he called "unilateral survival measures" such as shifting to genuinely mobile missiles. Complicating the "aim points" for the Soviet Union in this way would, he said, "have much the same effect as strategic defense, except it's cheaper." This course would also have the real political advantage, according to British strategist Michael Howard (in the same issue of the *Jour-*

nal), of staying within the framework of deterrence on which the NATO security posture is premised.

The mindless quality of tit-for-tat weapons responses is what has led Western governments in the past to overlook or downplay the critical factor of systems vulnerability. The largest share (more than half) of Soviet long-range nuclear armaments has been in highly vulnerable, fixed-missile systems. America's nuclear forces are predominantly (more than two-thirds) in relatively invulnerable, airborne and submarine systems. That gives the Soviets an edge in vulnerability, nothing else—and it can make no sense to engage in a race to become equally vulnerable.

Sensible, MIND-based policy would move in the other direction, uncoupled from Soviet weapons dispositions. A MIND set of U.S. deployments—shelving SDI, drawing down the MX, replacing Minuteman fixed missiles with truly mobile surface weapons, going forward with air- and submarine-launched cruise missiles—would make the United States more secure, and also more solvent, whether or not it was matched by the Soviet Union. (Soviet deployments have in fact been moving in this direction, but it is not essential that they should.)

Such a development would also help open up a further course of achievement: deep quantitative reduction of nuclear warhead inventories. Again, this would be a matter not of unilateral disarmament but of independent *arm*ament—the determination and fulfillment by the United States of its own security requirements. To show the magnitude of what might be at stake, a MIND approach could allow the United States to move by considered stages from its present level of 26,000 nuclear warheads to something like 400 (Robert S. McNamara) or 1,000 (Richard Garwin of IBM), without regard to what the Soviets would do. There are obvious (and surmountable) objections to doing so, but before examining them we should take account of the advantages this could bring:

1. "Nuclear winter"—the incineration of the atmosphere— would more likely be avoidable at a 1,000-warhead (or lower) exchange than at higher levels.
2. Reduction of nuclear warhead inventories to a level of minimum invulnerable deterrence would deprive idle hands of the surplus weaponry with which to concoct first-strike and

counterforce scenarios—thereby provoking SDI-type responses, and so on.

3. Lower levels of inventory would be likely to force real, not
   just rhetorical, attention to repairing the documented deficiencies in command and control that presently degrade
   the survivability of U.S. nuclear weapons.

4. Some cost savings would be realizable at once from the
   curtailment of present weapons programs, and more from
   the foregoing of future systems.

5. If the Soviets responded, and the cutbacks to minimum
   levels on both sides were suitably verified, the contribution
   to establishment of a guarded mutual trust would be addi-
   tionally beneficial to security.

This last point deserves further consideration, to see whether
it is (as suggested) a bonus or (as others might contend) a precondition. At a senior-level consultation on international security held
at Emory University in the Spring of 1985, under the joint chairmanship of former Presidents Ford and Carter, a consensus of the
participants favored the 1,000-warhead level proposed by Richard
Garwin, but only if it was *mutual* and *stabilizing;* General Brent
Scowcroft warned that the adoption of this weapons level, without
more, "would place an unbearable strain on verification and compliance." With respect, there is reason to believe that further reflection may turn up a different answer to these reservations.

First we must ask, what is deterrence? It has been described,
persuasively, as "dissuasion of a potential adversary from initiat-
ing an attack or conflict, often by the threat of unacceptable
retaliatory damage." What then is "unacceptable"? We have the
experience of the Berlin crisis (in 1959) and the Cuban missile
crisis (in 1962), when the Soviets had very few deliverable nuclear
warheads, and certainly far fewer than we, to show that even a low
level of nuclear weapons can threaten unacceptable damage to the
country that is looking at them. The U.S. was dissuaded on those
occasions, as the Soviets would be in future, by a lower-than-
Garwin or -McNamara level of deliverable nuclear warheads.

A MIND inventory of 1,000 warheads could actually be more
dissuasive than a non-MIND inventory very much larger. MX and
Minuteman and SDI all have the unfortunate characteristic of
inviting attack, whereas invulnerable weapons systems baffle it.

That is a pivotal difference, and it works in the direction of improved security.

What this suggests is that "unilateral survival measures" (General Kent's phrase) on the part of the United States, moving to a less vulnerable nuclear-deterrent posture at lower but still sufficient warhead levels, should prove stabilizing and security-strengthening no matter what the Soviets chose to do. MIND is stabilizing; it is mindlessness that has been destabilizing.

In practice, for appearances' sake, we and the Soviets would probably choose to proceed in tandem once a new policy direction had been set. This is what happened in the period 1958–63, preceding the Limited Test Ban Treaty. Progress could again be made by way of challenge and response, deferring negotiation of a full-scale agreement. The procedural sequence is important. The attempt to resolve by negotiation all issues of symmetry and balance, as between basically asymmetrical force structures, is what doomed the SALT process (including its initial START component) to ineffectuality. During the 15-year SALT negotiation period, while technology outpaced the draftsmen and the political climate for agreement dwindled, the level of nuclear warheads on both sides actually tripled. That is not arms limitation by any useful measure.

Room must be left, all the same, for *qualitative* prior agreements, of the kind that bar the door to new dimensions of the arms race. Examples include the ABM Treaty, now ready for a negotiated updating; a broadened Test Ban Treaty, taking advantage of new techniques in seismological verification; and a ban on deployment of Anti-Satellite weapons, which can also be made fully observable.

That leads us to verification, which remains a necessary element of any arms-reduction regime whether achieved by formal agreement or by challenge and response. The difficulty here is that invulnerability, a plus for security generally, will often take the form of elusiveness, a minus for verification. Ship-Launched Nuclear Cruise Missiles (SLCMs), for example—which look to an observer like conventional weapons—tend to defy inspection by established means. The same is true of mobile land-based missiles. There is concern, accordingly, that the mutually agreed upon counting rules and procedures developed during the period of the SALT negotiations may soon become obsolete.

This is a problem, it bears stressing, that exists independently of any shift in arms-control doctrine. Ways must be found in any case to substitute for satellite or on-site observation when these will not do the job. Technology can make up part of the deficiency but probably not all of it. Here again the MIND approach may make a difference. If we are satisfied that the right mix of, say, 1,000 warheads will protect American security no matter what, then verification is no longer the grimly vital matter for either side that we have previously considered it to be. We can always be sure of verifying, fully, the number and location of the most destabilizing weapons, because these are by definition the ones that are fixed and vulnerable. We can also be sure of verifying the observance of qualitative constraints (ABM, A-Sat, Test Ban), because these will be written at the level of observability. What are left, then, for some play in the verification joints, are only the stabilizing weapons systems; and on balance the trade-off of stability for verification seems positive for both American and global security.

All this must be made the subject of detailed prior consultation with our allies, of course, particularly in NATO. They still rely, doctrinally, on U.S. nuclear weapons to deter a land attack by the Soviet conventional forces facing NATO's borders. In practice there may be other factors deterring a Soviet land attack, just as there may be doubts about the credibility of a U.S. nuclear response; but the U.S. cannot restructure NATO nuclear doctrine unilaterally. Here again, a MIND approach could make a persuasive contribution, by focusing clearer attention on what actually deters and by inducing qualitative improvements in deterrent capability.

As of 1990, the NATO doctrine of "flexible response" is a quarter of a century old. Its origins, functions, and future viability are all ripe for reconsideration, given the general perception today that there is no such thing as a containable nuclear response to any level of attack. The protocol for nuclear weapons use needs to be re-examined with this in mind.

What must not be re-examined, at any time in the near future, is NATO's possession of some form of effective theater nuclear deterrent. Mr. Gorbachev's suggestion that all European-based nuclear weapons might one day be eliminated is an appeal whose blandishments, for now, should be resisted. One day the prophet Isaiah may be vindicated and all military weapons may be converted into plowshares. Until that happens, or draws appreciably closer to happening, NATO Europe will need a nuclear deterrent.

This is not just a matter of offsetting the Soviet Union's nuclear superiority, or even of counterbalancing the conventional force advantage the Soviets hold in the region. Both of these might be eliminated, as one hopes they will be, without removing the perceived need for a NATO nuclear deterrent.

As the Europeans see things, no nuclear-weapons drawdown can be countenanced that would make that continent "safe" again for the ravages of conventional war. This precept unites leadership opinion throughout Western Europe, even if popular manifestations sometimes obscure the view of that unity from across the ocean. The reality European leaders remember is that Adolf Hitler sent his forces into the Rhineland in 1938 when they were numerically far smaller than those of France, and he drove his tanks across the low countries in 1940 when those tanks were outnumbered four to three by the tank armies of France and Britain. Conventional deterrence alone, against this history, will not suffice; and Americans who wish to avoid being drawn into a third world war must accept and support this judgment.

Mikhail Gorbachev has conceded that the West Europeans, and therefore NATO, are free to pursue a policy of nuclear minimum deterrence. Speaking to the Council of Europe in Strasbourg in July of 1989, Gorbachev nevertheless proposed that the nuclear-weapons countries of NATO and the Warsaw Pact, along with those "on whose territories nuclear weapons are stationed" (that is, Germany), should meet to negotiate the upper boundaries of minimum deterrence. This invitation was disregarded, as it should have been. MIND and its attributes are a matter in the first instance for Western determination, free from divisive external intrusion.

On the conventional front, also, NATO has matters to settle apart from the negotiating table. West German General Wolfgang Altenburg, chairman of NATO's Military Committee, told a meeting of NATO defense ministers in late 1987 that the allies need to improve their weapons compatibility, battlefield communications, and identification systems. War games had shown that up to half of NATO aircraft might be shot down in combat by NATO troops unable to identify them. Essential military supplies need also to be assured for basic Western forces, cutting back selectively on the more exotic weaponry if need be to fund that availability. In the coming era of budget stringency and negotiated force reductions, attention to these points of qualitative readiness assumes a heightened importance.

As NATO reviews the quality of its forces, on the other hand, it must not slight the margin of superiority it has long enjoyed in troop training, morale, and weapons technology. Much of the Soviet weaponry is aging, and many of the troops on that side still have their missions in Eastern rather than Western Europe. This must be kept in mind, as it has not always been, in assessing an acceptable East-West balance.

There is a political agenda for Reciprocal Security as well. It is to avoid raising unnecessary fears or uncertainties about movements or intentions in areas of high security interest, whether in Central Europe where East-West forces are now arrayed against each other or in Third World "trouble spots" where they might be drawn into contention. This is the intricate, but manageable, task of future security politics.

To begin with, American politicians must give up the luxury of complaining about the "undue burden" of America's contribution to European security. U.S. troops and equipment stationed in or committed to Europe are there for the common defense, not just the defense of that continent. U.S. defenses begin at the NATO frontier, in concert with its allies, rather than alone on the East Coast of the United States. The reason for that is to keep this country from being dragged into another European war, as has happened twice in this century when the American East Coast was our perimeter. U.S. forces in Europe represent a sober, self-interested, security investment.

According to figures compiled by the independent Defense Budget Project, U.S. defense expenditures in the 1980's ran about 6.5 percent of national output, whereas for the larger NATO allies (France, West Germany, the U.K., and Italy) the comparable figure was 3.7 percent. The U.S. total, however, included the entire defense budget, not just the portion committed to Europe. If NATO-only figures are used, the U.S. expenditure came to roughly 3.9 percent, comparable to the contribution of its larger allies. There was no significant disparity.

The European allies could perhaps be asked to take on a share of America's global burden. But the North Atlantic Treaty, at U.S. insistence, very carefully limited NATO's defense role to its own territory; and one of the conspicuous achievements of the postwar era has been to move the European colonial powers out of the regions for which they used to assume security responsibility. Americans should not wish to repeal this historical evolution, to which their own efforts so substantially contributed.

With the lessening of East-West tensions, there will be temptations to lower U.S. defense spending unilaterally. For some kinds of costly armaments, particularly those that provoke rather than deter Soviet offensive preparations, this can make good sense. For basic forces in Europe, however, it does not make sense. Reductions in these forces must be achieved in concert with the Soviets and with allied forces of both East and West. Otherwise, on the NATO side, the armies of Germany could emerge as the largest in Europe—a perverse and politically unacceptable outcome to the war of German aggression that began some 50 years before.

The decade of the 1990's will be a period of delicate adjustment in the forces and antagonisms of the previous decades. To secure needed confidence, there will have to be some superintendence of the drawdown by the Soviet Union and the United States. Their troop removals must come last for this to happen, not first.

Politically, at home, this will require the formulation of a new mission statement to cover the ongoing role of American forces in Europe. At its simplest, that role must be to stabilize the process of regional reductions and realignments now underway. While the Soviets have renounced the capability to launch a rapid offensive thrust into Western Europe, the likelihood of that kind of assault was never very high; nor was its prospect ever the sole or even controling reason for a U.S. military presence in Europe. American troops have served throughout as a visible assurance, to allies and adversaries alike, of the U.S. commitment to a stable regional settlement—which is not yet in sight. It would be a plain contravention of the American sacrifices made in World War II, and of the peacekeeping burdens borne since then, for the U.S. now to walk away from Europe while the disruptive potential of that continent remains uncomposed. A continuing U.S. force presence in the region, at reduced but still significant levels, is what will assure this country a place in the councils where the instruments of settlement are forged.

That forging, to begin with, must proceed from a political interaction between Eastern and Western alliances. The aim of these two security groupings should include, as a priority, the bargaining down of the level of German forces in both East and West so as to achieve an acceptable balance with diminishing U.S. and Soviet forces. The two alliances should also concern themselves, politically, with the process of economic integration, recognizing that neither Comecon nor the European Community now offers an acceptable home for this enterprise; modulation of the discourse on this subject, by the two security alliances, should prove helpful.

Beyond that, it is not clear how far, institutionally, to go. Some believe that the 35-nation CSCE (Conference on Security and Cooperation in Europe) could take on the function of developing a general European settlement. The CSCE does have a wide jurisdiction, along with a record of accomplishment in arms reduction and confidence-building. It can serve as a good meeting ground for both formal and informal explorations. As a forum for germinating new settlement proposals, however, it suffers from the limitations of its consensus principle, which could allow the Soviet Union or, say, a neutral nation like Malta to block a Western initiative before it is formed. For the near future, at least, it seems wiser to look to the two security alliances or to the four wartime Allies for development of settlement ideas, which can then be brought to the CSCE if desired.

The main diplomatic challenge for the Western countries, during this period, will be to encourage the further evolution of Eastern Europe without undoing the stability procured by the preceding balance of East-West alignments. If the movements toward autonomy begun in Eastern Europe are to succeed, it is essential that the Soviet leadership should feel unthreatened by them. In this, the role of Germany will again be pivotal.

The Soviet concern, as some see it, is that the "Great Patriotic War" that cost them 20 million lives could turn out merely to have delayed, and not prevented, the final achievement of German hegemony in Central Europe. West Germany is already the largest Western trade partner, investor, and creditor to both Hungary and Poland, and to all other Eastern bloc countries apart from Czechoslovakia. East European leaders are concerned that these trends, if not offset by an active policy of engagement on the part of the United States, could lead to the substitution of Germany for Russia as the prevailing regional power. "It would be much better," says Polish political scientist Wojciech Lamentowitz, "if we could develop strong bilateral relationships between East European countries and the United States and the European Community as a whole, with Britain and France playing a strong role."

The U.S. has had difficulty, however, finding funds in its treasury to commit for this purpose, as President Bush made plain in his state visits to Hungary and Poland in 1989. The Economic Summit at Paris in July of that year assigned a clearinghouse role to the European Community for aid to these countries, but this too was slow to turn up new commitments. George F. Kennan, expressing his view of the subject in the spring of 1989, urged that it should "fall to the Community, rather than any of its individual members, to assume the main responsibility for designing the response to East European demands for a closer relationship with Western Europe." This was not quick to happen, however and in September 1989 Lech Walesa, the chairman of Poland's Solidarity party, felt obliged to appeal to West Germany for assistance.

The West Germans themselves were focusing their attention in this period increasingly on East Germany. Separated since 1945 by Allied occupation forces and then by the Cold War, the two Germanies had grown apart both economically and politically, each at the heart of a major contending alliance. Their peaceful unification had long been a proclaimed goal of the West, ostensibly frustrated by Soviet intransigence. The official Soviet position was that the West was to blame for the division, and that the Berlin Wall was an initiative of East Germany's. Now as the 1990's dawned the Wall was open, East Germans were streaming by the thousands into the West, and the grip of the Communist Party on East Berlin was visibly giving way.

The question this precipitated—perhaps the pivotal issue for East-West security—was that of German reunification. This was not quite the simple proposition many pundits and politicians seemed to think it. Even after the anticipated relegation of the GDR communist party to minority status, there would still be two separate political personalities within greater Germany—one with 40 years of democratic experience and one without, one with a classless ideal and one without. No doubt the coming years would witness an intensifying integration of the two economies; but the same had been true for decades of the U.S.-Canadian relationship, without producing political integration.

How far and how easily German unity might proceed would depend to a fair degree on external memories and apprehensions. A union of the two Germanies would produce a new nation with a population of some 78 million people, well beyond that of either Britain or France. Its Gross National Product would at once rival that of the two countries combined. The new nation would also have the strongest military force in Europe, and would contain the NATO/Warsaw short-range missiles theretofore pointed at parts of itself.

Those missiles might be removed, and a neutralized Germany perhaps withdrawn from the two alliances; but this would do little more by itself than recreate the external trappings of the Third Reich. All of the postwar measures designed to prevent this from happening would need to be re-examined and dealt with. As George F. Kennan described the problem, it was

> . . . tremendous in scope and difficulty. It involves the relation-ship of Eastern Europe, economically and politically, to the European Community. It involves the future of both NATO and the Warsaw Pact. It involves the military arrangements now pertaining in the center of the European continent. It involves the various negotiations now in progress over the conventional arms balance in Europe. . . .
>
> These problems are all of a part. None of them can be solved, or usefully treated, independently of the remainder of them.

Nor can either of the two Germanies consider itself free simply to throw out the conventional and nuclear forces positioned there by their respective allies:

> These forces are there not by the will of the German authorities alone but by elaborate and long-standing agreements with other powers, and particularly with other groups of powers organized in the two alliances. The Germans could not unilaterally . . . disregard, nor would they want to disregard, the contractual framework by which the presence of these forces is supported.

That framework was given its due emphasis in President Bush's statement to NATO on the subject, delivered on December 4, 1989—the day after his meeting at Malta with Chairman Gorbachev. Drafted with obvious care, the statement read in essential part as follows:

> One, self-determination must be pursued without prejudice to its outcome. . . .
>
> Two, unification should occur . . . with due regard to the legal role and responsibility of the Allied powers.
>
> Three, in the interests of general European stability, moves toward unification must be peaceful, gradual, and part of a step-by-step process.
>
> Four, on the question of borders, we should reiterate our support for the principles of the Helsinki Final Act.

Helsinki of course is a porous document: It is not a binding treaty, and its applicability to the inner-German border is open to debate. The pace and harmony of German integration is also difficult to regulate from the outside. If the German populations should genuinely insist on immediate reunion—a matter left undecided by the statement—then the only real barrier would be the "legal role and responsibility of the Allied powers."

That is not an inconsiderable factor. While none of the World War II allies would presumably wish to interpose its arms against a considered exercise of German sovereignty, the fact is that no peace treaty has ever been concluded with Germany, and that accordingly all of the sacrifices borne by the combatant powers on both sides in World War II and since have yet to be rewarded with a firm or durable outcome. The 600,000 or more outside troops now stationed in East and West Germany, and the web of postwar arrangements governing their status, are a potent symbol of the unfinished business in which all interested parties must take a hand.

Those outside forces may and probably will be drawn down by East-West consensus in the coming years, but they are unlikely to be withdrawn altogether until a generally acceptable final settlement is reached. The Soviets have given no signs of leaving before then. France and Britain have announced that their forces will remain for as long as needed. A European Community statement, issued in December 1989 and subscribed to by the West Germans as well as the French and British, set out acceptable conditions for unification and therefore for ultimate force withdrawal:

> This process should take place peacefully and democratically, in full respect of the relevant agreements and treaties and of all the principles defined by the Helsinki Final Act, in a context of dialogue and East-West cooperation. It has also to be placed in the perspective of European integration.

This closing idea, of a Germany whose unity would be subsumed within—and rendered innocuous by—a Europe-wide integration, is one that holds substantial appeal. Its realization, however, is something that will be slow and uncertain in coming. The countries of Eastern Europe that have shaken off Stalinism have not necessarily taken up Western democracy. Transitional East-West arrangements, looking toward a new economic and political and military dispensation, will be intricate and perhaps elusive. For the former Allied powers who will have to oversee this process, and for the others involved, it will be important not to suppose (1) that there is a clear and present avenue leading to harmonious European integration; or (2) that the U.S. or those other nations can devise it. The role of the Allied powers must be to let solutions emerge and not to force them—which means that they must stay around until the horizon clears.

Yet it is necessary to have a long-range goal, and to articulate it. Bush and Gorbachev each expressed a part of the necessary aim in 1989—Gorbachev calling for a "common European home," to the possible discomfiture of non-Continental powers like the United States; and Bush describing a "Europe whole and free," with an implied exclusion of non-democratic countries like the Soviet Union. A combining vision would be one that pointed toward a "Europe open, peaceable, and just, both in itself and with its outside partners." A formulation like that would establish a goal to which all interested parties, including the two Germanies, could feel comfortable addressing themselves.

In accepting such aims, America and its allies would not by any means be opting for the interests of the Soviet Union over those of the Federal Republic of Germany. The fact is that any sharp destabilization of alignments, such as might arise from a premature effort to settle European divisions, could set a chain reaction in process whose end results would not be positive for anyone's interests. Security here as elsewhere must be reciprocal to endure.

The Western alliance needs to agree more generally within itself on the essentials of a Reciprocal Security policy. Not all of the particulars need to be concerted. There can be strength in the diversity that characterizes the Western democracies. If one member's idea misses, another's may usually be tried. Recognizing and allowing for this fact should make it easier to summon unity of policy among NATO members on truly essential matters.

America's special role within the alliance should be to make use of its established, bilateral, political and military channels to consult with the Soviet Union about non-threatening modes of European rapprochement. Such talks can be structured—so as to avoid any appearance of superpower condominium—by making regular reports back to the alliance and by encouraging East-West European discussions on parallel themes. Acceptable change, with responsibility, should result.

In the Third World, too, as the Soviets have recognized, undisciplined behavior by either East or West can damage Reciprocal Security. It can breed miscalculation of the outside parties' intentions and, at worst, can catapult them into hostilities against each other. It can also serve as an obstacle to progress toward a more general stability between East and West. For these reasons a sober restraint, coupled with continuing "trouble spot" consultations, is advisable.

The problems and potential of the Third World invite attention on their own merits, of course, quite separate and apart from East-West rivalries. The burdens of debt-service payment, for example, or of the narcotics trade, press on the poorer countries without regard to U.S.-Soviet relations. Likewise, the age-old antagonisms of the Middle East flare up and recede without connection to West or East, none of whose countries even existed at the time those antagonisms were first bred. The major powers cannot resolve such problems easily, perhaps, or very far; but they can at least stop injecting extraneous complications.

For decades now, unfortunately, America has pursued perverse and often unattainable goals in its development assistance programs. It has sought to build clients or allies rather than nations. America's basic interests in a stable and harmonious world order would be better served by a process of economic and social development, steadily pursued, without regard to such temporary returns as votes in the UN or the allowance of base rights or other indicia of a client or alliance status. What is needed today is a fundamental rethinking of American development assistance, in the national interest and not as a short-term quid pro quo or handout.

Development is security, as Robert S. McNamara put it in a remarkable speech in Montreal in 1966 when he was Secretary of Defense:

> The security of the United States is directly related to the security and the stability of the other nations of the world, particularly those in the southern half.
>
> In a modernizing society, security means just one thing—development. Security is not military hardware—though it may include it. Security is not military force—though it may involve it. Security is not traditional military activity—though it may encompass it.
>
> For these nations, security is just one thing—development. Without development there can be no security. The trouble is that we have been lost in a semantic jungle for too long. We have come to identify "security" with military strength, with exclusively military phenomena; as military hardware. . . .
>
> But is just isn't so. And we need to accommodate to the facts of the matter, if we want to see security survive and expand in the southern half of the globe.
>
> Development means economic, social, and political progress. . . . Assistance in the purely military sphere is not enough. Economic aid is far more important.

This excellent advice, regrettably, has never yet been taken. American aid patterns have instead become deeply skewed toward security assistance and the payment for U.S. base rights. Just two countries, Israel and Egypt, now absorb $5 billion each year in aid monies, or one-third of the 1987 total. Another $2 billion goes for base rights, to countries like Spain and Turkey, which are part of the First World and not the Third. As budgetary constraints have clamped down on assistance funding, these and a handful of other politically "earmarked" payments have been spared the reductions. The effect has been to impose severe curbs on genuine economic development assistance, which is where the affirmative emphasis should be placed.

Paradoxically, perhaps, the economic squeeze on American resources may now force a review of what the national interest demands. The House Foreign Affairs Committee has already found the U.S. assistance program to be in serious disarray, with a welter of conflicting objectives and priorities and no comprehensive review of its mission for the past 20 years. A task force headed by Representatives Lee Hamilton and Benjamin Gilman has recommended a repeal of the basic statute and its replacement by a new law with freshly considered objectives.

The U.S. today lacks the funds to play a solo or commanding role in Western aid-giving, as it may once have done. Japan has emerged as the "new America" for this purpose, with large budgets and tied loans and the other familiar accoutrements of interested assistance. America ought now to share its experience and to pool its resources with such programs, and with the multilateral enterprises of the UN system, in the long-term interest of global stability and peaceful growth.

18

Constructive Detachment

Fashions die slowly. For decades now it has been intellectually easy, and attractive, to paint the struggle between East and West as a contest of ideologies. Zbigniew Brzezinski, the former U.S. national security advisor, addressed a late-1980's book to what he called "the grand failure . . . of communism," in China and the Soviet Union. But communism as such has never truly been tried in either of those countries, or elsewhere, on any scale, so it is hard to think of it as having any "grand" distance to fall. The condemnations voiced in the spring of 1989 at the opening sessions of the new Soviet Party Congress substantially exceeded in vituperation most of what is contained in Brzezinski's pages.

What is at issue today in Moscow and Beijing is less the persistence of "communism" than it is the staying power of absolutism, as bequeathed by the ages to both Russia and China. Russia at least has been making a determined effort to break loose from its feudal moorings. It has been drawn to this goal less by the attractions of Western ideology than by the needs of it own modernization.

Russia, as history shows, was never a good candidate for the application of Marxist theory. It had no developed capitalist system, which Marx posited as the precondition for socialism, and it had no "enlightened proletariat" equipped to take its place in the revolutionary system. What it had instead was mainly a vacuum, created by the decay and decline of the Tsarist regime. When that regime fell, leaving behind it no disciplined ruling alternative, the cohorts assembled under Lenin's inspired direction were able, quite simply, to take charge.

Stalinism, as Brzezinski notes, grew out of this beginning. Its ruthless despotism served to consolidate the possession of illegitimate power. But Stalinism also laid down a challenge, as the historian Arnold Toynbee might have put it, upon the Soviet people and culture to come up with a better alternative. The response was slow in coming; but first the partial reforms under Khrushchev, and then the systemic reforms under Gorbachev, have been elements of that alternative.

It is customary to speak of these reforms as issuing from a removable, impermanent top. In a sense this is accurate. But the "top" has been driven toward reform by the needs and demands of the "bottom." Soviet society has been evolving for decades out of its subservient origins. The complexities of modern life are today obliging the new, more urban, and better-educated Soviet populace to become increasingly more self-directed and autonomous. The process of social change is by no means complete, but it is authentic and by most signs enduring.

Brzezinski along with others has been tempted to see this as a vindication of Western values: "Democracy, not Communism," he writes, "will dominate the 21st century." Perhaps so; it is an appealing possibility. Certainly the attraction of old-style Soviet autocracy has faded around the world. But the news photographs from Beijing in the spring of 1989, showing Chinese students reading their Gorbachev next to the Tiananmen goddess of freedom, should give one pause before pronouncing on the inevitability of future ideological models.

There are more people by far to be found today in reform-prone socialist societies than there are in societies on the brink of constitutional democracy. To the great majority, for now, the reformer Gorbachev may have the most to say. The underlying strength of the Western democracies can be seen in the fact that it is to them that Gorbachev himself turns for practical confirmation. Connecting constructively with him for this purpose—and with Lech Walesa, and with other reform mediators yet to emerge from the windings of transitional "communism"—may be the most valuable contribution the West can now make to an orderly social progress.

What this means in agenda terms is that the West must de-link ideology from its security relationship with the East. Differences in political governance, economic opportunity, and social freedom exist and will continue. Their diminution, along the lines we are now witnessing, is an outgrowth of long-run historical forces over which neither side can exert much direction. What the two sides can do, and what they owe to history, is to take the small steps that together can improve their mutual understanding and relations. We know enough by now to say what these should be.

Diplomatically, to begin with, the United States and the Soviet Union should extend their military-to-military and trouble-spot consultations. These should continue to be, not negotiations but information exchanges—about forces, movements, plans, and behavior. Quietly and without great expectations, Latin America and Eastern Europe should be added to the subjects of discussion.

At the other end of the scale are Presidential summit meetings—ponderous and overly publicized affairs, which as Reykjavik showed are ill-suited to the settlement of complex international problems. Summits do have their uses, primarily to start or to ratify a diplomatic process carried out by others. When they take place infrequently, in this age of insistent publicity, they generate popular expectations out of all proportion to what they can deliver. Perhaps the best solution is to hold regularly scheduled, annual meetings between the U.S. and Soviet leaders—precisely in order to take the pressure off the meetings. The Economic Summit among Western leaders is an annual affair, no matter what the state of the agenda; the same could be done with superpower summits, setting no goal for them beyond a regular review of outstanding matters. Such meetings could be held in a neutral capital, reserving visits to each other's countries for more special occasions. The burden of carrying out negotiations on particular subjects would then fall to foreign ministers, who would also prepare the annual summit.

Diplomatic activity by the U.S. Secretary of State, his assistants, and other cabinet officers, should become the regular and unremarkable conduit through which most business with the Soviets is done. Congressional delegations and hostings, in Moscow and Washington, should be as frequent as useful. Both executive and legislative participants would do well to educate themselves on a systematic and continuing basis, through resort to inside and outside expertise—laying particular stress on consultation with qualified independent specialists on the Soviet Union whose views owe nothing to the government of the moment.

These specialists should include American business leaders— traders and investors whose dealings engage officials on both sides. There is, by virtue of governmental licensing, an inevitable overlap between U.S.-Soviet business and politics. As a result, American businessmen often know or understand Soviet political developments before they come to Washington's attention. It would be idle not to cultivate this resource.

Trade is a form of commercial and political conversation. It engages practical people in the pursuit of mutual benefit. Trade has undoubted value commercially, as a generator of foreign revenue; the U.S., as it happens, enjoys a tidy surplus in its current, small, trade account with the Soviet Union. But beyond that, trade and investment involve the carrying out of agreements in the joint interest of the contracting parties. Business experience has something to say, accordingly, about Soviet reliability and respect for agreements. So, as a factor of continuity and as a "reality" counterweight to the play of political fashions, business enterprises that want to deal with the Soviet Union should as a rule be allowed to do so.

How far ought this permission to carry? President Eisenhower used to say that we should sell anything to the Soviets they can't fire back. To return somewhere near to that common-sense standard, there are four simple steps to be taken.

The Jackson-Vanik amendment, to begin with, should be flatly repealed. There is no real point in issuing short-term waivers; they will not provide the planning framework needed for business decisions, or release the Soviet Union from what it considers the untenable premise of American social tutelage. Jewish emigration from the Soviet Union had already reached such proportions, by the summer of 1989, as to force the United States to close its doors to most of the flow—thereby disabling itself as a political matter from further attempts at control.

A normalized trade relation should also include the allowance of customary export credits. This is not a question of "subsidies" for the Soviet Union or for its program of *perestroika*. It is instead a return to the ordinary incidents of international commerce. The author of the Stevenson amendment, curtailing Export-Import Bank assistance for business transactions with the Soviet Union, today believes that facility should be restored.

Contracts once entered into with the Soviet Union should likewise be sheltered from domestic political cancellation. Present American law and practice make the United States an unreliable supplier, and undermine the commercial pillar that might otherwise help sustain normal relations. As Mikhail Gorbachev told the U.S.-USSR Trade and Economic Council in 1985: "Guarantees are needed that some political wind chill does not once again begin to erode business ties."

The fourth necessity is a slimming down, and tightening, of the overblown export control system operated by the U.S. and its Western allies. Soviet access to material or technology of direct military utility—to devices they can "fire back"—is a matter distinct from the conduct of general trade. Confusing the two, or using military controls to wage economic warfare, has made the allied system and its U.S. component leaky and ineffective. There is a need, as some describe it, for higher walls to defend a smaller territory. Reducing the export control list to otherwise unobtainable items of direct military utility would heal Western divisions and put our relations with the Soviet Union on a more sustainable footing.

Sustainable East-West relations would also be strengthened by de-politicizing educational and cultural exchanges. These have done much in the past 30 years to break down stereotypes and to promote greater realism about how life is lived on "the other side." Scholarly exchanges, while their volume is small, have managed over the years to survive both Soviet bureaucracy and American impatience; the quality of the resulting scholarship has been high. Undergraduate exchanges have gained a recent boost from the Reagan-Gorbachev summits: In the fall of 1988, the Soviets began allowing their students to spend a full unchaperoned year at American colleges, with American roommates.

Both countries stand to benefit from such exchanges, without regard to exact reciprocity. American audiences exposed to the Kirov ballet, or American poets introduced to Ukrainian audiences, carry away an impression of the other culture that has value even in the absence of counterpart bookings. Of course it would be best to remove all barriers, as expanded exchanges over time can be expected to do. But President Reagan's USIA director, Charles Z. Wick, seemed clearly in error when he threatened to cut off exchanges unless a mathematical balance was maintained.

The more serious problems with two-way exchanges have been their uncertain funding and political vulnerability. A review by the Kennan Institute for Advanced Russian Studies, in 1985, found that inadequate funding and political interruptions were most often cited by participants as defects of the exchange program. In the aftermath of the Geneva summit, later that year, U.S. Soviet exchanges were expanded. But no one could say with assurance when they might again be cut, or what the next cause of dissatisfaction would be. The history has been one of curtailments—after the Afghanistan invasion, after the KAL downing— so that precisely when Soviet behavior has seemed most perplexing we have cut back our capacity to understand it.

One thing that has come along to compensate for this vulnerability is a steady movement of exchange agreements away from governmental and toward private or unofficial sponsorship. Today, private-sector exchanges predominate at least on the U.S. side. But the Soviets still think that an intergovernmental agreement is necessary; they use it internally, they told an Eisenhower Institute conference in 1988, to make plans and to secure funding. To accommodate that view, and still move exchanges away from politics, there is a legislative initiative (H.R. 3500, in 1983), introduced by U.S. Representative Lee Hamilton and Senator Richard Lugar, that would create an endowment of perhaps $80 million, the annual income from which would be distributed through private hands to pay for the governmental share of U.S.-Soviet educational and cultural exchanges. Such an arrangement would allow exchanges to go forward in good times and in bad, effectively insulating them from the vagaries of the moment.

The purpose of such arrangements, overall, is not of course to remove the differences between the two societies but to improve our understanding of them. History can judge which is the better system. This cautionary point needs particularly to be kept in mind when looking at the related field of cooperative endeavors.

Projects of cooperation aimed at breaking down myths and

stereotypes are almost certain to be useful. The joint symposia now being sponsored on the U.S. side by the American Council of Learned Societies and the International Research and Exchanges Board give promise of correcting the adversary reading of history that has tended to dominate texts and pronouncements on both sides.

Joint economic and technical projects are, however, a different matter. These were a hallmark of the détente policies of the Nixon period. From 1972 to 1974, when that administration was in deepening difficulty from the Watergate revelations, it signed eleven agreements for cooperation with the Brezhnev regime in the Soviet Union. Most of these fell by the wayside in later years, as America's policy shifted from détente to confrontation; and since the agreements had been given a high degree of political visibility, their downfall accentuated the decline in the relationship.

Headlined cooperation on matters of substance between significant political rivals is inevitably affected by the ups and downs of the surrounding relationship. It was not therefore surprising when, following the Soviet invasion of Afghanistan in December 1979 and the later imposition of martial law in Poland, activities under most of the détente agreements were curtailed. Some were allowed to expire by their terms, while others were sharply pared. Overall, according to estimates by the Department of State, U.S. funding and man-hours devoted to the carrying out of these agreements declined after 1981 to approximately 20 percent of their previous level—a highly visible shift.

There were aspects of the détente agreements that made them particularly susceptible to this reversal. First, they were signed by the President or the Secretary of State or a senior cabinet officer in all cases, regardless of the subject matter (artificial heart research, in one instance). This made their execution seem more an act of political commitment than of technical cooperation— which, in the circumstances, may have been what Nixon wanted. Second, the agreements were entrusted for their execution to intergovernmental committees, which gave the Reagan administration a convenient lever by which to reduce the level of cooperation. Finally, five of the agreements contained automatic expiration clauses, meaning that, in these cases (among them Space, Science and Technology, and the Peaceful Uses of Atomic

Energy), a successor administration could cut off cooperation by the simple device of doing nothing.

Toward the end of the first Reagan term the climate for cooperative activities began to shift again. In January 1988 a new five-year agreement on scientific cooperation was signed, this one between the two Academies of Science. Other non-official or private entities then entered the cooperation field, including (on the U.S. side) such enterprises as the Overseas Development Council and the Natural Resources Defense Council. In 1987, the Soviet Council of Ministers chartered the first non-governmental, non-profit charitable foundation in that nation's history, giving the new International Foundation for the Survival and Development of Humanity authority to cooperate with foreign counterparts on projects involving the environment, energy, human rights, education, culture, government, and international security.

What now should be done with these opportunities is open to reflection. In the Bush administration, starting in 1989, the Department of State put new emphasis on a so-called "fifth basket" of cooperative enterprises it hoped to pursue with the Soviet Union. These included, to begin with, environmental protection, counterterrorism, and measures to combat the narcotics trade. A working group was established to examine these issues and to propose the addition of other topics from time to time as circumstances warrant.

What might such topics include? Gorbachev proposed to the Western Economic Summit in July of 1989 that there be Soviet participation in global economic development. This came at a time when the Western leaders were considering assistance to Poland and Hungary, and for that purpose Gorbachev's offer was much more positive than Stalin's response (outright rejection) had been to the Marshall Plan. In other regions of the world, however, the Gorbachev initiative has to be read against a history of essentially zero Soviet assistance since World War II for nation-building among the uncommitted nations.

Today of course the fiscal constraints on both Soviet and American development budgets rule out any large program of cooperative assistance. The Soviets also suffer from other limitations, such as an inconvertible currency and inappropriate technology. Even if all such barriers were to be lifted, it is at least not clear that the two major rivals for influence in the Third World are in the best position to design development programs keyed to objective local need. Multinational organizations like the World Bank and the UN Development Program may be better suited to that purpose.

Environmental protection is another field, this one already entered into the "fifth basket," where the need for global stewardship is great but the capacity of the two superpowers may not be. The Soviets, like the Americans, are substantial contributors to global warming, and the air and water of their cities and coastlines are in places severely degraded; they have taken steps both national and international to counter these trends. Soviet budgets and bureaucracies are, however, largely unequal to the clean-up responsibilities they have been given. The new State Committee for the Protection of Nature cannot, for example, issue cease-and-desist orders. The costs and incentives for environmental repair are, on the whole, overwhelmed by the priorities of economic renewal in the Soviet Union. It is unlikely—even leaving aside the comparable shortcomings of the United States—that the USSR can be more than a rhetorical partner in the environmental arena in the coming years.

Rhetorical cooperation is probably not a good idea. To contribute to global needs, and to sustain a posture of Constructive Detachment between the two great powers, agreements to cooperate on non-security matters should be limited to those that (1) make sense on the merits, and have a chance of succeeding, apart from any supposed political significance or symbolism; (2) are carried out wherever possible by competent private or unofficial groups; and (3) are insulated to the maximum feasible extent from the ups and downs of the political relationship. That way lies sense, and usefulness.

On the security side, America needs to change the way it conceives its objectives—beginning with the Truman Doctrine. As a general policy, standing up to the Russians made eminent good sense in 1950 and it still does, provided it is keyed to security concerns and not to mere disagreements. If there were ever a sign, for example, of a Soviet base for offensive military operations being established in Central America, the U.S. would clearly be moved to intercede as it did in the Cuban missile crisis of 1962. The same does not follow, however, from the existence of an ill-mannered Marxist regime in Nicaragua, which—by itself—was never a security threat to the United States. The absorbing distractions of Central America in the 1980's could all have been disposed of in quite short order with an acceptance of that distinction.

The problem is that the Truman Doctrine, as interpreted, has often been more concerned with ideology than with security. That was not plainly so at the beginning. One section of the founding document, NSC-68, sounding a theme associated with George F. Kennan, said that the purpose of U.S. military and related constraints on the Soviet Union should be to "deter an attack upon us while we seek by other means to create an environment in which our free society can flourish." Even if the Soviets did not change their aims, this passage asserted, coexistence on these terms "would be a triumph for Western values."

That strand or aspect of the policy has been successful, and ought in good measure to be continued. At an appropriately reduced level of arms, America still needs to deter aggression and still wants its free society to flourish. When that is understood as the objective, the importance of ideology can fade.

But there has been another strand to the Truman Doctrine, especially as applied in the 1950's and 1980's, and that is the strand of ideological confrontation. Certain passages in NSC-68, impossible to reconcile with straight deterrence, display this theme:

> The Soviet Union, unlike previous aspirants to hegemony, is animated by a new fanatic faith, antithetical to ours, and seeks to impose its absolute authority over the rest of the world. . . . *It is not an adequate objective merely to seek to check the Kremlin design, for the absence of order among nations is becoming less and less tolerable.* (Emphasis added.)

This italicized intolerance of diversity, this Manichean reduction of reality—to good versus evil, believers versus infidels—is the strand of the Truman Doctrine that came to prevail in the early Reagan era, and it helps to account for the excesses of that period. The lineage is easy enough to trace: From "fanatic faith" in the 1950's to "evil empire" in the 1980's is a straight oratorical shot.

All that was really needed for American security, then as now, is the straightforward doctrine of deterrence. Deterrence is a policy that draws on elements of both firmness and flexibility to bar the realization of Soviet geopolitical aims that threaten vital American interests. Deterrence in this basic sense, with its supportive armory of military and economic and political strengths, must once again be seen and pursued for what it is: an essentially conservative doctrine, one that obliterates no rival creeds, but that keeps the world and its divisions alive for future evolutions. We need once again to adopt that understanding.

Doing so will require the review and reformulation of a whole series of Presidential doctrines, decrees, dispositions, and authorizations that have followed the wrong strand. Among the candidates for this revision will be National Security Decision Memorandum 242, endorsing (in 1974) the concept of limited nuclear warfare; Presidential Directive 59, calling (in 1980) for the capability to wage protracted nuclear war; and National Security Decision Directive 172, offering (in 1985) a comprehensive rationale for SDI, or "Star Wars." A refocused sense of America's objectives should serve to thin out the more extravagant of these preoccupations.

Also ripe for reformulation is the process by which American security determinations are made. The allocation of authority between President and Congress is one unsettled question, which has not been satisfactorily resolved by the War Powers Act. Enacted over President Nixon's veto in 1973, that Act has never been effectively applied and is now accounted by most Congressional leaders to be a dead letter. The law holds that the President must report to Congress whenever U.S. troops are introduced "into hostilities or into situations where imminent involvement in hostilities is clearly indicated." Once the report is made, the President is given 60 to 90 days to withdraw the troops unless Congress affirmatively authorizes them to stay.

The procedure as adopted is both ineffective and unwise. The idea of having to cease hostilities after a set number of days, but of being free to initiate them without limitation, has placed both too large and too lax a constriction on the war-making power. Presidents have responded by refusing to report "hostilities" even when American forces (as in the Persian Gulf) are receiving and causing casualties. The obligation to make a report is unenforceable, both because the courts will not hear "political controversies" and because it has seemed fruitless to Congress to pass a new law enforcing one already on the books.

The answer is not to give up but to frame a different kind of War Powers Resolution, setting out common-sense substantive criteria for Presidential, Congressional, and shared decision-making. Procedural prescriptions as such could disappear. The aim would be to hold the President *politically* accountable for his actions, risking his office if necessary for the security of the nation as Abraham Lincoln did during the Civil War. A well-drafted bill along these lines was submitted in 1973 by Representative Robert Eckhardt of Texas, and gained substantial support from both conservatives and liberals. It ought now to be reintroduced.

There is a need also for process improvements within the Executive branch. U.S. policy toward the Soviet Union must from now on be characterized by firmness, flexibility, and also consistency. The Executive must speak with one voice. The role of the National Security Council staff should be returned by Presidential directive to one of coordination and support, leaving the choice and conduct and articulation of U.S. policy entirely to the Chief Executive and his NSC principals. Those named as responsible for U.S. policy must in fact exercise that responsibility. No one but the President himself, the Secretary of State, and duly authorized officers in the accountable departments, should act or speak on matters of foreign policy—vis-a-vis the Congress, the press, the public, or foreign governments. This limitation is so important, and its disregard so frequent, that its enforcement may have to be policed by the President himself.

A unified Executive must know where it is heading. At present there are many more competent Americanists participating in the formulation of Soviet foreign policy than there are Sovietologists advising on U.S. policy. That should be changed, by enlisting the counsel of capable outside scholars and negotiators, and by reinstating the foreign-service training program that, in an earlier era, produced America's excellent wartime and immediate postwar ambassadors to the Soviet Union.

It is also time, however, to return security judgments—as opposed to policy advice—to the seasoned career professionals who know what is realistic in the world: the uniformed military, that is, in tandem with the foreign service, both presided over by elected officials. The day of the "defense intellectual" as the principal architect of U.S. security policy is, or should be, over. The academics have made their contribution and it is there to be judged. Irreverently, one might ask, if war is too important for the generals, whether it is not perhaps too unimportant for the professors. Scholars can serve a cardinal role as policy critics, but decisions henceforth should be taken by a politically accountable President and Congress drawing on the resources of real-world experience available to them in the career services.

Those judgments must be guided by a professional and dispassionate intelligence. Security decisions are inevitably, and properly, political, but if the politics drive the intelligence process rather than resting on it the country will be ill-served. Former Secretary of State Dean Rusk described the risks to the Senate Intelligence Committee in 1985:

> There is a temptation for some in the intelligence community to arrange the information they furnish in such a way as to affect policy decisions in one direction or another. This factor played a major role in the tragic mistake of the Bay of Pigs. The duty of the intelligence community is to furnish information with as much integrity as possible, letting the chips fall where they may in terms of policy process. Correspondingly, the policy officers of the government should not expect the intelligence community to prepare a report aimed at producing a particular result from the point of view of policy. This surrenders the right of the policy officers of the government to know with as much accuracy and fidelity as possible what information the intelligence community has which should be taken into account in policy formulation.

On that occasion Rusk joined other distinguished users and contributors of security information who were providing advice on the aims and methods of intelligence. As summarized for the Senate Committee, the proper aims should be to:

—Assure the *quality* of information (accuracy, reliability), which is not the same as its secrecy;
—Insure the rigorous *evaluation* and *interpretation* of the information; and
—Enhance the *shareability* and *persuasiveness* of policy-relevant information in a democratic society.

For this purpose, the means suggested for strengthening the intelligence process were to:

—Entertain a presumption in favor of reliance for policy judgment on unclassified or declassified materials;
—Complement official U.S. government services with regular recourse to independent specialists;
—Aim to objectify the U.S. understanding of Soviet dynamics; and
—Consider the economic, political, military, and cultural dimensions of Soviet behavior all together, along with the internal roots of external conduct.

The diplomat and historian George F. Kennan was especially insistent on this latter point, advising the Senators that the objects of political intelligence must "embrace the whole spectrum of conditions and considerations which influence the behavior of the Soviet Union in its relations with us. These have to include, of course, not just contemporary happenings but also traditional methods and reactions."

Kennan added:

I stress all this, because there seems to me to be a tendency in our governmental statements and our public discussions to see these various impacts on Soviet decision-taking as being largely limited to actions *we* take, and things *we* do, that affect Soviet interests. It is my impression that, concerned as the Soviet leaders may be with us and our actions, there are many other factors affecting and partly determining their behavior which are slighted in the view we commonly take of their motivation. I would hope that a proper intelligence effort would bring out more sharply the true pattern of the environmental influences that work on them, in all its richness and diversity.

Beyond and beneath a responsive intelligence, an effective military, and a focused diplomacy, there lies the untapped strength of an enlightened public opinion. It is no longer enough to disdain or manipulate this resource. A democratic society will sustain a major shift of policy only with the support of public opinion. America proclaims itself a government resting on the "consent of the governed," but unless the consent is informed it will not hold. Our elected officials and career professionals must therefore exert themselves in unpracticed ways to demystify a foreign and security policy that is not, at bottom, terribly complex. They will need, and can get, some help along the way.

Some aid can come from a core of responsible news media, which fortunately exists, ready to explore the larger picture and the longer range; also a few politicians willing to bet on the underlying good sense of the electorate. A new generation of candidates for public office, unshackled from the policy formulations of the past, will have to be prepared to make their own judgments and forge their own constituencies. The nation's educational system must also join in: No longer can the average high school or college student be left uninformed about the rudimentary ingredients of international relations. The language, culture, and history of the major powers, including the Soviet Union, must be offered by the schools and to some degree required.

With the help of such changes, the American political system has within itself the capacity to renew its vision and its grasp of basic interests. It should not take another catastrophe like Pearl Harbor to awaken the nation to its proper course. One vehicle that could stimulate the needed recognition is a high-level Blue Ribbon Commission on U.S.-Soviet Relations. The membership and procedures of such a commission would have to be thoughtfully considered. Its chairman should be someone of unquestioned breadth and integrity, a respected figure like George F. Kennan. A majority of the other members, however, should probably be well-connected political generalists, ready to learn and to lead in the search for a sustainable new consensus.

The work of such a commission could engage from the outset the political and educational processes of the country. Perhaps half of its budget might be earmarked for exploration and discussion of the commission's report, whose summary section should be kept short enough to fit on the editorial pages of the nation's newspapers. Television presentations, debates, and speaking tours could all be authorized, capped by a special Presidential address to Congress, submitting for endorsement a brief statement of the principles that should guide future policy. That way could a new beginning be marked.

No policy statement by itself can guarantee smooth relations with a nation as self-determining as the Soviet Union. The American public, together with the peoples of other democratic societies, may have occasion in the future to want to rebuke Soviet behavior they find offensive. Political leaders should give some quiet, advance attention to a selection of measures that can be taken in these circumstances without damage to the West. In 1979, when the USSR invaded Afghanistan, a hurried call went out from the National Security Council staff for a comprehensive list of imposable retaliatory actions. One item that made it onto this list was cancellation of Soviet press privileges. By chance, the people in the government charged with promoting global press freedom found out about it and got the item dropped. There needs in the future to be a more thoughtful tabulation.

Traditional measures exist by which to express disapproval of Soviet behavior—like the KAL shoot-down, the Sakharov imprisonment, or the Afghanistan invasion—that American opinion finds objectionable. One is to call back the U.S. ambassador "for consultations." Another is to deliver and publicize a stiff note of protest. A third is to consult, visibly, with allies and like-minded countries. A fourth is to suspend high-level contacts, and a fifth is to alert the private sector to perceived instabilities. Steps of this sort could appropriately serve as the foundation elements of a Presidential "sanctions kit"—a list of measures to be kept up to date and discussed in advance with Congressional and Executive bodies. If the President chose, such a kit might even be carried along on his travels side by side with the fabled "black box."

The President himself, in conclusion, will want a few points of basic guidance to carry around as his own mental framework. The points that occur are these:

1. The security of the United States cannot be achieved, in today's world, by isolationism; nor can the world be obliged to become more secure by any exercise of purely American power.
2. There are no magic cures or instant technological fixes for deep-seated political problems. These must be addressed with patience, firmness, and an educated insight.
3. Ideological approaches can complicate the East-West secu-

rity balance but cannot improve it. Whenever realism is pushed away from Washington's inner councils, we can be reasonably sure it will be pushed away in Moscow as well.

4. Policy depends on priorities. America's leadership must pick a set of authentic foreign-policy priorities—nuclear and conventional arms reductions, a stable and constructive balance of power, orderly growth and development among the newer nations, strengthened world trade and financial structures—and concentrate resources on them without undue distraction from lesser annoyances.

5. Priority must also be given to recovering America's economic strength, so as (among other things) to restore weight and credibility to U.S. leadership in the world.

6. On global policy matters, the Western alliance presents itself as not just a necessary nuisance but a source of strength. The field of action of the North Atlantic Treaty is restricted to the territory of it members. But its field of consultation is universal, and the other members of the alliance bring to the enterprise of world order a wider and longer experience than that of the United States.

7. America has its own agenda and its own vocation in the world, apart from and beyond its relations with the Soviet Union. America is still the granary of ideas and talents and capacities the world has need of. Development, innovation, harmony, and growth all find a place in the American experience. To act out its role in this larger setting America does not need to preach very much; it just has to be itself.

Acknowledgments

This book grew out of a project conducted for the American Committee on U.S.-Soviet Relations, a non-profit and non-partisan membership organization headquartered in Washington, D.C. The work profited considerably from its members' advice and encouragement, beginning (at the conceptualization stage) with George F. Kennan and concluding (at the manuscript stage) with McGeorge Bundy.

The project was launched by Jeanne Vaughn Gayler, then the American Committee's director, and was continued by her successor, William Green Miller.

First-year funding came from the W. Alton Jones Foundation, in Charlottesville, Virginia. Principal support thereafter was provided by the Alfred P. Sloan Foundation in New York City, through the offices of its senior vice president, Arthur Singer. Additional funding was provided by various church groups that took an interest, including the Catholic Conference (Joseph Cardinal Bernardin), the Presbyterian Office of International Affairs (Reverend Robert Smylie), the Methodist Board of Global Ministries (Joyce Hamlin), the United Church of Christ (Reverend Theodore Erickson), and the United Church Board for World Ministries (Kenneth Ziebell).

An informal board of advisers helped to identify qualified

specialists and to design a meeting format for their discussions. Its members included Professor Stephen Cohen, of Princeton University; Bradford Johnson, formerly of the Kennan Institute for Advanced Russian Studies; and Professor Vladimir Petrov, of George Washington University.

Several persons in government contributed to the shape of the proceedings. Among these were Secretary of State George Shultz, Congressman Lee Hamilton, and Senator Dave Durenberger—the last two serving as chairmen, at the time, of their respective Intelligence Committees. Senator Sam Nunn, chairman of the Armed Services Committee, met separately with us, as did Deputy Secretary of State John Whitehead and Under Secretary Michael Armacost.

All of the American Specialists on the Soviet Union deserve full recognition. Those who were architecturally helpful, offering advice as well as engagement, included Harold Berman, Lawrence Caldwell, Mark Garrison, Loren Graham, Ed Hewett, Gail Lapidus, Robert Legvold, Ellen Mickiewicz, Frederick Starr, and Robert Tucker.

Structural advice and encouragement from our media participants, beyond the confines of the meeting table, were forthcoming from Charles Corrdry of the *Baltimore Sun*, Hedrick Smith of the *New York Times*, Henry Trewhitt of *U.S. News & World Report*, Frederick Kempe of the *Wall Street Journal*, and Ted Clark of National Public Radio.

Within the American Committee staff, I am grateful to those doctoral and postdoctoral fellows who guided me to the pertinent literature and corrected or refined my understanding of Soviet developments as they occurred. These included Linton Bishop, Defense; William Brazier, Foreign Policy; Gerald Easter and Joel Hellman, Internal Politics; and Eric Green and Timothy Smith, Economics.

To my Committee colleagues, Margaret Chapman and Shirleen Lewis, and to my patient assistant, Patricia Donnelly, I express a warm and thankful *do svidanya*.

Outside the Committee, Stan Windass and his Foundation for International Security sharpened the arms-control discussions in the book by organizing two sets of consultations, a year apart, in

Moscow and London and Oxfordshire, with Soviet and West European counterparts.

In America, Judith Geller and her Potomac Speakers Bureau helped to round out the political insights of the book by exposing them, and their author, to a series of lecture audiences ranging from Maine to Oklahoma, and from Dallas to Seattle. She also read and commented thoughtfully on the manuscript.

The book's editor, Cornelia Bessie, who earlier had published Mikhail Gorbachev's *Perestroika,* showed in her attentions to this work the high intelligence and ready tact that must have been offered to that busy leader. I am grateful to her, as to all others who have lent encouragement.

American Specialists on the Soviet Union

Specialists

Gordon Adams
Director, Defense Budget Project
Doctorate in European History
Specialty: Comparative Defense
Spending

Harold Berman
Professor of Law, Emory University
Visiting Professor at Moscow Law
School
Specialty: Soviet Legal System

Robert Byrnes
Professor of History, Indiana
University
Former Director, Soviet-
East European-American Academic
Exchanges
Specialty: Russia and Eastern Europe

Lawrence Caldwell
Professor of Political Science,
Occidental College
Chairman, Political Science
Department
Specialty: Soviet Foreign and Military
Policy

Robert Campbell | Professor of Economics, Indiana University
Author, *After Brezhnev: "The Economy"*
Specialty: Soviet Economic and Resource Policies

Alexander Dallin | Professor of History and Political Science, Stanford University
Author, *The Domestic Sources of Soviet Foreign Policy*
Specialty: Soviet Foreign Policy

Karen Dawisha | Professor of Government and Politics, University of Maryland
Author, *Kremlin and the Prague Spring*
Specialty: Soviet foreign policy, Eastern Europe

Murray Feshbach | Center for Population Research, Georgetown University
Specialty: Soviet Demographics and Statistics

Mark Garrison | Director, Center for Foreign Policy Development, Brown University
Former U.S. Chargé d'Affaires, Moscow
Specialty: Soviet Foreign Policy

Raymond Garthoff | Senior Fellow, Brookings Institution
Former U.S. Ambassador to Bulgaria
Author, *Détente and Confrontation*
Specialty: U.S.-Soviet Relations, SALT

Paul Goble | Bureau of Intelligence and Research Department of State
Specialty: Soviet Nationalities

Seymour Goodman | Professor of Management Information Systems, University of Arizona
Adviser on Technology Transfer Policy
Specialty: Information Systems in East-West Trade

Loren Graham — Professor of History of Science, MIT
Author, *Red Star*
Specialty: Soviet Science and
Technology

John Hardt — Assistant Director, Congressional
Research Service
Senior Soviet specialist
Specialty: Soviet Foreign Economic
Policy

Ed Hewett — Senior Fellow, Brookings Institution
Editor, *Soviet Economy*
Author, *Reforming the Soviet Economy*
Specialty: Soviet and East European
Economies

Richard Judy — Head, "USSR as an Information
Society" Project
Hudson Institute
Specialty: Information Technologies

Donald Kendall — Chairman, PepsiCo, Inc. Executive
Committee
Chairman, American Committee on
U.S.-Soviet Relations
Specialty: East-West Trade

Gail Lapidus — Professor of Political Science, Berkeley
Chair, Center for Slavic and East
European Studies
Specialty: Soviet Domestic/Foreign
Policy

Robert Legvold — Director, Harriman Institute, Columbia
University
Author, *The Soviet Union and the Other
Superpower*
Specialty: Soviet Foreign Policy

Ellen Mickiewicz   Professor of Political Science, Emory
                          University
                          Editor, *Soviet Union*
                          Author, *Split Signals: Television and
                          Politics in the Soviet Union*
                          Specialty: Soviet Information Practices

Condoleezza Rice   Assistant Professor of Political Science,
                          Stanford University
                          Former Adviser to Joint Chiefs of Staff
                          Specialty: Soviet Military Affairs

Robert Scalapino   Professor of Government, Berkeley
                          Director, Institute of East Asian Studies
                          Specialty: Soviet-Asian Affairs

Dimitri Simes   Senior Associate, Carnegie Endowment
                          Adjunct Professor, Columbia University
                          Specialty: Soviet Security Policies

Frederick Starr   President, Oberlin College
                          Founder, Kennan Institute for
                          Advanced Russian Studies
                          Specialty: Soviet Society

Sarah Terry   Professor of Political Science, Tufts
                          University
                          Author, *Poland's Place in Europe* (AHA
                          Prize)
                          Specialty: Soviet Policy in Eastern
                          Europe

Robert Tucker   Professor of Politics (emeritus),
                          Princeton University
                          Author, *Political Culture and
                          Leadership in Soviet Russia*
                          Specialty: Soviet History and Politics

Nina Tumarkin   Professor of Political Science, Harvard
                          University
                          Author, *The Cult of Lenin*
                          Specialty: Soviet History and Ideology

Members of Congress

House Committee Leadership

Lee Hamilton	Chairman, Intelligence Committee
William Broomfield	Ranking, Foreign Affairs Committee
Benjamin Gilman	Ranking, European Subcommittee
Sam Gibbons	Chairman, Trade Subcommittee

House Democratic Caucus

Richard Gephardt	Chairman
Steny Hoyer	Chairman, Helsinki delegation
Charles Hayes	
William Hughes	

House Republican Research Committee

Thomas Coleman	Chairman, Foreign Policy Task Force

Senate Intelligence Committee

Dave Durenberger	Chairman
Bill Bradley	
Frank Murkowski	
Chic Hecht	
Thomas Eagleton	

Executive Branch

State Department

Seventh Floor	James Timbie, Steven Coffey, Eric Edelman
Soviet Affairs	Thomas Simons, Mark Parris, John Evans, Richard Johnson, Louis Sell
Central Europe	Pierre Shostal
Policy Planning	Richard Solomon, Sherrod McCall, Jeremy Azrael,

State Department

| | John van Oudenaren, Karen Galatz, Peter Hauslohner, Dale Herspring, Raymond Smith, Richard Kauzlarich |
| Intelligence & Research | Martha Mautner, Robert Baraz, Don Graves, Robert German, Jack Sontag, Morton Schwartz, Leslie Steinberg, Wayne Limberg, John Parker |

Defense Department

| International Security | Robert Joseph, Kenneth Katzner, Kenneth Smock, Rebecca Joyce, Peter Sullivan, Mark Schneider, Beth Masters, Frank Dellerman |

National Security Council Staff

Soviet Affairs	Peter Rodman
European Affairs	Lisa Jameson
Soviet Economy	John Herbst

Joint Chiefs of Staff

Plans and Policy	MAJ Alan Stolberg
International Security	CAPT Richard Davis, COL Wade Williams, LCOL Kevin Cullane, MAJ Robert Boudreau
European Theater	COL Verner Pike, COL Richard Naab, COL Richard Edwards

Central Intelligence Agency

| Soviet Analysis | Robert Leggett, Kay Oliver, Douglas MacEachin, Mark Zlotnick, Thomas Bjorkman, Benjamin Rutherford, Nancy Heer, Mary Des Jeans, Mal Helgesen, Martin Singer, Derk Swain, Peter Nyren, George Simmons, John Davidson, Ira Campbell, Grace Managan, Robert Pringle, Ann Crocker, Brian McCauley, Thomas Behling |

Media

Print

Associated Press	Henry Gottlieb, Barry Schweid
Baltimore Sun	Charles Corrdry, Stephens Broening
Chicago Tribune	Terry Atlas, David Evans
Christian Science Monitor	Gary Thatcher, Linda Feldman
Los Angeles Times	Robert Toth
Milwaukee Journal	Jack Kole, Richard Foster
New York Times	Hedrick Smith, Michael Gordon
Reuters	Michael Battye, Tony Barber
Scripps-Howard	Walter Friedenberg
St. Louis Post-Dispatch	Bob Adams
UPI	Dan Gilmore
U.S. News & World Report	Henry Trewhitt, Douglas Stanglin
Wall Street Journal	Frederick Kempe
Washington Post	Michael Getler

Broadcasting

ABC News	John McWethy, Rick Inderfurth
CBS News	Wyatt Andrews, Bill McLaughlin
MacNeil/Lehrer	David Shapiro
National Public Radio	Allan Berlow, Ted Clark
Voice of America	Joan Beecher Eichrodt

Sources

The text and context of this book are derived very largely from the observations of our American Specialists on the Soviet Union, in conversation with their policy-making and diplomatic and media audiences. The summaries of those 50 conversations, reviewed and approved by the participants, are listed by subject matter at the close of this section and are on file at the American Committee on U.S.-Soviet Relations, 109 11th Street, N.W., Washington, D.C. 20003.

The daily American press for the period 1984–89 was a source of regular information and perspective. The principal newspapers consulted were the *New York Times,* the *Wall Street Journal,* and the *Washington Post,* with further recourse to the *Los Angeles Times,* the *Christian Science Monitor,* and the *Chicago Tribune.* Public broadcasting was an instructive resource, particularly "All Things Considered" (National Public Radio) and "The MacNeil/Lehrer News Hour" (PBS). Special broadcasts on the commercial networks, for example, the NBC interview with Mikhail Gorbachev before the 1987 Washington Summit, were also useful.

The younger scholars and linguists at the American Committee conducted a systematic review of Soviet developments as reported in the general and professional Russian literature. Their summaries and text translations, coded by subject matter in computer-retrievable form, formed a valuable source of anecdotal information, particularly for the year 1987.

The principal Soviet publications brought under this review were *Pravda,* the official organ of the Communist Party, and *Izvestia,* the organ of the Soviet government. Both were outdistanced in reform enthusiasm by the weekly *Moscow News,* available in several languages, including English, and the weekly magazine *Ogonyok* ("Little Flame"). Other useful journals included the *Literary Gazette,* the weekly newspaper of the Writers' Union; *Novy Mir* ("New World"); the *Economic Gazette,* a Party weekly; and *Red Star,* the military journal of the Ministry of Defense.

American official organs concerned with Soviet developments include the CIA-directed Foreign Broadcast Information Service (FBIS), which publishes daily translations of selected Soviet broadcasts, press reports, and major speeches. Also, Radio Free Europe and Radio Liberty, funded by the U.S. government, publish periodic research papers on developments in the Soviet Union and Eastern Europe.

Non-governmental organizations that contribute to informed understanding of the USSR, and whose work has been useful to this book, include the following:

- The Kennan Institute for Advanced Russian Studies, through symposia and talks by both Soviet and American experts.
- The Aspen Institute for Humanistic Studies, through its Soviet discussion series with a bipartisan group of U.S. Senators.
- Emory University and its Carter Center, through a 1985 review of policy choices with senior American and Soviet political figures.
- The Brookings Institution, through a day-long review conference on the publication of Raymond Garthoff's book *Détente and Confrontation.*
- The Carnegie Endowment for International Peace, through its "Face to Face" series of dinner meetings on Soviet developments.
- The Johns Hopkins School for Advanced International Stud-

ies, through its series of informal brown-bag luncheon discussions on Soviet affairs.
- The Institute for Soviet-American Relations, through its publication *Surviving Together,* which summarizes pertinent meetings and publications.

American Specialists on Soviet Union

Summary Minutes, 1984–89

December 1984	Senior State Department: *Strategic Parity, Soviet Economy, Human Rights*	Mark Garrison, Robert Byrnes, Robert Tucker
April 1985	House Committee Leadership: *The Gorbachev Succession*	Lawrence Caldwell, William Griffith
May 1985	House Democratic Caucus: *Soviet Human Rights*	Robert Tucker, Ellen Mickiewicz
June 1985	House Committee Leadership: *Third World Activism*	Raymond Garthoff, Dimitri Simes
October 1985	Senate Intelligence Committee: *Informing U.S. Policy*	Ed Hewett, Lawrence Caldwell, Mark Garrison
October 1985	House Committee Leadership: *Soviet Domestic Turbulence*	Gail Lapidus, Frederick Starr

March 1986	Senate Intelligence Committee: *Prospects for Eastern Europe*	Sarah Terry, Ed Hewett
April 1986	House Republican Caucus: *27th Party Congress*	Lawrence Caldwell, Ed Hewett
May 1986	Executive Branch Group: *Gorbachev Succession*	Lawrence Caldwell, Ed Hewett
September 1986	Executive Branch Group: *Soviet Third World Aims*	Arthur Cox, Dimitri Simes
December 1986	Executive Branch Group: *"New Political Thinking"*	Mark Garrison, Raymond Garthoff
March 1987	Senior Media Group: *Soviets and the Persian Gulf*	Karen Dawisha, Raymond Garthoff
April 1987	Executive & Media Groups: *USSR and Asia*	Robert Scalapino, John Hardt
April 1987	Executive & Media Groups: *Gorbachev's Reforms*	Archie Brown (Oxford University)
May 1987	Executive & Media Groups: *Soviet Legal Reform*	Harold Berman, Frederick Starr

July 1987	Executive & Media Groups: *Soviet Military Policy*	Lawrence Caldwell, Condoleezza Rice
September 1987	Executive & Media Groups: *Soviet Economic Reform*	Robert Campbell, Ed Hewett
October 1987	Executive & Media Groups: *Soviet Science & Technology*	Loren Graham, Seymour Goodman
November 1987	Executive & Media Groups: *Glasnost and Infotech*	Ellen Mickiewicz, Richard Judy
February 1988	Executive & Media Groups: *Ideology in Foreign Policy*	Alexander Dallin, Robert Legvold
March 1988	Executive & Media Groups: *Political Uses of History*	Robert Tucker, Nina Tumarkin
April 1988	Executive & Media Groups: *Human Face of the USSR*	Frederick Starr, Murray Feshbach
May 1988	Executive & Media Groups: *Nationality Stresses*	Paul Goble, Sarah Terry

| September 1988 | Executive & Media Groups: *Soviet Political Reform* | Harold Berman, Gail Lapidus |
| September 1989* | Executive & Media Groups: *The German Question* | Karen Dawisha, Gordon Adams |

*Summarized directly in Chapter 17 of this book.

Documentation

Preface

POSTWAR PERIOD: Isaacson & Thomas, *The Wise Men.*

DISQUALIFICATION OF OTHER POTENTIAL WORLD LEADERS: A *Wall Street Journal* centennial series in January 1989 surveyed the leadership strengths and limitations of the USSR, China, the European Community, and Japan.

WASHINGTON'S FAREWELL ADDRESS: Commager, *Documents of American History*, 9th ed., Volume I, 169–75.

WARTIME PUBLIC ATTITUDES TOWARD THE RUSSIANS: *Life* magazine, as recounted in Gaddis, *The U.S. and the Origins of the Cold War*, 38–39, 57–58.

THE NEED FOR AMERICAN NEW THINKING: Steinbruner, Introduction, in Steinbruner, ed., *Restructuring American Foreign Policy*, 1–11.

SUMMARY MINUTES: A complete set is on file with the American Committee on U.S.-Soviet Relations, Washington, D.C.

Chapter 1

SCOPE OF SOVIET REFORM: Gorbachev, *Perestroika.*

SOVIET COUNTER-REFORMATION: Adam Michnik, interview with Lawrence Wechsler, *The New Yorker,* August 29, 1988.

CHANGES IN CONCEPTUAL DIRECTION: Lapidus, "Gorbachev and the Reform of the Soviet System," *Daedalus,* Spring 1987.

NO HABIT OF DEBATE: Vitaly Korotich, editor of *Ogonyok,* speaking at the Kennan Institute for Advanced Russian Studies, January 19, 1989.

SIBERIAN BEAR STORY: Letters to the Editor, *Britain-USSR* newsletter, January 1989.

Chapter 2

SENIOR KREMLINOLOGIST: Fritz Ermarth, National Security Council staff, at a Harvard-Columbia conference in March 1987.

"THE SOVIETS ARE OUT TO CONQUER THE WORLD": Statement by Eugene Rostow in 1982 to Admiral Noel Gayler (USN-Ret.), recounted to the author.

POWER AND DIPLOMACY: George Shultz speech at the Waldorf-Astoria Hotel, reprinted in the *New York Times,* December 10, 1984.

ALLIES' ATTRACTION TO GORBACHEV: *Chicago Tribune* opinion survey, April 1987.

AMERICAN CONSERVATIVES' REJECTION OF REAGAN DOCTRINE: Ted Galen Carpenter, Director of Foreign Policy Studies,

Cato Institute, "How Now to Counter Moscow?" *Wall Street Journal*, October 13, 1987.

CONFLICT AND CONVERGENCE: de Tocqueville, *Democracy in America*, quoted and discussed by the author in "Ideologies and Inevitabilities," *East-West Outlook*, September 1985.

TRUMAN DOCTRINE: Quoted and discussed in Fitzgerald, "Reflections: The American Millennium," *The New Yorker*, November 11, 1985.

MORALE OF MOSCOW EMBASSY: Interview with Martha Mautner, Bureau of Intelligence and Research, Department of State, 1986.

TAFT AND VANDENBERG POSITIONS: Acheson, *Present at the Creation.*

HAZARDS OF "HINDRANCE": Gaddis, "How The Cold War Might End," *Atlantic Monthly*, November 1987, 88, 92.

A GATHERING OF "HELPERS": Institute for East-West Security Studies, "Report of the Task Force on Soviet New Thinking"; MacMillan & Ullman, "America's Self-Interest in Helping Gorbachev," *New York Times*, October 7, 1987.

THE BRADLEY IDEA: *New York Times*, op-ed page, October 15, 1987.

"ANOTHER MAN'S MONASTERY": Mikhail Gorbachev, NBC interview with Tom Brokaw, *Washington Post*, December 1, 1987; *Perestroika*, 131–32.

LIPPMANN ALTERNATIVE: Lippmann, "The Cold War" (1947), reprinted in *Foreign Affairs*, Spring 1987.

INTERESTS VS. VALUES: Tonelson, "The Real National Interest," *Foreign Policy*, Winter 1985–86.

TRADING AND WARRING: Robin Gray, former Deputy Secretary, British Department of Trade and Industry, conference on "USSR Participation in the GATT," September 20, 1988.

McCARRAN-WALTER ACT: *Washington Post,* December 17, 1987.

KENNAN CONTRIBUTION: Kennan, "The Sources of Soviet Conduct" (1947), reprinted in *Foreign Affairs,* Spring 1987.

SIMULATED DANGER: Richard Perle, quoted in Aaron, "Verification: Will It Work?," *New York Times Magazine,* October 11, 1987.

RESUME THE WORLD WAR II ALLIANCE: Gorbachev NBC interview, *Washington Post,* December 1, 1987.

PUBLIC AGENDA SURVEY: "U.S.-Soviet Relations in the Year 2000: Americans Look to the Future," a report of the Public Agenda Foundation and the Center for Foreign Policy Development at Brown University, 1988.

BLUE RIBBON COMMISSION: Response by the author to Henry Kissinger, *Washington Post,* op-ed page, October 20, 1984.

DISDAIN FOR THE PUBLIC: Eberstadt, book review, *Wall Street Journal,* July 22, 1987.

Chapter 3

GORBACHEV'S FIRST PARTY CONGRESS: Political Report of the CPSU Central Committee to the 27th Congress of the Communist Party of the Soviet Union, February 25, 1986.

FARM FAILINGS: Diamond, "Soviet Agricultural Plans for 1981–1985," in Bialer & Gustafson, eds., *The 26th Congress of the Communist Party of the Soviet Union;* Vladimir Tikhonov, Soviet Academy of Agricultural Sciences, speaking at the Kennan Institute for Advanced Russian Studies, February 17, 1989.

WORKPLACE MORALE: Bialer, "Will Russia Dare Clean Up Its Economic Mess?," *Washington Post,* April 21, 1985.

GORBACHEV ON TECHNOLOGICAL SELF-SUFFICIENCY: Speech at space complex in Kazakhstan, May 14, 1987, reported in *Pravda.*

SOVIET BUDGET DEFICIT: Vladimir Tikhonov, speaking at the Kennan Institute for Advanced Russian Studies, February 17, 1989.

PENT-UP INFLATION: Lead editorial, *The Economist,* March 11, 1989.

LINGERING FEUDALISM: "Dangerous Stalemate," report of a 1983 U.S. Senate delegation visit to the Soviet Union, 39–45.

JOSEPH BRODSKY: Remnick, "The Poet of Independence," *Washington Post,* October 23, 1987.

ARTHUR'S ANT COLONY: White, *The Once and Future King,* 122.

DEMOCRATIC CENTRALISM: Bialer, "Gorbachev's Program of Change," in Bialer & Mandlebaum, ed., *Gorbachev's Russia and American Foreign Policy,* 231, 258.

"PARENTAL" LEGAL SYSTEM: Harold Berman, "The Struggle for Legality in the Soviet Union," speech at Emory University, February 19, 1985.

Chapter 4

"SWEEPING CHANGES" OF SOVIET LEADERSHIP: Brown, "Change in The Soviet Union," *Foreign Affairs,* Summer 1986.

LOCAL AND REGIONAL PARTY DIFFIDENCE: Bialer, "Gorbachev's Program of Change," above cited.

1987 ELECTION PROPOSALS: Central Committee Plenum on Reorganization, reprinted in *Foreign Broadcast Information Service (FBIS),* January 28, 1987.

WORKPLACE DEMOCRACY: Bialer, "Gorbachev's Program of Change," above cited.

LONG-TERM FARM LEASING: Brooks, "Gorbachev Tries the Family Farm," *Bulletin of the Atomic Scientists,* December 1988.

MEANING OF "GLASNOST": Luers, "A Glossary of Russia's Third Revolution," *New York Times,* July 7, 1987.

GLASNOST AS DIRECTED LICENSE: Statements by Mikhail Gorbachev and Alexander Yakovlev, in *Pravda,* April 1, 1987; by Victor Afanasyev, in *Dagens Nyheter* (Stockholm), January 30, 1987.

SAKHAROV COMMENTS ON CHANGE: Interview with John Hersey, *The New Yorker,* September 7, 1987.

STATUS OF CHURCHES: Homet, "East-West Church Diplomacy," *East-West Outlook,* September 1985; Tolz, "Church-State Relations Under Gorbachev," *Radio Liberty,* September 11, 1987; Antic, "Religious Policy Under Gorbachev," *Radio Liberty,* September 28, 1987.

LESS-FAVORED FREEDOMS: Laber, "The Moscow Book Fair: Glasnost Has Its Limits," *New York Times Book Review,* October 11, 1987.

THE DYNAMICS OF GLASNOST: Bialer, "Gorbachev's Move," *Foreign Policy,* Fall 1987.

1988 PARTY CONFERENCE: Central Committee Theses, *FBIS,* May 27, 1988; Mikhail Gorbachev Opening Speech, *New York Times,* June 29, 1988; Final Resolutions and Gorbachev Closing Speech, *FBIS,* July 5, 1988.

PUBLIC PARTICIPATION: *Moscow News* (English edition), No. 17, 1988.

CONSTITUTIONAL AMENDMENTS AND NEW ELECTION LAW: Reproduced in *FBIS,* October 24, 1988.

DEBATES AND ADOPTION: *FBIS,* November 21–22, 1988.

A SOVIET LAW-STATE *(RECHTSSTAAT):* Bialer, "Gorbachev's Program of Change," above cited.

Chapter 5

POPULAR RESENTMENT OF SOVIET ENTREPRENEURS: Alec Nove, Professor Emeritus of Economics at the University of Glasgow, speaking at the Kennan Institute for Advanced Russian Studies, November 3, 1987.

WORKER CONCERNS ABOUT *PERESTROIKA:* Vilan Ivanov, director of the Institute of Sociological Research, reported in *Izvestia*, May 5, 1987.

A RUN ON THE SHOPS: Feldstein, "Why Perestroika Isn't Happening," *Wall Street Journal*, April 21, 1989.

EDUCATIONAL DEFICIENCIES: Harley Balzer, director of Russian Area Studies at Georgetown University, speaking at the Kennan Institute for Advanced Russian Studies, October 29, 1986; Fyodor Burlatsky, adviser to Chairman Gorbachev, "The Process of Reform in Soviet Society," *Surviving Together*, Summer 1987.

ZASLAVSKAYA REPORT ON SOCIAL CHANGE: Miller, "The Relationship of U.S.-Soviet Arms Reductions and Human Rights," *U.S.-Soviet Outlook*, January 1989.

SOVIET "CIVIL SOCIETY": Pehe, "The New and Democratizing Soviet Middle Class," *New York Times*, May 25, 1987; Gustafson, "The Power of the People," *New Republic*, March 28, 1988; Bialer, "Gorbachev's Move," *Foreign Policy*, Fall 1987; Starr, "Soviet Union: A Civil Society," *Foreign Policy*, Spring 1988.

FRACTIONATING NATIONALITIES: Lapidus, "The Nationality Problem and the Soviet System," in Hoffman, ed., *The Soviet Union in the 1980s*.

ECONOMIC INCENTIVES TO FEDERATION: Konstantin Lubenchenko, chair of Supreme Soviet delegation to the United States, interview in the *Los Angeles Times*, September 1, 1989.

SOVIET VOLUNTARY GROUPS: Lyudmila Alexeyeva, exiled historian, "Informal Associations in the USSR," paper presented to the Kennan Institute for Advanced Russian Studies, October 24, 1988.

Chapter 6

ROOSEVELT RESEMBLANCE: Schlesinger, *Age of Roosevelt;* interview with Dr. Loren Graham of MIT, a fellow graduate student with Alexander Yakovlev at Columbia University in the 1950's.

"WE WILL NOT JUMP OVER PHASES": Gorbachev, NBC-TV interview, *New York Times,* December 1, 1987.

DEMOCRACY AND DISCIPLINE: *Pravda* editorial, February 2, 1987.

ZASLAVSKAYA AND SOVIET STATISTICS: Nahaylo, "A Heretic's Star Rises Under Glasnost," *Wall Street Journal,* October 14, 1987.

Chapter 7

"REGENERATION OF VINEYARDS": Aganbegyan, *Literary Gazette* (No. 8), February 18, 1987.

USSR AS A MOBILIZATION SOCIETY: Harley Balzer, speaking at the Woodrow Wilson Center, September 21, 1987.

URGENCY OF CHANGE: Helprin, "The Russian Reformation," *Wall Street Journal,* April 28, 1989.

"NO LONGER SETTING FIXED DEADLINES": Interview with Evgeni Primakov, director of the Institute of World Economy and International Relations (IMEMO), reprinted in *FBIS,* February 6, 1987.

HOLMES QUOTATION: *Hudson Water Co.* v. *McCarter,* 209 U.S. 349, 355.

POLITICS IN ESTONIA: Shipler, "A Reporter at Large (Estonia)," *The New Yorker,* September 18, 1989.

Chapter 8

ORDERED LIBERTY: Cardozo, J., in *Palko* v. *Connecticut*, 302 U.S. 319.

DEMOCRATIZED DISCIPLINE: *Pravda* editorial, February 2, 1987.

COMPARATIVE STANDARDS: Berman, "American and Soviet Perspectives on Human Rights," *Worldview*, November 1979.

FEDERALIST PAPERS: *The Federalist*, Clinton Rossiter, ed., 1961.

CULTURAL CONSTRAINTS ON SOVIET DEMOCRACY: Bialer, "Gorbachev's Program of Change," above cited.

"MAY I?": *Moscow News* legal correspondent, quoted in Butler, "Legal Reform in the Soviet Union," *Harriman Institute Forum*, September 1988.

Chapter 9

INTERNAL AND EXTERNAL SOVIET LEGITIMACY: Kennan, "The Sources of Soviet Conduct" (1947), reprinted in *Foreign Affairs*, Spring 1987.

LIMITS OF LEVERAGE: Clark, "Where Is Lord Macaulay Now That We Need Him?" *Wall Street Journal*, January 14, 1986.

PROSECUTORIAL CHARACTER OF HELSINKI PROCESS: Sussman, "In Defense of Helsinki," *Wall Street Journal*, August 1, 1985.

PELL ASSESSMENT: "Dangerous Stalemate: Superpower Relations in Autumn 1983," a U.S. Senate delegation report.

U.S. SUPPORT FOR *PERESTROIKA:* James Baker speech to the New York Foreign Policy Association, October 16, 1989, reprinted in *Surviving Together*, Fall/Winter 1989.

PEACEABLE DEMOCRACIES: Doyle, "Kant, Liberal Legacies,

and Foreign Affairs," *Journal of Philosophy & Public Affairs*, Fall 1983.

SOVIET ECONOMIC SURVEY: National Public Opinion Research Center, October 1989, translated and published in the *New York Times*, November 5, 1989.

"CALCULATED DISORDER": *Time* magazine, cover article, January 1, 1990.

CONSTITUTIONAL SETTLEMENT: *The Federalist*, No. 22 (Hamilton).

GATT MEMBERSHIP: Chapman, "International Experts Endorse Soviet Association with the GATT," *U.S.-Soviet Outlook*, November 1988.

Chapter 10

"INVOLUNTARY SIGHS" OF MARXIST IDEOLOGY: Adam Ulam, director of Harvard University's Russian Research Center, talk to Harvard alumni in Washington, D.C., April 1983.

SS-20 AS A MILITARY NULLITY: Admiral Noel Gayler (USN-Ret.), conversation with the author.

ORIGINS OF RUSSIAN DIPLOMACY: Joseph G. Whelan, "Soviet Diplomacy and Negotiating Behavior," a report for the House Foreign Affairs Committee, 1979.

SOVIET "NEW THINKING": Caldwell, "XXVII CPSU Congress: The Security Dimension," *East-West Outlook*, May 1986.

CONVENTIONAL FORCE BALANCE: Mikhail Gorbachev, speech to the UN General Assembly, excerpted in the *New York Times*, December 8, 1988; NATO statement on arms control, excerpted in the *New York Times*, December 9, 1988; East-West arms tabulations, *New York Times*, May 31, 1989.

SOVIET VERSION: "East-West Tallies," *New York Times,* January 31, 1989.

FRANÇOIS DE CALLIÈRES: Quoted approvingly in Whelan, "Soviet Diplomacy and Negotiating Behavior," above cited.

OBJECTIVE LIMITS ON SUPERPOWER CONFLICT: Kennan, "The Gorbachev Prospect," *New York Review of Books,* January 21, 1988.

SOVIET DIPLOMATIC ACCOMPLISHMENT: Newsom, "The True Soviet Threat," *Christian Science Monitor,* September 9, 1987.

Chapter 11

THE WARMING OF WESTERN COLD WARRIORS: Nitze, "The Word and the Woods," *Wall Street Journal,* March 23, 1984.

GORBACHEV 70TH ANNIVERSARY SPEECH: *FBIS,* November 3, 1987.

BUSH SPEECH AT TEXAS A&M: *Washington Post,* May 13, 1989.

SHULTZ SPEECH: *New York Times,* December 10, 1984.

CATO INSTITUTE: Carpenter, "How Now to Counter Moscow?" *Wall Street Journal,* October 13, 1987.

Chapter 12

INTERNAL CONSTITUENCIES FOR SOVIET FOREIGN-POLICY CHANGE: Michnik, interview with Lawrence Wechsler, *The New Yorker,* August 29, 1988.

SHEVARDNADZE ON SOVIET ECONOMIC DIPLOMACY: Excerpted in *U.S.-Soviet Outlook,* March 1988.

THIRD WORLD REORIENTATION: Fukayama, "Gorbachev and the Third World," *Foreign Affairs*, Spring 1986.

Chapter 13

INTEREST SYMMETRIES: George, "Mechanisms for Moderating Superpower Competition," *AEI Foreign Policy and Defense Review*, Vol. 6, No. 1, 1986.

U.S. EXPORT LEVERAGE: "Gorbachev's Economic Plans," U.S. Senate Print 100–57, Vol. 2, 454–55.

POSITION OF AMERICAN BUSINESS LEADERS: Kendall, "Toward the Elements of a New Trade Policy," *East-West Outlook*, May 1986.

VLADIVOSTOK SPEECH: Reprinted in "News and Views from the USSR," Soviet Embassy, Washington, D.C., July 29, 1986.

THE NUCLEAR-ELIMINATION FOLLIES: "Reykjavik: A Reckoning," *U.S.-Soviet Outlook*, November 1986.

MILITARY-TO-MILITARY TALKS: Joint Statement by U.S. Admiral William J. Crowe, Jr. and Marshal of the Soviet Union Sergei F. Akromeyev, and transcript of joint press conference, issued at Washington, D.C., July 11, 1988.

Chapter 14

NON-PROVOCATIVE DEFENSE: Gareyev, "The Revised Soviet Military Doctrine," *Bulletin of the Atomic Scientists*, December 1988.

COMPLEXITY OF CONVENTIONAL FORCE REDUCTIONS: Jonathan Dean, former U.S. ambassador to the Mutual and Balanced Force Reduction Talks, recorded in *U.S.-Soviet Outlook*, July 1988.

SOVIET ARMS-CONTROL MOTIVATIONS: Holloway, *The Soviet Union and the Arms Race*.

COUNSELS OF DISRUPTION: Nixon, *1999: Victory Without War.*

KISSINGER'S SECOND YALTA: Kaufman, "U.S. Experts Ponder Approach to Changes in the Eastern Bloc," *New York Times,* April 2, 1989.

MODES OF INTEREST ADJUSTMENT: George, Farley & Dallin, eds., *U.S.-Soviet Security Cooperation.*

DÉTENTE-ERA CODES OF CONDUCT: Garthoff, *Détente and Confrontation,* 290–98, 316.

ARBATOV-COX REPORT: "The Requirements for Stable Coexistence in United States–Soviet Relations," reprinted in the *Congressional Record,* May 9, 1988.

SOVIET DIPLOMACY IN THE PERSIAN GULF: Walcott, "Washington Insight," *Wall Street Journal,* November 2, 1987.

GORBACHEV'S UN PROPOSALS: "The Reality and Guarantees of a Secure World," *Pravda,* September 16, 1987.

TRUSTING THE RUSSIANS: Kennan, "The State of U.S.-Soviet Relations," *East-West Outlook,* July 1983.

AGREEMENTS ARE NO BETTER THAN THEIR UNDERLYING INTERESTS: Gaddis, "The First Fifty Years," in Garrison & Gleason, eds., *Shared Destiny.*

MUTUALLY EFFECTIVE INFORMAL RESTRAINTS: Garthoff, *Reflections on the Cuban Missile Crisis* (revised edition).

CSCE CONFERENCE: Concluding Document of the Vienna Meeting, excerpted in the *New York Times,* January 17, 1989; Eggleston, "The Vienna Debate on the Proposed Moscow Human-Rights Meeting," *Radio Free Europe,* October 27, 1987.

COUNTERTERRORISM COOPERATION: Wright, "U.S., Soviets Seek Ways to Combat Terrorism," *Los Angeles Times,* January 27, 1989; Jenkins & Marks, "Talking Terrorism With Moscow," *Wash-*

ington Post, March 5, 1989; Kemp & Norton, "U.S.-Soviet Team-work on Terrorism," *Christian Science Monitor,* March 10, 1989.

VERIFICATION PROSPECTS: Homet, "Symbols and Strategies from the Washington Summit," *U.S.-Soviet Outlook,* March 1988.

Chapter 16

INAPPROPRIATENESS OF "TESTING" SOVIET INTENTIONS: Robert Legvold, director of Columbia University's Harriman Institute for the Study of the Soviet Union, interviewed in the *New York Times,* May 9, 1989.

"NO SEASON OF SUSPICION": Speech by President George Bush at Texas A & M University, reprinted in the *Washington Post,* May 13, 1989.

HEAVY-FOOTED AMERICAN ECONOMIC DIPLOMACY IN ASIA: Homet, "New Technologies and Intellectual Property Rights: The International Dimension," a report for the Congressional Office of Technology Assessment, October 1984.

ARMS-CONTROL "BARGAINING CHIPS": Correspondence with General Sir High Beach, director, The Council for Arms Control, London, May 1988.

Chapter 17

DEFINING DETERRENCE: "The Nuclear Dilemma," a report of the Episcopal Diocese of Washington, D.C.

GORBACHEV AT STRASBOURG: Speech to the Council of Europe, excerpted in the *New York Times,* July 7, 1989.

COMPARATIVE NATO DEFENSE BUDGETS: Defense Budget Project, "Burden Sharing and the NATO Alliance," July 1989; compare Hewett, *Reforming the Soviet Economy,* 67.

SOVIET VIEW OF GERMANY/BERLIN DIVISION: Gorbachev, *Perestroika*, 200.

KENNAN ON GERMANY: "Reunification? Not Yet," *Washington Post*, November 12, 1989.

"DEVELOPMENT IS SECURITY": McNamara, "Defining 'Security' in an Interdependent World," excerpted in *U.S.-Soviet Outlook*, September 1986.

AMERICAN AID DISTORTIONS: Ottaway, "Foreign Aid Largely A Failure," *Washington Post*, February 21, 1989; "The Week in Review," *New York Times*, January 21, 1990.

Chapter 18

IDEOLOGICAL SCOREKEEPING: Brzezinski, *The Grand Failure.*

BUSINESS DIPLOMACY: Remarks of Dwayne Andreas, co-chairman of the U.S.-USSR Trade and Economic Council, at a Forum on U.S.-Soviet Trade Relations, July 13, 1989.

TRADE AGENDA: Kendall, "Toward the Elements of a New Trade Policy," *East-West Outlook*, May 1986.

REMOVING IMPEDIMENTS TO ORDINARY TRADE AND INVESTMENT: Stevenson & Frye, "Trading With the Communists," *Foreign Affairs*, Spring 1989; Gorbachev, speech to the U.S.-USSR Trade and Economic Council, excerpted in *East-West Outlook*, January 1986.

RATIONALIZING COCOM: Congressman Lee Hamilton, ranking member, House Foreign Affairs Committee, Newsletter, September 1989.

SCHOLARLY AND EDUCATIONAL EXCHANGES: Kassoff, "The Status of Scholarly Exchanges with the USSR," *Humanities*, August 1984; "Educational Exchanges Deepen," *U.S.-Soviet Outlook*, May 1988.

POLITICAL VULNERABILITY: "U.S.-Soviet Exchanges," a conference report of the Kennan Institute for Advanced Russian Studies; "U.S.-Soviet Exchanges: The Next Thirty Years," The Eisenhower World Affairs Institute.

DÉTENTE-ERA AGREEMENTS FOR COOPERATION: Jamgotch, *U.S.-Soviet Cooperation;* Friends Committee on National Legislation, "Are U.S.-Soviet Scientific and Technical Exchanges Worthwhile?," August 1983.

INTERNATIONAL FOUNDATION FOR THE SURVIVAL AND DEVELOPMENT OF HUMANITY: "A New Foundation," *U.S.-Soviet Outlook,* May 1988; Midyear Report of the Foundation, August 1989.

OBSTACLES TO BROAD-SCALE COOPERATION: Green, "The Political Economy of Environmental Protection in the Soviet Union," American Committee on U.S.-Soviet Relations, February 1989.

DISPASSIONATE INTELLIGENCE: "Criteria and Process for Intelligence on the Soviet Union," a paper presented to the Senate Select Committee on Intelligence by the American Specialists on the Soviet Union, June 1985.

THE NEED FOR INFORMED PUBLIC SUPPORT: Lippmann, *The Phantom Public;* Rosen, "Phantom Public Haunts Nuclear Age," *Bulletin of the Atomic Scientists,* June 1989.

BLUE RIBBON COMMISSION: Homet, "U.S.-Soviet Relations: We Need a Consensus, Not Just a Commission," *Washington Post,* October 20, 1984.

Index

Roland Stevens Homet, Jr., has served in all three branches of our national government as well as the military and diplomatic services. He has negotiated treaties, moved legislation, and conducted Presidential policy reviews. His fields of particular engagement have included energy, communications, and nuclear armaments. In recent years he has focused on international economic and security relations.

Mr. Homet was educated at Harvard and the Harvard Law School, sandwiched around his service in the U.S. Navy as an operations and gunnery officer on destroyers and in amphibious operations. He was a law clerk to Supreme Court Justices Felix Frankfurter and John Marshall Harlan. He has served twice on diplomatic assignments (at NATO and in the UN system), twice in White House positions, and twice with Congressional committees (House Foreign Affairs and Senate Judiciary). His past publications include *Notes on The Nuclear Dilemma* and *Politics, Cultures, and Communication.* Mr. Homet lives in Washington, D.C.